T0358361

ENVIRONMENTAL POLICIES IN **ASIA**

Perspectives from Seven Asian Countries

ENVIRONMENTAL POLICIES IN **ASIA**

Perspectives from Seven Asian Countries

Editors

Jing HUANG

Lee Kuan Yew School of Public Policy, National University of Singapore, Singapore

Shreekant GUPTA

Delhi School of Economics, India & Lee Kuan Yew School of Public Policy, National University of Singapore, Singapore

 **World Scientific**

NEW JERSEY · LONDON · SINGAPORE · BEIJING · SHANGHAI · HONG KONG · TAIPEI · CHENNAI

Published by

World Scientific Publishing Co. Pte. Ltd.
5 Toh Tuck Link, Singapore 596224
USA office: 27 Warren Street, Suite 401-402, Hackensack, NJ 07601
UK office: 57 Shelton Street, Covent Garden, London WC2H 9HE

Library of Congress Cataloging-in-Publication Data
Environmental policies in Asia : perspectives from seven Asian countries / edited by Jing Huang
(Lee Kuan Yew School of Public Policy, National University of Singapore, Singapore) & Shreekant
Gupta (Delhi School of Economics, India & Lee Kuan Yew School of Public Policy, National
University of Singapore, Singapore).
    pages cm
  ISBN 978-9814590471 (hardback : alk. paper)
  1. Environmental policy--Asia. I. Huang, Jing, 1956– editor of compilation.
II. Gupta, Shreekant, editor of compilation.
  GE190.A78E586 2014
  333.7095--dc23

                                                          2014000054

British Library Cataloguing-in-Publication Data
A catalogue record for this book is available from the British Library.

In-house Editor: Chye Shu Wen

Typeset by Stallion Press
Email: enquiries@stallionpress.com

Printed in Singapore

Contents

Acknowledgements

The publication of this volume would not have been possible without generous funding from the S.T. Lee foundation (administered by the National University of Singapore). This funding supported the presentations by contributing authors at an international on Asia's environmental policies, conference convened by the Centre on Asia and Globalisation (CAG) in May 2012. The chapters in this volume are revisions of these presentations.

In addition, a number of people deserve acknowledgement for their valuable assistance in both the preparation of this volume's contributions for publication and for helping to run the research project that the volume stems from. The team at the Centre on Asia and Globalisation — Jasmin Kaur, Esther Yeoh, Yang Fang and Wang Runfei — played an essential role in ensuring that conference held in May 2012 was of a great success as desired. Our deep appreciation also goes to Sandhya Venkatesh at World Scientific Publishing for her helpful and timely correspondence and coordination with us in the process of publication. Further, we thank the copy editors who have scrutinised the chapters for consistency.

Last but not least, Sharinee Jagtiani is indispensable for the publication of this volume. As a researcher at CAG, not only did she carry out the painstaking task of copy-editing, but she also acted as the "gate-keeper" for all the chapters to make sure the analysis is factually accurate and logically sound. Kaammini Chanrai, our intern at CAG, was also helpful in her assistance to Sharinee. Their contribution, albeit mostly invisible, is greatly appreciated by the authors and editors of the volume.

About the Contributors

Jing HUANG is a Professor and Director of the Centre on Asia and Globalisation at the Lee Kuan Yew School of Public Policy. He is an internationally recognised expert on Chinese politics, China's foreign relations and security issues in Asia-Pacific. He has written two books and numerous journal articles, book chapters, policy papers, and op-eds on Chinese politics, China's foreign policy, the military, US-China relations, and security issues in the Asia-Pacific. His book, *Factionalism in Chinese Communist Politics* (Cambridge University Press, 2000), won the prestigious Masayoshi Ohira Memorial Prize in 2002. Huang received his PhD in Political Science from Harvard University.

Shreekant GUPTA is an Associate Professor of Economics at the Delhi School of Economics and Adjunct Associate Professor at the Lee Kuan Yew School of Public Policy. He has worked as a researcher, policymaker and consultant on environment, natural resources, energy and urban issues. His teaching and research interests are in applied microeconomics and econometrics in these contexts. He has been a Fulbright Fellow at the Massachusetts Institute of Technology and Shastri Fellow at Queens University, Canada. He has served on several national and international committees on environmental and urban issues including the Intergovernmental Panel on Climate Change that was awarded the Nobel Peace Prize in 2007. He received his PhD from the University of Maryland in 1993.

Ryuzo YAMAMOTO is a Professor in the Faculty of Business Management, Tokoha University. His current research interests include the economics of global warming, projects for reducing GHG, policy for energy and electricity supply and decision making for overseas projects. He has been involved in several environmental projects, both in Japan and overseas, including Indonesia, India, China, Ukraine and Russia.

NGUYEN Huu Ninh is Chairman of the Centre for Environment Research, Education and Development and Lecturer at Vietnam National University. He is also Co-Founder of the International Programme on Climate Change and Variability Risk Reduction based in the Pacific Disaster Centre, and Adjunct Faculty of the San Diego State University. He has conducted a series of projects and programmes on environment and climate change in Vietnam and a wider Southeast Asia region and contributed to various international programmes. He is a contributor in the UNDP Human Development Report 2007/2008 as author of Occasional Paper on Flooding in Mekong River Delta, Vietnam, and co-author of *Living with Environmental Change: Social vulnerability, adaptation and resilience in Vietnam* (Routledge, London, 2001). He is also a Lead Author Member of the Fourth Assessment Report of the Intergovernmental Panel on Climate Change. He is Professor, Doctor (Hon.) of the University of Pécs (Hungary), Doctor of Science (Hon.) of the University of East Anglia (U.K.)

ZHU Shou-xian is Associate Professor in the Institute for Urban and Environmental Studies & Research Centre for Sustainable Development, Chinese Academy of Social Sciences. His research interests lie in resources exploitation and regional development. He has been an Associate Professor at the Institute for Urban and Environmental Studies, Chinese Academy of Social Sciences since 2010 and was Postdoctoral Fellow from 2008–2010 in the same Institute. He received his PhD from the Graduate University of the Chinese Academy of Sciences in 2008.

WU Fuzuo is an Oxford-Princeton Global Leaders Fellow (2012–2014). Her research areas focus on China's energy diplomacy, climate change, non-proliferation and export control policy, in addition to South Asian affairs. She has published a book in Chinese and a few articles in both Chinese and English on some peer-reviewed journals such as *Asian Survey* and *Journal of Contemporary China*. She received her PhD in International Relations from Fudan University and was Postdoctoral Research Associate at International Security Studies at Yale University (2010–2011). She has also worked as a Research Fellow at Sichuan University (2001–2004) and Fudan University (July 2007–April 2014).

CHEE Yoke Ling works on sustainable development issues, with a focus on social justice and equity issues and the effects of globalisation on developing countries. She is Director of Programmes of Third World Network, an international non-government organisation with its secretariat in Malaysia, and is currently based in Beijing.

LIM Li Ching is a Senior Researcher at Third World Network, focusing mainly on biosafety and sustainable agriculture issues. She was a lead author in the East and South Asia and the Pacific sub-global report of the International Assessment on Agricultural Science, Technology and Knowledge for Development, a multi-United Nations agency initiative. She is co-editor of *Biosafety First: Holistic Approaches to Risk and Uncertainty in Genetic Engineering and Genetically Modified Organisms* (Tapir Academic Press, 2007), and *Climate Change and Food Systems Resilience in Sub-Saharan Africa* (Food and Agriculture Organisation, 2011).

Sudhir Chella RAJAN is Professor at the Department of Humanities and Social Sciences at the Indian Institute of Technology (IIT) Madras. He is also Coordinator at Indo-German Centre for Sustainability, IIT Madras. He is broadly concerned with the interactions among social, political, technological and environmental factors relating to sustainable development. His research has included energy and environmental scenario analyses, studies on the politics of power sector reform in developing countries, and analysis of institutional reform measures to reduce corruption. He is the author of *The Enigma of Automobility: Democratic Politics and Pollution Control* (University of Pittsburgh Press, 1996) and co-author of *The Suicidal Planet: How to Prevent Global Climate Catastrophe* (Thomas Dunne Books, 2007). He was awarded his Doctorate of Environmental Science and Engineering from University of California, Los Angeles.

Shakeb AFSAH is an environmental economist and is currently the CEO of Performeks LLC—a Bethesda MD based consulting firm that he founded in 2002. He is also the creator of the popular climate management site, CO2 Scorecard (www.CO2Scorecard.org), and his analyses on climate policies are reported by top media outlets. He is globally recognized for implementing environmental rating and disclosure programs in developing countries. His current research focuses on policy communications and applications of big data and natural language processing to understand public perception and sentiment on key policy issues expressed in tweets, blogs and news reports. He holds a US patent on a methodology for measuring environmental performance. He has a Bachelor of Technology from IIT Delhi and a Masters in Public Policy from Harvard's Kennedy School of Government.

Nabiel MAKARIM is the former State Minister of Environment (2001–2004) for the Republic of Indonesia, and is globally recognised for creating a new brand of environmental programmes based on the principles of performance rating and public disclosure. He helped launch flagship initiatives like ADIPURA, PROKASIH and PROPER that successfully cut industrial pollution, improved urban environmental management and abated worsening water quality in the national river system of Indonesia. He now serves as an advisor to several private companies, and is working on three books — a political thriller, an environmental treatise and a fictional story.

LYE Lin-Heng is Associate Professor at the Law Faculty, National University of Singapore and Director of its Asia-Pacific Centre for Environmental Law (APCEL). She teaches and researches on Environmental Law and Property Law. She is an Advocate & Solicitor of the Supreme Court of Singapore, and Visiting Associate Professor at Yale University's School of Forestry & Environmental Studies. She also chairs the NUS multidisciplinary MSc (Environmental Management) [MEM] program, hosted by the School of Design & Environment. She is Vice-Chair and on the Board of Governors for the International Union for Conservation of Nature Academy of Environmental Law and has published and presented papers on environmental law, governance and management at conferences worldwide.

Keigo AKIMOTO is currently the Leader of the Systems Analysis Group, chief researcher at the Research Institute of Innovative Technology for the Earth (RITE) and a guest professor at the Graduate School of Art and Science, University of Tokyo. His scientific interests are in modelling and analysis of energy and environment systems including the costs, risks and public perceptions. He is also a lead author for the Fifth Assessment Report of IPCC, and a member of several committees of the Japanese Government. He received PhD degree from Yokohama National University in 1999. **Dr Fuminori Sano, Dr Takashi Homma, Junichiro Oda, Kenichi Wada and Dr Miyuki Nagashima. Dr Ayami Hayashi and Kohko Tokushige** are senior researchers and **Dr Toshimasa Tomoda** is a chief researcher at RITE.

INTRODUCTION

Environmentally Sustainable Development in Asia: Challenges and Choices

Jing HUANG

The deterioration of the global ecosystem, noticeably indicated by climate change, poses an unprecedented threat to human security. According to a recent report by the Intergovernmental Panel on Climate Change (IPCC) of the UN, "(W)arming of the climate system is unequivocal, and since the 1950s, many of the observed changes are unprecedented over decades to millennia" (IPCC, 2013 p. 3).[1] Of equal concern is the finding that "(H)uman influence on the climate system is clear" (*op. cit.*, p. 10) as evidenced by rising concentrations of greenhouse gases (GHGs) in the atmosphere emphasised the need for immediate global action to reverse the current trend in climate change. Such concerns had also been raised by the Bali Action Plan of 2007 which stated that a delay in action would "significantly ... [increase] the risk of more severe climate change impacts."[2]

However, despite growing global convergence on the need for urgent action on a range of environmental issues, there is substantial divergence especially between the developed (North) and developing (South) countries on actions that need to be taken to deal with these burgeoning problems. This divergence ranges over a number of issues from environmental standards to greenhouse gas mitigation targets and from financial arrangements to technology transfer, to name a few. These differences arise from differing perceptions and explanations of the causes, and hence responsibility, for our worsening ecological environment, and also substantial conflicts of interest, caused essentially by the gap between the North and South in socio-economic and political developments.

The developing countries, especially relatively rapidly growing economies like China and India, argue that the North has to shoulder major responsibility in reversing the decay of the ecosystem. This is not only because of their lion's share in consumption of energy and other natural resources but also because the post-industrialised, developed countries are responsible for most of carbon dioxide emission since the dawn of industrialisation. The South insists that the developed countries, given their predominance in technology, finance, and capacity of research and development, should provide assistance, rather than shifting the responsibility, to the developing countries in our endeavour to improve the ecological environment. While the dramatic increase in carbon emissions in the developing countries, especially China and India, may be a cause for future concern, their demand that the North should shoulder the main responsibility in addressing the ecological degradation, especially climate change, is morally and economically justified in terms of poverty eradication and human development. The South demands that the North should adopt a higher emission standard or equitable allocation of global atmospheric commons (carbon space), provide more financial and technical assistance to developing countries and alter their consumerist life style.

Developed countries (especially the European Union (EU) and Japan) on the other hand, argue that the North has already endeavoured to combat ecological degradation. Moreover, policy initiatives and increasing commitment by countries such as EU countries and Japan to greater energy efficiency and tougher environmental policy standards have helped to generate a global momentum to reverse — or at least contain — the decay of ecosystem. As emerging economic powers, China and India are large carbon emitters in the aggregate (though not in per capita terms). They are also increasingly large consumers of other natural resources such as minerals and there is a growing concern that their formula of rapid development will aggravate environmental degradation. Hence, the North urges the South, especially countries like China and India, to be 'responsible stakeholders' in the global effort to improve the ecological system.

Essentially, the difference between North and South on the ecological challenges reflects a fundamental dilemma in the effort to achieve economic modernisation, which is an inalienable goal for human development. Since industrialisation has been the only way for a human society to achieve this goal effectively, virtually all the developing countries have, to various degrees, embarked on the path of industrialisation in their efforts to modernise their societies as well as economies. Ironically, while the developed countries are trying to upgrade their industries to the high-tech, high value-added and low energy-consumption sections, high energy-consumption but (usually) low value-added manufacturing and processing industries have been outsourced to developing countries and have become an integral part of the economic development of the latter countries. The consequence is an explosive increase in consumption of coal and other fossil fuels and minerals in developing countries during the process of industriali-sation accompanied by rampant urbanisation, which in turn has aggravated the ecological environment.

Such a situation seems to have created an impasse between the North and South on the ecological issue, wherein both see the other side as the "irresponsible" party. The North urges the South to be responsible for the future in its development; and the South, while beating on the old path of the developed countries, blames the North for the consequence caused by its past behaviour and present "luxury" life style.[3]

The difference between the North and South on preserving the ecological environment is not one in kind but in degree, for the dispute does not root in ideological or even conceptual confrontations. Both sides have keenly realised that human industrial activities, especially irresponsible energy consumption, are the major causes for the decay of ecosystem, and that only through international cooperation can we effectively prevent the dete-riorating of ecosystem evolving into an irrevocable catastrophe. The issue between the North and South, given their different levels of socio-economic development, is essentially about the distribution of costs and benefits in our effort to improve the ecosystem. As such, both the North and South would be losers should they enter a zero-sum game on this critical issue. But the international community can, and should reach an agreement and make a joint effort to reverse the current trend of worsening environmental degradation.[4]

Asia at Crossroads in Environmentally Sustainable Development

In Asia, there is a mix of developed and developing countries with different levels of socio-economic and political developments. While countries like Japan and Singapore have been focusing on energy efficiency and regime building for preservation of the ecosystem, policymaking in China and India, which represent the developing countries, still prioritises energy security in order to sustain development. Hence a close examination of how the environmental policy is produced in various Asian countries, given their varied priorities in dealing with ecological challenges, will provide us with essential insights for assessment of the ecological stakes shared by the developed and developing countries in Asia and, more importantly, how the North and South can work together to preserve the ecosystem in economic development.

Indeed, although the re-emergence of Asia, centred on fast developments in China and India, is so impressive that some pundits have postulated the current century as the 'Asian century', it remains questionable whether fast development in Asia is environmentally sustainable. These countries are also witnessing large-scale environmental impacts in various sectors ranging from forests and fishing to mining and manufacturing. In addition, massive and rapid across Asia is causing serious concern about air and water pollution and congestion in its cities. While it is well observed that the environmental footprint generated by economic activities is concentrated in urban areas, it is uncertain if this has been internalised in policymaking in Asia, especially in the developing countries.

In particular, it remains unclear to what extent the unaccounted costs of environmental degradation (air and water pollution, soil erosion and deforestation to name some key problems) are negating economic growth in a long run. For example, early estimates of the cost of environmental degradation in China ranged from 3.5 to 8 per cent of gross domestic product or GDP (World Bank, 1997). More recent studies continue to highlight significant health and other costs of air and water pollution in China (World Bank, 2001, 2003 and 2004). Similar figures have also been derived at for India. Subtracting the median estimate of these costs, i.e., 4–5 per cent of GDP, from a growth rate of 9–10 per cent approximately halves the latter figure. Furthermore, netting out population growth at the rate of 1–2 per cent per annum implies that after adjusting for the cost of ecological degradation and population growth, environmentally sustainable per capita incomes in the fast growing economies in Asia may be growing much more slowly than commonly perceived by as little as 3–4 per cent per annum. A long-term and more serious concern is whether Asia is 'eating up' its natural capital (forests, mineral wealth, water resources, and etc.) and converting it into GDP growth that will not sustain into the future.[5]

Moreover, various industries tend to free-ride on the environmental issue despite obvious deterioration of the ecosystem, of which the effort of preservation can never have an equal distribution of cost and benefit.

Thus, a strong leadership and effective state intervention are necessary to overcome the challenges to the environmentally sustainable development. Policy interventions can not only improve the environment across Asia, but can also offer win-win opportunities and yield positive net benefits in economic development. For example, investments in improving air and water quality (controlling air and water pollution) lead to significant health benefits (reduced mortality and morbidity) and also improve productivity of the labour force.

Given the enormous stake and inevitable conflicting interests, environmental policymaking always involves various stakeholders and vested interests. Thus, a good understanding of the environmental policy and its implications requires a close examination of not only the policymaking process, but also interactions among various stakeholders in a given policy structure. Moreover, policymakers need to explore the available policy options that can optimise the incentives and mitigate conflicting interests in our effort to sustain the development. After all, environmentally sustainable development could not be achieved but for a sustainable policy that reflects the joint effort of the international community.

With this in mind, the Centre on Asia and Globalisation of the Lee Kuan Yew School of Public Policy convened an International Workshop on environmental policies of seven different Asian countries, namely China, India, Japan, Singapore, Indonesia, Malaysia and Vietnam. This group of countries is representative and captures the essence of Asia with regard to its growing economic clout, population and its environmental and natural resources — between them, these seven countries account for approximately 30 per cent of world GDP (in PPP) and 44 per cent of world population. Four of them (China, Japan, India and Indonesia) rank 2nd, 3rd, 4th and 15th, respectively, in the world in terms of size of their economies and are also among the world's ten most populous countries — ranking 1st, 2nd, 10th and 4th, respectively.[6]

With regard to environmental and natural resource endowments and policy challenges, these countries are again highly representative of Asia. They encompass a wide range of unique ecosystems and biodiversity and of mineral wealth. Indonesia and Malaysia, for example, are 'megadiverse' countries (a select group of 17 countries that harbour the majority of the world's plant and animal species).[7] Two-thirds of Malaysia (and about 60 per cent of Indonesia) is forested. It is estimated Malaysian forests contain 20 per cent of the world's animal species, notable since it has only 0.002 per cent of the world landmass, a little smaller than Germany (Alexander, 2006). The rainforests of Indonesia and Malaysia date back to 130 million years and are the oldest in the world. On the island of Borneo, shared between these two countries and Brunei, a 25-acre plot of rainforest can contain more than 700 species of trees — a number equal to the total tree diversity of North America.

What this suggests is that planners and policymakers in Asia (as represented by these seven countries) face a number of challenges as the continent undergoes rapid economic growth. At the workshop, experts from these countries deliberated upon the environmental challenges Asia faces. Instead of the black-and-white reading of the North-South environmental debate, this workshop aimed to examine the more complicated policymaking process, which involves not just various views and positions of Asian policymakers but, more importantly, the internal debates, constrains of the policymaking structure, and interactions of various stakeholders in the endeavour to overcome the environmental challenges they confront in their respective countries. The aim is to channelize the North-South debate in the Asian country-specific context, placing major focus on policymaking, implementation and implications on development. The volume hence remains empirically heavy, with each chapter focusing on a different country and an assessment of its environmental challenges within a given policy framework.

Structure of the Volume

Based on the above mentioned themes, the volume has been broken into three main sections for the sake of structure and coherence. The first part assesses key issues involved in combating environmental concerns. Shreekant Gupta's chapter on 'Environmental Policy and Governance in a Federal Framework: Perspectives from India' and Ryuzo Yamamoto's chapter on 'Japan's Role in Climate Change Issues' and fall within this section. The former throws light upon the question of how national governments should respond to what has been dubbed a 'race to the bottom', which describes the tendency of businesses to move to places where wages are lowest and laws are weak. He explores this notion in the Indian context and discusses environmental policy and its role in intergovernmental relations in India. Yamamoto on the other hand, discusses the challenges facing Japan's aim to reduce its carbon emissions, especially in the wake of the Fukushima mishap. The decision to reduce its dependence on nuclear energy would invariably mean a rise of carbon dioxide emissions from thermal power plants. Yamamoto asserts that there is a need to "reduce [Green House Gas] emissions domestically, to assist the growth of developing countries internationally with more effective energy use and less emission." Both chapters hence focus on how the source and solution of environmental concerns lie within the policymaking agendas of people in power and how they need to be addressed in the light of economic development.

The second part of the book discusses the inevitable environmental outcomes of fast development in countries through chapters on Vietnam and China. In his chapter titled 'Policy for Environmentally Sustainable Development: Perspectives from Vietnam' Nguyen Huu Ninh states that the Vietnamese economy has grown remarkably in the past decade. This however, has put a major strain on its natural resources and had an adverse environmental impact due to the knock-on effects of deforestation, land degradation, water pollution, overfishing, pollution and so on. Similarly in the case of China, both Zhu Shou-xian and Wu Fuzuo raise similar concerns in relation to its development in their respective chapters. Zhu's chapter on 'Resource-Environmental Foundation for Green and Low-Carbon Development in China', states that poor management of resources and environment protection can, in fact, become a stumbling block for the next stage of the country's economic development, if left unchecked. The author exemplifies the need for stronger policy making mechanisms and technology innovations to hasten China's transition to a green and low-carbon society. Wu's chapter, 'China's Environmental Governance: Evolution and Limitations', identifies three key limitations for this phenomena: the mind-set that prioritises economic development over environmental protection; institutional limitations, especially those faced by local Environmental Protection Bureaus and the Cadre Evaluation System; and legislative barriers in terms of penalty for noncompliance, and weak public involvement. She contends that addressing these limitations is critical for the improvement of China's environmental policy.

Chee Yoke Ling and Lim Li Ching express a similar concern as Wu's first limitation in the Malaysian context. In their chapter titled 'Fragmentation to Integration: Environmental and Sustainable Development Challenges in Malaysia', they argue that despite Malaysia's intention to maintain the three dimensions of sustainability i.e., environmental, social and economic, the policy framework in practice remains economic-heavy. The failure to integrate the environmental dimension into development planning is a key concern and this is reflected in Malaysia's ministerial set-up. For instance the 'macro' branch of Malaysia's Economic Planning unit has an Environment and Natural Resource section; however its influence remains weak. The authors also discuss the environmental challenge posed by Free-Trade Agreements (FTAs), with particular emphasis to the asymmetry between North-South FTAs like the Trans-Pacific Partnership

Agreement and the European Union FTAs. Interests of companies that are investing in these FTAs are prioritised and protected by private international tribunals. These may rule out any act, policy or law (including those in place for public health or environment) if it expropriates or threatens to expropriate its investments and real or predicted profits. While developing countries have policy frameworks in place to deal with environmental challenges, their effectiveness remains highly limited and are often overruled by economic agendas. Authors in this section raise the need to take action to ensure environmental agendas are brought to the forefront for the sustainability of their respective countries' development.

The last section of this volume evaluates the implementation of environmental policies in certain countries. It consists of a mix of environmental challenges of varying degrees that developing India and Indonesia and developed Singapore face. Sudhir Chella Rajan identifies how small firms can be a significant source of pollution given that they are difficult to track, license and regulate in India. In his chapter titled 'Governing the Common Firm: The Evolution of Environmental Policy for Small Businesses in India', he enumerates crisp policy recommendations, including the need to design macro-policies to encourage technology innovation and training for small firms. This would be effective, in sectors where motives of self-interest such as cost reduction and improved workplace safety may be easy to identify. Furthermore, he states that guild-like networks to help technology transfer ought to be developed, along with the provision of finance and other support mechanisms.

The Indonesian case study has been discussed at length in the chapter titled 'Environmental Management 3.0: Connecting the Dots between Pollution, Sustainability, Transparency and Governance in Indonesia'. Authors Shakeb Afsah and Nabiel Makarim discuss creative attempts made by the Suharto government to manage environmental concerns such as the Clean City Programme (ADIPURA) and the PROPER programme that used a system of colour codes to reflect the quality of environmental compliance demonstrated by industry players. Despite these, Indonesia needs to retool its environmental management to deal with trans-boundary environmental concerns like climate change. To conclude the section, the final chapter focuses on the comparatively successful Singapore case. In her chapter 'Environmental Law, Policy, Governance and Management for Cities: Getting it Right for a Sustainable Future — The Singapore Experience', Lye Lin-Heng focuses on the importance of an effective Environmental Management System (EMS) to regulate a city's activities and ensure that its citizens have an enhanced quality of life. The author expresses her concern over the lack of laws mandating environmental impact studies/assessments and lack of laws on recycling. She states that progress needs to be made on these two fronts to enhance Singapore's ability to confront future environmental challenges.

The final multi-authored chapter of the volume titled 'Trade-offs and Synergies for Sustainable Development and Climate Stabilisation in Asian Regions' analyses multiple income, climate and environmental indicators to look at the trade-off between sustainable growth and reducing poverty. It discusses the complexity of these trade-offs. For instance, the authors state, "while economic growth can advance many of the indicators for sustainable development, it can also lead to environmental degradation such as ocean acidification under a non-intervention or baseline scenario. On the other hand, any excessive emission cuts may derail sustainable development, particularly in some Asian regions". They argue that balanced measures are required for sustainable development. They hence call for the need for more balanced measures to achieve sustainable development that might differ from country to country.

In the past few decades, several international conventions have formulated an international normative framework for sustainable growth. Different countries have adopted this notion domestically and attempted to build policy-frameworks to implement them. These have been fraught with challenges and met with varying levels of success and failure. The need to strengthen these frameworks and establish effective checks and balances to ensure the effectiveness of their implementation has been a consistent plea of most authors in this volume. By presenting the plight between environment and development in the Asian context, this volume highlights the circumstances that often amount to the preference of the latter over the former. This is likely to have a perverse impact upon the socio-economic fabric of these countries, making sustainable development a dangerously distant goal.

Endnotes

[1] See the Intergovernmental Panel on Climate Change Report (2013) for full text.

[2] See Bali Action Plan 2007. Full text available at UN (2007).

[3] In his bestseller *Hot, Flat, and Crowded: Why We Need a Green Revolution — And How It Can Renew America*, Thomas Friedman has provided a compelling analysis of the seemingly impasse between the North and South amidst the global environmental crisis. The solution he proposed is a "green revolution," led by the United State, not just to save the mother earth, but also to sustain America's overall supremacy.

[4] This section was published in a varied form in Huang (2009).

[5] Partha Dasgupta and Karl-Goran Mäler (1994) were among the first economists
to forcefully propound this view: "The quality of the environment is part of our
capital stock, just like bridges and buildings. There is every reason to treat the
environment along with other capital as a relevant input in a firm's production
function."

[6] See http://en.wikipedia.org/wiki/List_of_countries_by_population.

[7] See http://en.wikipedia.org/wiki/Megadiverse_countries.

References

Dasgupta, Partha and Karl-Goran Mäler. *The Environment and Emerging Development Issues.* Oxford: Clarendon Press, 1997.

Friedman, Thomas. *Hot, Flat, and Crowded: Why We Need a Green Revolution —
And How It Can Renew America.* New York: Picador, 2009.

Huang, Jing "A Leadership of Twenty (L20) within UFCCC: Establishing a Legit-
imate and Effective Regime to Improve Our Climate System." *Global Governance: A Review of Multilateralism and International Organizations* 15,
No. 4 (2009): 435–442.

IPCC (Intergovernmental Panel on Climate Change). "Summary for Policymakers, IPCC Fifth Assessment Report, Working Group I, September
2013." 2013. Available online at http://www.ipcc.ch/report/ar5/wg1/#.
UlJIp9KnqX6. Last accessed on 7 October, 2013.

James, Alexander. *Malaysia, Brunei & Singapore.* London: Cadogan Guides,
2006.

UN (United Nations). "Report of the Conference of the Parties on its thirteenth
session, held in Bali from 3 to 15 December 2007." 2007. Available online at
http://unfccc.int/resource/docs/2007/cop13/eng/06a01.pdf#page=3. Last
accessed on 7 August, 2013.

World Bank. *Clear Water, Blue Skies: China's Environment in the New
Century.* Washington, DC: The World Bank, 1997. Available online at:
http://siteresources.worldbank.org/INTEAPREGTOPENVIRONMENT/
Resources/Clear_Water_Blue_Skies.pdf.

World Bank. *China: Air, Land, and Water — Environemental Priorities for
a New Millennium.* Washinton, DC: The World Bank, 2001. Available
online at: http://siteresources.worldbank.org/INTEAPREGTOPENVIRON
MENT/Resources/china-environmental.pdf.

World Bank. "China Country Assistance Strategy (2003–2005)", World Bank
Report, 2003. Available online at: http://www.wds.worldbank.org/external/
default/WDSContentServer/WDSP/1B/2002/12/14/000094946_021128041
84941/Rendered/PDF/multi0page.pdf.

World Bank. *Clean Development Mechanism in China: Taking a Proactive and
Sustainable Approach.* Washington, DC: The World Bank, 2004.

KEY ISSUES IN COMBATING ENVIRONMENTAL CONCERNS IN ASIA

1. Environmental Policy and Governance in a Federal Framework: Perspectives from India

Shreekant GUPTA

The pollution haven hypothesis which posits that investors from industrialised nations are attracted to developing countries with weak environmental laws has been a recurring theme in the literature on trade and environment, particularly in the context of competitiveness and environmental regulation (Birdsall and Wheeler, 1993; Copeland and Taylor, 2004). The basic question is whether differences in environmental standards and enforcement provide an unfair competitive advantage to some countries, and how this should be addressed. Similar questions could also be asked in the sub-national context for large federal countries: does interjurisdictional competition for investment, both domestic and foreign, manifest itself through differences in environmental standards and enforcement? If so, how should national governments respond in what has been dubbed a "race to the bottom"? This chapter attempts to address these issues by examining the legislative and institutional framework for environmental protection in the context of India's federal structure and the Indian experience with the so-called "race to the bottom" which describes the tendency of businesses to move to places where the wages are lowest and laws are weak?

The bulk of economic literature on federalism in India has focused on fiscal federalism (Singh and Srinivasan, 2008; Rao and Singh, 2007). There has been little work in the area of environmental policy and its role in intergovernmental relations in India. To keep the chapter focused, environmental problems related to natural resource degradation such as soil erosion, deforestation, biodiversity, or desertification are mentioned in passing, and are not dealt with explicitly.

Environmental Policy and Federalism in India

The regulatory regime for environmental protection in India is a picture of sharp contrast. The country has elaborate statutes and regulations on almost every conceivable area from hazardous waste to forests and wildlife. Yet, monitoring and enforcement capabilities remain weak. This section examines the division of environmental policymaking between national, state, and local governments in India. Much of the discussion focusses on the *de jure* division rather than the *de facto* situation. However, since much of the latter follows from the former, it is important to understand how the division is supposed to work.

Constitutional provisions vis-à-vis environment: accident or design?

The division of responsibility between different tiers of government, including environmental matters is governed by the Indian constitution. The sharing of environmental policy formulation between the central, state and local governments reflects the manner in which the constitution was originally framed and the way in which it has subsequently been interpreted and amended.[1] In this context, it should be kept in mind that the division of power *vis-à-vis* the environment between the centre and the states in India is simply a by-product of the overall devolution of power. The Indian constitution provides for a federal structure within the overall framework of a parliamentary form of government. While states have some degree of autonomy, ultimate authority rest with the central government. For instance, the centre can create new states; alter the boundaries of existing states (Article 3) and under special circumstances, even take over their governance (Article 356). Part XI of the Constitution ("Relations Between the Union and the States") governs the division of legislative and administrative authority between the centre and states. Article 246 divides the subject areas for legislation into three lists: Union List, State List, and Concurrent List[2] (see Table 1.1). The Union List comprises 97 subjects over which parliament has exclusive powers to make laws. Apart from defence and foreign affairs, the list also includes environmentally relevant subjects such as inter-state rivers and river valleys,[3] mines and minerals, oil fields, atomic energy, air traffic, and so on. The State List gives state governments exclusive jurisdiction over areas such as public health and sanitation, agriculture, land improvement and water management.[4] Under the Concurrent List,

Table 1.1: Constitution of India: Environment related subjects.

Union List

52	Industries
53	Regulation and development of oil fields and mineral oil resources
54	Regulation of mines and mineral development
56	Regulation and development of inter-state rivers and river valleys
57	Fishing and fisheries beyond territorial waters

State List

6	Public health and sanitation
14	Agriculture, protection against pest and prevention of plant diseases
18	Land, colonisation, etc
21	Fisheries
23	Regulation of mines and mineral development subject to the provisions of List-I
24	Industries subject to the provisions of List-I

Concurrent List

17A	Forests
17B	Protection of wild animals and birds
20	Economic and social planning
20A	Population control and family planning

both central and state legislatures can enact laws on subjects ranging from forests and wildlife[5] to factories and electricity.

In addition, the centre has the residual power to legislate on any subject not covered in the three lists (Article 248).[6] The balance is tilted further in its favour by three additional constitutional provisions: (i) a central law on any subject in the Concurrent List generally prevails over a state law on the same subject (Articles 251 and 254); (ii) it can legislate in the "national interest" on any subject in the State List (Article 249), and (iii) it can also pass laws on state subjects if two or more state legislatures consent to such legislation (Article 252).[7]

The centre has used another constitutional provision to take the lead in enacting environmental laws, namely, Article 253. This article empowers the national assembly to enact laws arising from not only treaties to which India is a signatory, but also decisions made at any international conference.[8] Particularly striking about this article is that it allows the central government to enact laws merely on the basis of decisions of an international conference or association, even though such decisions may not be legally binding upon India. This article in conjunction with other similar constitutional provisions such as Article 51(c), enables the centre to legislate on virtually any entry in the State List.[9] What this means in effect is that anything on the State List is fair game as far as the centre is concerned.[10] In fact, two major environmental statutes in India, namely, the Air (Prevention and Control of Pollution) Act of 1981 and the Environment (Protection) Act of 1986, have been enacted under this very provision by citing the United Nations Conference on the Human Environment at Stockholm (1972).[11] Similarly, the Biological Diversity Act 2002 and the National Green Tribuanl Act 2002 were enacted in the wake of the UN Convention on Biological Diversity signed in Rio de Janerio in 1992.[12] In February 2012, the state of West Bengal was directed to draft a policy for wetlands by the Kolkata High Court after India became a signatory of the Ramsar Convention for protection of wetlands.[13]

The Institutional Framework for Environmental Management

The UN Conference on the Human Environment in Stockholm in 1972 is a landmark in the evolution of environmental policy in India. Preparations for India's participation in the conference acted as a catalyst in the formation of a National Committee on Environmental Planning and Coordination (NCEPC). The committee was the forerunner of the Department of Environment (DoE) which eventually became the present Ministry of Environment and Forests (MoEF). Its main job was to plan and coordinate with the actual implementation carried out by the various government ministries and agencies (see Table 1.2).

In January 1980 the central government set up a committee chaired by N.D. Tiwari, then deputy chairman of the Federal Planning Commission, to recommend legislative measures and administrative machinery for environmental protection. The Tiwari committee made extensive recommendations including, *inter alia*, the establishment of a Department of Environment in November 1980 as an agency under the central government in charge of coordinating national policies for environmental protection and resource management, as well as administrative responsibility for pollution monitoring and regulations. In 1985, DoE was transferred to the newly created MoEF. It is currently the nodal agency in the administrative structure of the central government for the planning, promotion and coordination of environmental and forestry programmes. In tandem with these developments at the centre, almost all states and union territories

Table 1.2: Subjects under Ministry of Environment and Forests.

1. Environment and Ecology, including environment in coastal waters, in mangroves and coral reefs but excluding marine environment on the high seas.
2. Environment Research and Development, education, training, information and awareness.
3. Environmental Health.
4. Environmental Impact Assessment.
5. Forest Development Agency and Joint Forest Management Programme for conservation, management and afforestation.
6. Survey and Exploration of Natural Resources particularly of Forest, Flora, Fauna, Ecosystems etc.
7. Bio-diversity Conservation including that of lakes and Wetlands.
8. Conservation, development, management and abatement of pollution of rivers, which shall include National River Conservation Directorate.
9. Wildlife conservation, preservation, protection planning, research, education, training and awareness including Project Tiger and Project Elephant.
10. International co-operation on Issues concerning Environment, Forestry and Wildlife.
11. Botanical Survey of India and Botanical Gardens.
12. Zoological Survey of India.
13. National Museum of Natural History.
14. Biosphere Reserve Programme.
15. National Forest Policy and Forestry Development in the country, including Social Forestry.
16. All matters relating to Forest and Forest Administration in the Union territories.
17. Indian Forest Service.
18. Wild Life Preservation and protection of wild birds and animals.
19. Fundamental and applied research and training including higher education in forestry.
20. Padmaja Naidu Himalayan Zoological Park.
21. National Assistance to Forestry Development Schemes.
22. Indian Plywood Industries Research and Training Institute, Bangalore.
23. Afforestation and Eco-Development, which shall include National Afforestation, and Eco-Development Board.
24. Bio-fuel plantations in forest, wastelands and environmental issues concerning bio-fuels.
25. Desert and Desertification.
26. Forest Survey of India.
27. Indian Institute of Bio-diversity, Itanagar.
28. Central Pollution Control Board.
29. G.B.Pant Institute of Himalayan Environment & Development.
30. Wildlife Institute of India and Indian Board for Wildlife.
31. Indian Institute of Forest Management.

(Continued)

Table 1.2: (*Continued*)

32. Central Zoo Authority including National Zoo Park.
33. Indian Council of Forestry Research & Education.
34. Andaman and Nicobar Islands Forest and Plantation Development Corporation Limited.
35. Prevention of cruelty to animals.
36. Matters relating to pounds and cattle trespass.
37. Gaushalas and Gausadans.
38. The Prevention of Cruelty to Animals Act, 1960 (59 of 1960).
39. The National Environment Tribunal Act, 1995 (27 of 1995).
40. The National Environment Appellate Authority Act, 1997 (22 of 1997).
41. The Water (Prevention and Control of Pollution) Act, 1974 (6 of 1974).
42. The Water (Prevention and Control of Pollution) Cess Act, 1977 (36 of 1977).
43. The Air (Prevention and Control of Pollution) Act, 1981 (14 of 1981).
44. The Indian Forest Act, 1927 (16 of 1927).
45. The Wild Life (Protection) Act, 1972 (53 of 1972).
46. The Forest (Conservation) Act, 1980 (69 of 1980).
47. The Environment (Protection) Act, 1986 (29 of 1986).
48. The Public Liability Insurance Act, 1991 (6 of 1991).

Note: The Ministry of Environment and Forests will be responsible for overall policy in relation to forests, except all matters, including legislation, relating to the rights of forest dwelling Schedule Tribes on forest lands.
Source: Cabinet Secretariat (1961).

have established environmental boards similar to those of the national committee. Most of these have since been converted into environment departments.

There is another important set of environmental institutions in India that were established even before the DoE. These are the central and state pollution control boards (CPCB and SPCBs) initially created under the Water (Prevention and Control of Pollution) Act. Unlike MoEF, the pollution control boards are statutory bodies which have main functions of monitoring pollution and taking the neccessary measures to improve air and water quality. In other words, their mandate is to implement and enforce the major pollution control laws (Jasanoff, 1986). State pollution control boards are found in all states now. The central board coordinates the activities of the state boards as well as the federally administered union territories. Its role includes the compilation of data on air and water pollution, and more importantly to lay down ambient and emission standards for both air and water.

Evolution of the Legal Framework for Environmental Protection

Antecedents to current legislation

Unlike the recent origin of the institutional framework discussed in section II, environmental statutes in modern India date back at least to the mid 19th century (Ramakrishna, 1984) with laws such as the Indian Forest Act of 1865 and 1878. Other environmental aspects such as air and water pollution as well as wildlife were also covered. For example, the Shore Nuisance (Bombay and Kolaba) Act of 1853, was one of the earliest laws to address water pollution and had authorised the Collector of Land Revenue in Bombay to order the removal of any nuisance in Bombay harbour. Similarly, under the Oriental Gas Company Act of 1857, fines could be imposed on the Oriental Gas Company and compensation paid to anyone whose water was "fouled" by its discharges. The Indian Easement Act of 1882 guaranteed the property rights of riparian owners against "unreasonable" pollution by upstream users. The division of responsibility between states and the central authorities was also introduced by the Government of India Act (1935). Some of the earliest statutes aimed at curbing air pollution include the Bengal Smoke Nuisance Act of 1905 and the Bombay Smoke Nuisance Act of 1912. The Elephants' Preservation Act of 1879 and the Wild Birds and Animals Protection Act of 1912 are among the earliest pieces of legislation in the field of wildlife protection. After independence in 1947, laws such as the Factories Act of 1948 and the River Boards Act of 1956 contained further provisions for water pollution controls.[14] These early legislative efforts, however, tend to have limited territorial reach and it would, thus, be fair to characterize them as generally piecemeal and inadequate.

Legislation on water pollution

It was not till the 1970s that the federal government started enacting more wide-ranging and comprehensive environmental laws starting with the Water (Prevention and Control of Pollution) Act of 1974,[15] which was notable for the degree of consensus between the centre and the states. Six states had passed resolutions in 1969 urging parliament to legislate on water pollution.[16] By the time the Act came into force in 1974, a total of 12 states had joined the consensus in a remarkable instance of voluntary surrender of legislative authority to the central government.[17]

The Act is very much in the nature of a "command and control" regulation: it prohibits the discharge of pollutants into water bodies beyond established standards (Section 24) and requires generators of all new and existing sources of discharge into water bodies get the prior consent of pollution control boards (Sections 25 and 26). It also lays down penalties including fines and imprisonment for non-compliance. Prior to 1988, enforcement was through criminal prosecutions initiated by state boards and by seeking injunctions to restrain polluters. After amendments to the Act in 1988, boards were given more teeth in that they can shut down errant factories or cut off their water or electricity by administrative orders.

As mentioned in this chapter, the Act created a regulatory apparatus in the form of central and state water pollution control boards. These boards have the power to establish effluent standards which are enforced by approving, rejecting, or modifying applications for consent to discharge effluents. However, since this Act was enacted through Article 252, states had discretion in setting up water pollution boards and as of 1982, six states had not established these boards. However, the 1988 amendments increased the power of the central board *vis-á-vis* the state boards under Section 18 of the Act, enabling the central government take over the functions of a state board that has failed to comply with its directions.

A major gap in the Act was, however, the absence of any provision for the funding of boards, despite the range of functions they were expected to perform. Thus, the Water (Prevention and Control of Pollution) Cess Act of 1977 was passed to help meet the expenses of the central and state water boards. The Act requires designated industries[18] and local governments such as municipalities to pay a water consumption tax (see Table 1.3).

Legislation on air pollution

The primary statute in this area is the Air (Prevention and Control of Pollution) Act of 1981. In direct contrast to the Water Act which was justified on the basis of decisions by subnational entities, the Air Act was based on the decisions of a supranational body, namely, the 1972 UN Conference on Environment (see Section 2). The Act is nationwide in its scope and states that had not set up pollution boards under the Water Act were now required to establish them. Under this Act all industries have to obtain consent from state boards to operate within air pollution control areas

Table 1.3: Water Cess Rates.

Purpose for Which Water is Consumed	Maximum Rate Under Sub-Section 2 of Section 3	Maximum Rate Under Sub-Section 2(A) of Section 3
	(All figures in paise per kilolitre)	
Industrial cooling, spraying in mine pits or boiler feeds	5.00	10.00
Domestic purpose	2.00	3.00
Processing whereby water gets polluted and the pollutant are easily bio-degradable and are toxic	10.00	20.00
Processing whereby water gets polluted and the pollutants are not easily bio-degradable are toxic	15.00	30

Source: Water (Prevention and Control of Pollution) Cess Act, 1977 (as amended up to 2003).

delineated by the boards.[19] In practice, however, all states have declared themselves as entirely air pollution control areas. Thus, the whole of India is *de facto* an air pollution control area.

A legislation to end all legislation?

The Environmental Protection Act of 1986 (EPA) was enacted in the aftermath of the Bhopal tragedy. It takes a comprehensive definition of environment[20] and arms the centre with extensive powers "to take all measures as it deems necessary or expedient for the purpose of protecting and improving the quality of the environment and preventing, controlling and abating industrial pollution." (EPA, 1986, Section 3). Under the Act the central government has set nationwide ambient air quality standards as well as standards for vehicle emissions and discharge of effluents.

Thus, EPA *prima facie* appears to be an "umbrella" legislation. When introducing the bill in 1986, the Minister of State for Environment and Forests, Z.R. Ansari stated that "although there are existing laws dealing directly or indirectly with several environmental matters, it is necessary to have a general legislation for environmental protection, which, *inter alia*, should enable coordination of action of the various regulatory authorities, creation of an authority or authorities with adequate powers for environmental protection, regulation of discharge of environmental pollutants and handling of hazardous substances, speedy response in the event of accidents threatening the environment and deterrent punishment to those who endanger human environment, safety, and health" (as quoted Hadden, 1987: 719 en:38). The long wish list notwithstanding, there is little in EPA that is really new. Also, despite its all-encompassing title, it focuses narrowly on "brown" issues such as pollution and hazardous substances at the expense of other serious environmental problems such as deforestation.

From the viewpoint of environmental federalism, however, the EPA is quite significant since it tilts the balance firmly towards the centre: the states can have standards that are more (but not less) stringent than the centre. Section 3(2) of the Rules clearly states, "the central board or a state board may specify more stringent standards from those provided in Schedule I to IV of the EPA rules." Similarly, the states can reduce but not increase the time allowed for an industry to comply with standards. In recent years, environment regulations have taken a step further to set up administrative and judicial bodies with more teeth. The National Green Tribunal has been set up as an appellate body for environment cases. Laws have also been enacted specifically for hazardous waste management[21] under which organisations have to seek authorisation from the appropriate state pollution control boards.

Rationale for the dominance of the centre in environmental regulation

As argued in section II earlier, the centripetal tendencies in environmental legislation are largely a by-product of the dominance of the centre in the constitutional set-up, as well as characteristics of the Indian polity and economy. In fact, India had a closed and controlled economy in which the centre had a very dominant role *vis-à-vis* the states and the private sector until 1991, when major economic reforms were launched. It not only played a key role in determining the pattern and location of resource allocation in large scale projects in a wide range of industries such as steel, power and chemicals, but also dictated the private investment quantum. States were only bit players and hence it seems unlikely that the interstate competition for investment or the "race to the bottom" played any significant role in environmental regulation. The marginalisation of states in investment decisions may partly explain two puzzling aspects of the legislation on water and air pollution mentioned above. In both cases states yielded more power to the centre than they had to. Several states voluntarily asked the centre to legislate on water pollution and all states voluntarily designated the entire country as an air pollution control area under the Air Act.

"Race to the Bottom": Conceptual and Empirical Issues

Normative aspects

Two quite distinct issues are involved here: Firstly, should environmental standards vary spatially? And who should set these standards? These issues are conceptually quite separate: a single standard setter does not necessarily imply a single standard, and *vice versa*. Thus, a central agency (such as CPCB) could in principle set different standards for different regions based on carrying capacity, or some other criteria. By the same token, if subnational agencies were to set standards for their jurisdictions, they could still converge to the same standard due to interjurisdictional competition. Here, I address these issues purely from a normative perspective of economic efficiency. Thus, the answer to the first question is an unambiguous yes, and to the latter "it all depends."

For local pollutants, that is, those not generating any externality outside the jurisdiction, it stands to reason that environmental standards can vary spatially. Given jurisdiction-specific marginal social damage (MSD) and marginal abatement cost (MAC) functions as shown in Figure 1.1, pollution emission standard $P(i)^*$ should be set so that $MSD_i = MAC_i$ for any jurisdiction $i(i = 1, \ldots, n)$. A uniform standard, P^*, would lead to welfare losses as indicated by the shaded triangles. While the magnitude of welfare loss will depend on the shapes and location of the different MSD and MAC curves, it seems plausible that these curves will vary considerably among jurisdictions. With respect to the former, since the MSD curve for each jurisdiction i, is the vertical summation of individual willingness-to-pay for environmental quality, it will depend on the number of people and their preferences for environmental quality. The curve will also be a function of the assimilative capacity for pollution in that jurisdiction.

In other words, the aggregate demand for environmental quality in a jurisdiction (as reflected in the shape and position of the MSD curve) will depend, *inter alia*, on its population density, income levels and geographical

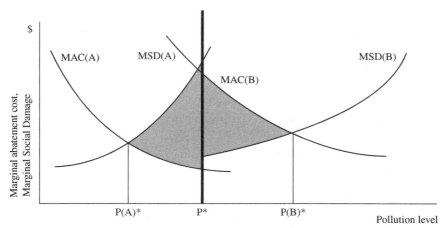

Figure 1.1: Uniform Versus Differentiated Standards (Baumol and Oates, 1988).

factors. It is also likely that abatement costs will vary across regions depending on the composition of industrial activity and the age of the plants and equipment, among other things. In sum, as Baumol and Oates (1988: 287)[22] point out, "the optimal level of environmental quality in one jurisdiction is unlikely to coincide with that in another."

The conclusion above would obviously not hold if the effects of the pollutant extend to other jurisdictions. In such cases, environmental standards would have to be set such that the externality was internalised.[23] This implies that in the presence of interjurisdictional externalities: (i) the optimal level of environmental standards would be more stringent than otherwise, and (ii) standard setting at the local level may not take these externalities into consideration. There are, however, a large number of pollutants that are local in character, and for which local environmental standards are appropriate.

An answer to the question of *who* should set environmental standards has to be sought in the larger context of interjurisdictional competition. If such competition is perceived as harmful, then environmental standards should be set by the national government. On the other hand, if such competition is viewed as beneficial, then standards should be set by local governments.

The case for harmonisation of environmental standards is based on the perception that competition among jurisdictions is harmful and can lead to sub-optimal levels of public goods including environmental quality

(Spatareanu, 2007; Oates 2001; Gray and Shadbegian, 1998). Proponents of this view advocate national minimum standards for environmental quality to avoid 'destructive interregional competition.' The problem with this approach, however, is that if environment is a normal good, then there is a trade-off between environmental degradation and bringing more jobs and economic activity into the jurisdiction by relaxing environmental standards.

Looking at the issue of harmonisation of environmental standards from a different angle of trade and environment, there have been opposing arguments on whether trade would lead to a "race to the bottom" or a "race to the top". On one hand, setting standards could lead to a "regulatory chill" or weak enforcement of standards in developing countries. On the other, a school of thought in public finance regards interjurisdictional competition as a disciplining force that forces public agents to make efficient decisions (Tiebout, 1956; Brennan and Buchanan, 1980; Stigler, 1957). This has also been supported by empirical evidence (Wheeler, 2001; Dasgupta *et al.*, 2002). Evidence from empirical work looking at cross-country data, FDI trends from USA and Europe and WTO trade negotiations suggestes that along with environmental regulation, factors like heterogenous preferences and/or differences in endowments and technology across economic entities, level of pollution of industry, size of export market, as well as whether trade is North-South or South-South will affect optimal environmental standards (Xing and Kolstad, 2002; Wagner and Timmins, 2009; Chau and Kanbur, 2006; Dinda 2004). It may hence not be appropriate to strictly link environment with trade issues (Bhagwati, 2000; Bhagwati and Srinivasan, 1996).

In this sense, what might be perceived as a race between states is merely the logical outcome of heterogenous preferences and/or differences in endowments and technology. To clarify, I am not arguing that a deliberate "race to the bottom" is a good thing. It certainly is not. What I am trying to say is that differences in environmental standards across states are not undesirable, and that all such differences should not be attributed to a "race to the bottom" phenomenon. The conclusion then is a mixed one: while there is an unambiguous case for spatially varying environmental standards, there is only qualified support for the beneficial effects of interjurisdictional competition. However, even if harmonisation of environmental standards were desirable, *a priori*, given the absence of a "race to the bottom" in any meaningful sense in India, such harmonisation has not been required so far.

Is There A "Race to the Bottom" in India?

From the discussion of the Environment Protection Act earlier in this chapter, it is evident that Indian states cannot compete by lowering environmental standards. In this sense, environmental standards in India are already harmonised at some minimum levels. It is, of course, possible that states may get around this *de jure* restriction by *de facto* lax enforcement. By an analogous argument, states may leverage the powers devolved to them post-1991 liberalisation (Rudolph and Rudolph, 2001) to enforce higher than national environmental standards. For instance, states like Kerala which are heavily dependant on tourism revenues would have a greater incentive to be stricter than national norms. Given the scope of this chapter, a rigorous empirical examination of this proposition is not attempted here. Research along these lines should be quite fruitful and interesting.[24]

Short of an econometric approach, however, it is difficult to disentangle the effect of environmental regulations *per se* from the other factors that also influence location decisions. While it may be possible to order states in terms of the stringency of their environmental regimes and expenditure on environment (see Table 1.4), location decisions may be influenced by a host of other factors such as availability of transport and communications infrastructure, power, access to markets and raw materials, and amicable labour relations, to name a few. With respect to infrastructure, states in India differ greatly and this is made worse by its overall inadequacy. A comprehensive index for infrastructure also reveals a wide disparity among Indian states — from around 70 for Arunachal Pradesh and Jammu and Kashmir to above 180 for Punjab and Goa (see Table 1.5).[25] It is interesting to note that the performance of states in terms of infrastructure has not changed considerably over time. This can be seen by looking at break-up of physical infrastructure indicators. For instance, the density of the rail and road network and teledensity varies considerably across states, even at per square area and per capita terms (see Table 1.6). This variation could be a key factor in influencing location decisions. A simple comparative exercise shows that states with better transport and communication connectivity also experience higher growth and gross income. Hence, it is plausible that the policy levers in interstate competition for investment may comprise, *inter alia*, provision of better and/or subsidised infrastructure rather than an environmental "race to the bottom."

Table 1.4: Allocations by States and Union Territories for Environment and Ecology Sectors.

States/ Union Territories	*Figures in Rs million*		
	2007–2008 Actual Expenditure	2008–2009 Anticipated Expenditure	2009–2010 Annual Plan Outlay
States			
Andhra Pradesh	—	—	—
Arunachal Pradesh	1.2	2.0	4.0
Assam	0.8	5.0	10.0
Bihar	—	—	—
Chhattisgarh	7.3	—	10.0
Goa	22.7	30.6	33.6
Gujarat	30.9	50.0	100.0
Haryana	16.6	15.0	15.5
Himachal Pradesh	1.3	—	—
Jammu & Kashmir	—	10.6	16.6
Jharkhand	—	—	100
Karnataka	65.0	109.6	109.6
Kerala	3.2	100	101.5
Madhya	147.0	110.7	119.8
Maharashtra	—	—	—
Manipur	35.6	53.5	65.0
Meghalaya	7.2	9.5	12.5
Mizoram	0.4	0.4	0.5
Nagaland	0.7	—	—
Odisha	65	114.3	104.3
Punjab	48.1	153	104.5
Rajasthan	4.7	2.6	2.0
Sikkim	5.6	5.5	17
Tamil Nadu	29.5	90.1	17.2
Tripura	12.6	8.4	10.9
Uttar Pradesh	477.2	445.5	114.7
Uttaranchal	—	—	—
West Bengal	86.0	130.0	200.0
Union Territories			
Andaman and Nicobar Islands	—	—	—
Chandigarh	30.2	24.0	24.2
Dadar and Nagar Haveli	—	—	—
Daman and Diu	0.2	5.0	2.8
Delhi	165.7	100.2	150.0
Lakshadweep	5.5	7.2	16.7
Puducherry	5.5	5.5	7.5
Total	**1275.7**	**1588.2**	**1473.2**

Source: Planning Commission, Government of India (2008).

Table 1.5: Index of Economic and Social Infrastructure: Indian States.

States	1994 Index	1994 Rank	1999 Index	1999 Rank
Andhra Pradesh	99.19	12	103.30	11
Arunachal Pradesh	48.94	25	69.71	25
Assam	81.94	15	77.72	17
Bihar	92.04	13	81.33	15
Goa	192.29	3	200.57	1
Gujarat	123.01	7	124.31	6
Haryana	158.89	4	137.54	5
Himachal Pradesh	80.94	16	95.03	13
Jammu & Kashmir	76.07	17	71.46	24
Karnataka	101.20	11	104.88	10
Kerala	205.41	2	178.68	3
Madhya Pradesh	65.92	23	76.79	18
Maharashtra	121.70	8	112.80	7
Manipur	70.38	22	75.39	22
Meghalaya	73.75	19	75.49	21
Mizoram	61.85	24	82.13	14
Nagaland	70.92	20	76.14	19
Odisha	74.46	18	81.00	16
Punjab	219.19	1	187.57	2
Rajasthan	70.46	21	75.86	20
Sikkim	104.62	10	108.99	9
Tamil Nadu	149.86	5	149.10	4
Tripura	83.55	14	74.87	23
Uttar Pradesh	111.80	9	101.23	12
West Bengal	131.67	6	111.25	8
All India	**100.00**		**100.00**	

Source: Anant *et al.*, 1994; 1999.

In general, it seems more logical for state-level policymakers to induce investment with more substantive "carrots" than those afforded by lax environmental standards. This is not only due to the fact that other factors loom large in location decisions, but also because enforcement of environmental laws is quite weak in India. Therefore, these regulations are often perceived as non-binding constraints. Weak enforcement is partly due to the precarious finances of the SPCBs. For instance, the funds made available to the West Bengal SPCB "in the first year of its operation hardly even covered the expenses of the chair and member-secretary of the Board" (Ramakrishna,

Table 1.6: Infrastructure Indicates Across Selected Indian States and Union Territories.

States/Union Territories	State Income		Roads in States			Railway in States			Phones
	State GDP in '000s 2010–2011	Growth of State GDP 2010–2011	Total Road Length (in km) March 2011	Per 100 sq. km of Area March 2011	Per One Lakh of Population (March 2011)	Rail km in 2010–2011	Rail km Per 100 sq. km of Area (March 2011)	Rail km Per Lakh Population (100,000) (March 2011)	Tele-density* (March 2012)
Andhra Pradesh	382	9.96	2,38,001	86.53	281.11	5,264	1.91	6.22	80.87
Assam	74	7.34	2,41,789	308.26	775.73	2,434	3.10	7.81	46.61
Bihar	144	14.77	1,30,642	138.74	125.85	3,612	3.84	3.48	48.9
Chhattisgarh	79	11.16	93,965	69.51	367.91	1,187	0.88	4.65	
Delhi	192	10.92	29,648	1,999.18	176.97	183	12.34	1.09	238.6
Goa	21	8.3	10,627	287.06	729.01	69	1.86	4.73	
Gujarat	365	10.47	1,56,188	79.68	258.66	5,271	2.69	8.73	91.14
Haryana	166	9.59	41,729	94.38	164.59	1,540	3.48	6.07	89.42
Himachal Pradesh	39	8.8	47,963	86.15	699.53	296	0.53	4.32	120.67
Jammu & Kashmir	39	6.63	26,980	12.14	215	256	0.12	2.04	54.82
Jharkhand	78	6.01	23,903	29.99	72.51	1,984	2.49	6.02	
Karnataka	280	8.87	2,81,773	146.92	460.94	3,073	1.60	5.03	97.22
Kerala	193	9.13	2,01,220	517.77	602.68	1,050	2.70	3.14	106.61
Madhya Pradesh	183	8.17	1,97,293	64.01	271.76	4,955	1.61	6.83	53.88
Maharashtra	775	10.47	4,10,521	133.41	365.32	5,602	1.82	4.99	96.83
Odisha	128	8.6	2,58,836	166.23	617.05	2,461	1.58	5.87	65.84

(Continued)

Table 1.6: (*Continued*)

States/Union Territories	State Income		Roads in States			Railway in States			Phones
	State GDP in '000s 2010–2011	Growth of State GDP 2010–2011	Total Road Length (in km) March 2011	Per 100 sq. km of Area March 2011	Per One Lakh of Population (March 2011)	Rail km in 2010–2011	Rail km Per 100 sq. km of Area (March 2011)	Rail km Per Lakh (100,000) Population (March 2011)	Tele-density* (March 2012)
Punjab	149	7.04	84,193	167.18	303.9	2,134	4.24	7.70	112.9
Rajasthan	204	10.97	2,41,318	70.51	351.67	5,784	1.69	8.43	73.11
Tamil Nadu	391	11.74	1,92,339	147.89	266.62	4,062	3.12	5.63	116.47
Uttarakhand	51	7.37	49,277	92.14	487.08	345	0.65	3.41	60.91
Uttar Pradesh	394	7.86	3,90,256	161.98	195.54	8,763	3.64	4.39	79.91
West Bengal	318	7.06	2,99,209	337.13	327.55	3,937	4.44	4.31	
NORTH-EAST States excluding Assam	55	54	14,420	804.68	337.65	168	1.53	1	65.92
ALL INDIA	4886	8.39	46,90,342	142.68	387.57	64460	1.96	4.31	

* Teledensity numbers: Bihar includes Jharkhand figures, UP includes Uttarakhand. GDP at constant 2004–2005 prices.

Note: GDP indicators greater than median in text color red; transport infrastructure indicators greater than Median in Green. States with transport infrastructure greater than median in 3 or more categories highlighted.

Sources: Indian Railways (2011), Ministry of Statistics and Programme Implementation (2012), Ministry of Road Transport and Highways (2012) and TRAI (2012).

1984). Moreover, most SPCBs have very few lawyers on their payrolls to initiate and follow up on litigation.

In the Indian context, one can go even further and question the "race to the bottom" hypothesis. In fact, it has been observed to the contrary that state agencies often work at cross purposes and at loggerheads over environmental issues. For instance, back in 1990s, the government of Tamil Nadu had gone to the Supreme Court to seek a relaxation of the effluent standards for tanneries set by the Tamil Nadu Pollution Control Board (TPCB)![26] On the other hand, the Karnataka Pollution Control Board (KPCB) was taken to task by the state legislature for not enforcing environmental regulations stringently[27] while in Orissa, it was the SPCB that "expressed its dismay over the (state's) inaction to the problem of high fluoride pollution by the National Aluminium Company Limited (NALCO) at Angul identified by the board" (The Financial Express, 1996). These cases suggest that state governments are pluralistic in nature with competing interest groups such as the SPCBs, individual departments or ministries each pursuing its own agenda. The objectives of SPCBs in particular, are quite different from those of state governments. Given the tight budgetary positions of SPCBs mentioned earlier, revenue considerations often dictate their actions when it comes to implementing environmental laws.

Another interesting aspect is the extent of judicial activism, particularly by the Supreme Court and state High Courts in enforcement. With the establishment of the National Green Tribunal, this is expected to further strenghtened. The Supreme Court[28] for example, decided in a landmark judgment in 1995 that the right to environment was a part of the Right to Life of Indian citizens, as enshrined in the Constitution. On the basis of this judgment, there have been a series of court orders and injunctions leading to closures of polluting factories with civic bodies, environmental officials as well as central and state pollution control boards taken to tasks.

In a nutshell, courts in India, particularly the Supreme Court, are not only legislating from the bench but are also taking over the functions of the executive branch.[29] This will have far reaching consequences for environmental legislation as well as enforcement, across sectors and states. For instance, the Supreme Court asked the Union Government to implement 29 directives vide an order passed in 2003, (one of which led to the Hazardous Waste Management and Handling Rules 2003), and followed up on its implementation in October 2011 by asking the Government to file an affadavit on the compliance status with its directives.[30] I do not wish to go into the reasons for judicial activism. Much of it, however, has been triggered by public interest litigation which in turn may reflect frustration with the bureaucracy and lack of faith in it for managing the environment. Judicial activism adds another set of players in the making of environmental policy in India, and further complicates the analysis of a "race to the bottom." State governments have to now contend with SPCBs as well as the appropriate High Court, Supreme Court and the National Green Tribunal.

Conclusion

Based on secondary data of the nature examined in this chapter, there is not much evidence at the state level, to either support or reject a "race to the bottom" hypothesis *vis-á-vis* environmental regulations. It does appear though that a host of other factors such as the availability of infrastructure do play a major role in interstate competition for investment. Further, given the weak enforcement of environmental laws and regulations, it is quite plausible that they are not perceived as a major cost of doing business in India. This may, however, change given the high degree of judicial activism witnessed recently in many environmental cases.

In any event, there is a need to examine the data more carefully and collect primary data before the "race to the bottom" question can be answered conclusively. Further, even if the conclusion of the suggested exercise is in the negative at this stage, it is plausible that an environmental "race to the bottom" could surface in the near future as economic reforms and liberalisation and the trend towards coalition governments at the centre hasten the process of decentralisation. In such a situation, a *de facto* harmonisation of environmental standards would have to be considered seriously.

Endnotes

[1] The words "central" or "centre" in the Indian context refer to the federal government. According to Article 1 of the Constitution, India is a union of states. There are 28 states and 7 union territories at present. The latter are directly administered by the central government. The federal legislature, also known as Parliament, comprises two houses, Council of States (upper house) and Council of People (lower house). In the chapter, the words "centre", "central" and "Parliament" are used interchangeably.

[2] These are List I, II, and III, respectively, in the Seventh Schedule of the Constitution of India.

[3] "Regulation and development of inter-State rivers and river valleys to the extent to which such regulation and development under the control of the Union is *declared by the Parliament* by law to be expedient in the public interest." (7th Schedule, List I, entry 56, Constitution of India, emphasis added).

[4] "Water, that is to say, water supplies, irrigation and canals, drainage and embankments, water storage, and water power subject to the provisions of entry 56 of List I" (7th Schedule, List II, entry 17, Constitution of India).

[5] Forests and environment was shifted from the State List to the Concurrant list of the Constituion by addition of Article 48A to the Indian Constitution in 1976.

[6] To make things more explicit, the 97th and final entry in List I of the 7th Schedule (Union List) is: "Any other matter not enumerated in List II or List III including any tax not in either of those Lists."

[7] It was under this very provision that the first major federal environmental legislation, the Water (Prevention and Control of Pollution) Act of 1974, was enacted by the Indian Parliament Recall that "water" is otherwise a state subject. The role of Article 252 in the enactment of the Water Act was discussed in detail in section IV.

[8] "Notwithstanding anything in the foregoing provisions of this chapter, Parliament has power to make any law for the whole or any part of the territory of India for implementing any treaty, agreement or convention with any other country or countries *or any decision made at any international conference, association or other body*." (Article 253, Part XI, "Relations Between the Union and the States," Constitution of India, emphasis added).

[9] "The State shall endeavour to foster respect for international law and treaty obligations in the dealings of organised people with one another" (Article 51(c), Part IV, Directive Principles of State Policy, Constitution of India). In addition, entries 13 and 14 of the Union List empower the centre to respectively, "participate in international conferences, associations and other bodies and implement decisions made thereat", and sign and implement "treaties and agreements with foreign countries".

[10] Almost five decades ago a scholar predicted an "inevitable and irresistible invasion of the state list by the Parliament under Article 253 of the Constitution," because of "the vast range of subjects covered by the conventions, treaties, agreements and recommendations of various specialized agencies and international conferences" to which India belonged (Looper, 1957, p. 305–306). If anything, the variety of these subjects has only increased over time. Such division of power between the central and state governments was the main issue debated by the Constituent Assembly in the 1940s. See generally, Austin (1966), Rao (1968), and Seervai (1996), and also the debates of the Constituent

Assembly of India. The "debate over where to locate authority to regulate environmental matters was primarily a manifestation of this more fundamental power dispute" (Ramakrishna, 1984, p. 910).

[11] For example, the preamble to the act on air pollution states, "Whereas decisions were taken at the United Nations Conference on the Human Environment held in Stockholm in June, 1972, in which India participated, to take appropriate steps for the preservation of the quality of air and control of air pollution; *and whereas it is considered necessary to implement the decisions aforesaid in so far as they relate to the preservation of the quality of air and control air pollution;* be it enacted by Parliament in the Thirty-second year of the Republic of India." (Air Prevention and Control of Pollution Act, 1981, as cited in GOI 1995, p. 131). Similar wording is contained in the preamble to the Environment (Protection) Act, 1986, which also cites the Stockholm conference as its *raison d'etre* (see GOI 1995, p. 213).

[12] Under the Biological Diversity Act 2002, National and 25 State Biodiversity Authorities have been set up. Under the National Green Tribuanal Act 2010, 5 seats have set up throughout India to provide judicial and administrative remedies to victims of pollution and environment damage.

[13] Kolkata High Court, *Forum for Human, Legal and Ecological Rights, Bansdroni & Another v. The Union of India and Others., against Writ Petition No.606 of 2011.*

[14] Section 12 of the Factories Act requires all factories to make "effective arrangements" for waste disposal. It also empowers state governments to frame rules to implement this directive. River Boards established under the River Board Act for the regulation and development of interstate rivers and river valleys, also have powers to prevent water pollution.

[15] This Act has precursors such as the Orissa River Pollution Prevention Act of 1953 and the Maharashtra Prevention of Water Pollution Act of 1970. The latter Act emphasised negotiation of effluent standards with industry.

[16] It "was the culmination of over a decade of discussion and deliberation between the centre and the states" (Rosencranz *et al.*, 1991, p. 65).

[17] Water is a state subject in the 7th Schedule of the Indian Constitution.

[18] These 16 "dirty" industries include *inter alia*, industries such as ferrous and non-ferrous metallurgical, mining, ore processing, petroleum and petrochemicals, cement, textile, paper, fertilizer, coal, etc.

[19] Section 19 (1) of the Air Act states quite explicitly that, "the state government may, after consultation with the state board, by notification in the official gazette *declare in such manner as may be prescribed, any area or areas within the state as air pollution control area or areas for the purposes of this Act*" (GOI 1981).

[20] "Environment" includes water, air, and land and the inter relationship which exists among and between water, air, and land, and human beings,

other living creatures, plants, micro-organisms and property" EPA, 1986, section 2(a).

[21] 29 directives issued by Supreme Court of India in order dated 14 October 2003, in the matter of Writ Petition (Civil) No. 657 of 1995, Research Foundation for Science, Technology and Natural Resource Policy vs. Union of India and others: one of the directives proposed changes in Hazardous Waste Management Rules (2003).

[22] This conclusion is also valid in an *inter-temporal* sense. In other words, for the reasons cited above not only should standards vary spatially, but also over time, jurisdictions can get more crowded, incomes can rise, and so on.

[23] "From a supra-regional efficiency viewpoint, those creating the environmental impacts in a region should bear the social costs not only of the impacts within the region, but on those outside that region." (Harris and Perkins, 1985).

[24] Theoretical and empirical literature in recent years has explored the question of fiscal federalism for environmental issues, since the seminal paper by Oates and Schwab (1988) (Kruger *et al.*, 2007; Kunce and Shogren, 2005; Levinson, 2003; Oates, 2001). Some work suggests that like tax efficiency, pollution efficiency is also best left to the local administration, as in the case of EU which has given considerable flexiblity to member countries. Alternatively, it is argued that devolved environmental regulation is "second-best" as local citizens do not capture economic rents fully. Others have also highlighted the role of central governments in encouraging research in environmental science and efficient technology.

[25] Eight major sectors are covered under this index, namely, agriculture, banking, electricity, transport, communications, education, health, and civil administration. The first five are classified as economic infrastructure, the next two as social infrastructure, and the last one as administrative infrastructure. For details see Anant *et al.* (1994).

[26] "TN to move SC against TPCB", Financial Express, New Delhi, January 8, 1996.

[27] "Pollution Board comes under fire", Deccan Herald, Bangalore, March 2, 1996. In its interim report the State Legislature Subject Committee on Revenue, Forest, Ecology and Environment Department was very critical of the KPCB for not taking action against polluting industries, granting environmental clearance to firms without proper studies, and entering into an agreement with polluting industries in order to get a case withdrawn from the state High Court.

[28] *Supreme Court in Virulent Gar vs State of Haryana 1995(2) SCC 577.* The judgement also referes to Art. 48-A, Art. 47 and Art 51A(g), and Art. 21 of the Indian Constituion, and Principle 1 as laid down in the Stockholm Declaration of 1972: *"Enjoyment of life and its attainment including their right to life with human dignity encompasses within its ambit, the protection*

and preservation of environment, ecological balance free from pollution of air and water, sanitation without which life cannot be enjoyed. Any contra acts or actions would cause environmental pollution. Environmental, ecological, air, water, pollution etc should be regarded as amounting to violation of Art. 21."

[29] Focusing only on pollution for the moment, a sampling of recent headlines in Indian newspapers illustrate this point: "MP plant suitable for trial burning of Bhopal waste: Govt to SC" (Anand, 2013); "India Court Orders Pollution Agency on Sterlite Time Extension" (Patnaik and Shanker, 2012); "India: Supreme Court asks where Yamuna river cleanup money disappeared" (Overdorf, 2012); "Vedanta shares tumble as Indian court shuts smelter on pollution grounds" (The Economic Times, 2010); "Supreme Court seeks CPCB report on ground water contamination" (PTI, 2012); "Lower noise level around IGI Aiport: Delhi HC" (The Times of India, 2010); "SC asks Madhya Pradesh about action on safe water to gas victims" (The Times of India, 2012). As can be noted, the orders include interpretation of existing laws directions, directions to executive, monitoring of executive's compliance with previous directives, as well as resolving disputes. See Centre for Environment Law Education (2012).

[30] The Supreme Court passed an October 11, 2011: "We direct the respondent, Union of India/Government of India to consider the report of the Monitoring Committee prepared by Dr. D.B. Boralkar and Dr. Claude Alvares, the directions contained at page 541 of the aforesaid judgment and a copy of the submissions filed on behalf of the writ petitioner on 21st September, 2011, and to prepare a note as to what steps have been taken to implement the directions and, if the same have not been implemented, as to why the same have not been implemented. While considering the aforesaid report and judgment, the Government of India shall also consider the other judgment in the same matter reported in (2005) 13 SCC 186. Let this matter be adjourned till 15th November, 2011...": in the Supreme Court of India, Civil Original Jurisdiction Writ Petition (C) No.657 of 1995, Research Foundation for Science, Petitioner Technology And Natural Resource Policy vs Union of India and others.

References

Agarwal, Anil, Sunita Narain and Srabani Sen. *State of India's Environment — The Citizens' Fifth Report.* New Delhi: Centre for Science and Environment, 1999.

Anant, T.C.A., K.L. Krishna and Uma Roy Chaudhry. "Measuring Interstate Differentials in Infrastructure." *A Study Undertaken for the Tenth Finance Commission.* New Delhi, 1994.

————. "Measuring Interstate Differentials in Infrastructure." *A Study Undertaken for the Eleventh Finance Commission.* New Delhi, 1999.

Austin, Granville. *The Indian Constitution: Cornerstone of a Nation.* 2nd ed. New Delhi: OUP India, 1999.

Baumol, William J. and Wallace E. Oates. *The Theory of Environmental Policy.* 2nd ed. Cambridge, U.K.: Cambridge University Press, 1988.

Bhagwati, Jadgish. "On Thinking Clearly About the Linkage Between Trade and the Environment." *Environment and Development Economics* 5, 4 (2000): 483–529.

Bhagwati, Jagdish and T.N. Srinivasan. "Trade and the Environment: Does Environmental Diversity Detract from the Case for Free Trade." In *Harmonization and Fair Trade,* edited by Jagdish Bhagwati and Robert Hudec. Cambridge, MA: MIT Press, 1996.

Birdsall, Nancy and David Wheeler. "Trade Policy and Industrial Pollution in Latin America: Where Are the Pollution Havens." *Journal of Environment & Development* 2, 1 (1993): 137–149.

Brennan, Geoffrey and James Buchanan. *The Power to Tax: Analytical Foundations of a Fiscal Constitution.* Cambridge, U.K.: Cambridge University Press, 1980.

Cabinet Secretariat, Government of India. "Allocation of Business Rules." 1961. Available online at http://cabsec.nic.in/showpdf.php?type=allocation_download. Last accessed on 15 August, 2013.

Centre for Environment Law Education, Research and Advocacy, National Law School of India University. "Green Decisions: Summary of some Important Judgments." Available online at http://www.ceeraindia.org/documents/greensummaries.htm. Last accessed on 16 December, 2012.

Chau, Nancy H. and Ravi Kanbur. "The Race to the Bottom, from the Bottom." *Economica* 73, 290 (2006): 193–228.

Copeland, Brian and M. Scott Taylor. "Trade, Growth, and the Environment." *Journal of Economic Literature (American Economic Association)* 42, 1 (2004): 7–71.

Cullet, Phillipe and Joyeeta Gupta. "India: Evolution of Water Law and Policy." In *The Evolution of the Law and Politics of Water,* edited by Joseph W. Dellapenna and Joyeeta Gupta, pp. 157–173. Dodrecht: Springer Academic Publishers, 2009.

Dasgupta, Susmita and others. "Confronting the Environmental Kuznets Curve." *Journal of Economic Perspectives* 16, 1 (2002): 147–168.

Dinda, Soumyananda. "Environmental Kuznets Curve Hypothesis: A Survey." *Ecological Economics* 49, 4 (2004): 431–455.

Gray, Wayne B. and Ronald J. Shadbegian. "Environmental regulation, investment timing, and technology choice." *The Journal of Industrial Economics* 46, 2 (1998): 235–256.

Hadden, Susan G. "Statutes and Standards for Pollution Control in India." *Economic and Political Weekly* 22, 16 (1987): 709–720.

Harris, Stuart and Frances Perkins. "Federalism and the Environment: Economic Aspects." In *Federalism and the Environment*, edited by R. L. Mathews. Canberra: Centre for Research on Federal Financial Relations, The Australian National University, 1985.

Indian Railways, Government of India. "Indian Railways Year Book 2010–11." 2011. Available online at http://www.indianrailways.gov.in/railwayboard/ view _ section . jsp?lang = 0 & id = 0,1,304,366,554,1165. Last accessed on 16 August, 2013.

Jasanoff, Sheila. "Managing India's Environment: New Opportunities, New Perspectives." *Environment: Science and Policy for Sustainable Development* 28, 8 (1986): 12–38.

Kruger, Joseph, Wallace E. Oates and William A. Pizer. "Decentralization in the EU Emissions Trading Scheme and Lessons for Global Policy." *Review of Environmental Economics and Policy* 1, 1 (2007): 112–133.

Kunce, Mitch and Jason F. Shogren. "On Interjurisdictional Competition and Environmental Federalism." *Journal of Environmental Economics and Management* 50, 1 (2005): 212–224.

Levinson, Arik. "Environmental Regulatory Competition: A Status Report and Some New Evidence." *National Tax Journal Part 1* 56, 1 (2003): 91–106.

Looper, Robert B. "The Treaty Power in India." In *British Yearbook of International Law (1956)*, edited by Claud H. M. Waldock. London: Oxford University Press. 1957.

MoEF (Ministry of Environment and Forests), Government of India, Central Pollution Control Board. "Pollution Control Acts, Rules and Notifications Issued Thereunder." Pollution Control Law Series New Delhi, 2010. Available online at http://www.cpcb.nic.in/NewItem_19_PollutionControlLaw. pdf. Last accessed on 15 August, 2013.

Ministry of Law and Justice, Government of India. "Constitution of India." 1950. Available online at http://lawmin.nic.in/coi/coiason29july08.pdf. Last accessed on 15 August, 2013.

Ministry of Road Transport and Highways, Transport Research Wing, Government of India. "Basic Road Statistics of India 2008–09, 2009–10 & 2010–11." 2012. Last accessed on 16 August, 2013.

Ministry of Statistics and Programme Implementation, Government of India. "State wise SDP 2004–05." 2012. Available online at http://mospi.nic.in/ Mospi_New/upload/State_wise_SDP_2004-05_14mar12.pdf. Last accessed on December 2012.

MoEF (Ministry of Environment and Forests), Government of India. "The India Forest Act 1927." New Delhi, 1927. Available online at http://moef.nic.in/ sites/default/files/Indian%20%20Forest.pdf. Last accessed on 15 August, 2013.

MoEF (Ministry of Environment and Forests), Government of India. "The Air (Prevention and Control of Pollution) Act 1981, amended 1987." New Delhi. No.14, 1981. Available online at http://www.envfor.nic.in/legis/air/air1. html. Last accessed on 15 August, 2013.

MoEF (Ministry of Environment and Forests), Government of India. "The Environment (Protection) Act 1986, amended 1991." New Delhi. No.29, 1986. Available online at http://moef.nic.in/sites/default/files/eprotect_act_1986. pdf. Last accessed on 15 August, 2013.

MoEF (Ministry of Environment and Forests), Government of India. "The Environment (Protection) Rules, 1986." New Delhi, 1986. Available online at http://moef.nic.in/sites/default/files/fellowships/THE%20ENVIRON MENT.pdf. Last accessed on 15 August, 2013.

Oates, Wallace E. "A Reconsideration of Environmental Federalism." Washington, DC: Resources for the Future, 2001. Available online at http://www.rff.org/documents/rff-dp-01-54.pdf. Last accessed on 12 August, 2013.

Oates, Wallace E. and Paul R. Portney. "The Political Economy of Environmental Policy." In *Handbook of Environmental Economics*, edited by Karl-Göran Mäler and Jeffrey R. Vincent, pp. 325–354. The Netherlands: Elsevier Sceince BV, 2003.

Oates, Wallace E. and Robert M. Schwab. "Economic Competition Among Jurisdictions: Efficiency Enhancing or Distortion Inducing?" *Journal of Public Economics* 35, 3 (1988): 333–354.

Pargal, Sheoli and Muthukumara Mani. "Citizen Activism, Environmental Regulation, and the Location of Industrial Plants: Evidence from India." *Economic Development and Cultural Change* 48, 4 (2000): 829–846.

Peltzman, Sam and Nicolaus Tideman. "Local Versus National Pollution Control: Note." *American Economic Review* 62, 5 (1972): 959–963.

Planning Commission, Government of India. "Environment and Forests." In *India's 11th Five Year Plan (2007–12)*: 467. New Delhi, 2008.

Prakash, Aseem and Matthew Potoski. "Racing to the Bottom? Trade, Environmental Governance, and ISO 14001." *American Journal of Political Science* 50, 2 (2006): 350–364.

Ramakrishna, Kilaparti. "The Emergence of Environmental Law in the Developing Countries: A Case Study of India." *Ecology Law Quarterly*, 12 (1984): 907–935.

Rao, M. Govinda and Nirvikar Singh. "The Political Economy of India's Fiscal Federal System and its Reform." *The Journal of Federalism* 37, 1 (2007): 26–44.

Rao, Shiva. *The Framing of India's Constitution: A Study.* New Delhi: The Indian Institute of Public Administration, 1968.

Rosencranz, Armin, Shyam Divan and Martha L. Noble. *Environmental Law and Policy in India: Cases, Materials, and Statutes.* Mumbai: Tripathi Private Limitied, 1991.

Rudolph, Lloyd I. and Susanne Hoeber Rudolph. "Iconisation of Chandrababu: Sharing Sovereignty in India's Federal Market Economy." *Economic and Political Weekly* 36, 18 (2001): 1541–1552.

Seervai, Hormasji M. *Constitutional Law of India: A Critical Commentary.* 4th ed. Mumbai: N.M. Tripathi, 1996.

Singh, Nirvikar and T. Srinivasan. *Federalism and Economic Development in India: An Assessment.* Munich: Personal RePEc Archive, 2008.

Spatareanu, Mariana. "Searching for Pollution Havens: The Impact of Environmental Regulations on Foreign Direct Investment." *Journal of Environment and Development* 16, 2 (2007): 161–182.

Srinivasan, T.N. "Interstate Competition for Private, Foreign and Domestic Capital: Some Analytical and Regulatory Issues." *Unpublished paper presented at IRIS-NCAER Conference.* New Delhi, January 9–10, 1996.

Stigler, George. "The Tenable Range of Functions of Local Government." In Joint Economic Committee, U.S. Congress, *Federal Expenditure Policy for Economic Growth and Stability.* Washington, DC: U.S. Government Printing Office, 1957.

The Financial Express. "Govt. inaction irks OPCB." April 10 1996.

Tiebout, Charles M. "A Pure Theory of Local Expenditures." *Journal of Political Economy* 64, 5 (1956): 416–424.

Tiwari, N. D. "Report of the Committee for Recommending Legislative Measures and Administrative Machinery for Ensuring Environmental Protection." Department of Science and Technology, Government of India, 1980.

TRAI (Telecom Regulatory Authority Of India). "Highlights on Telecom Subscription Data as on 29th February 2012." *Press Release No. 72/2012*, 2012. Available online at http://www.trai.gov.in/WriteReadData/PressRealease/Document / InfoPress-Telecom%20Subscription%20Data_%2029022012.pdf. Last accessed on 16 August, 2013.

Wagner, Ulrich J. and Christopher D. Timmins. "Agglomeration Effects in Foreign Direct Investment and the Pollution Haven Hypothesis." *Environmental and Resource Economics* 43, 2 (2009): 231–256.

Wheeler, David. "Racing to the Bottom? Foreign Investment and Air Pollution in Developing Countries." *The Journal of Environment Development* 10, 3 (2001): 225–245.

Xing, Yuquing and Charles D. Kolstad. "Do Lax Environmental Regulations Attract Foreign Investment?" *Environmental and Resource Economics* 21, 1 (2002): 1–22.

2. Japan's Role in Climate Change Issues

Ryuzo YAMAMOTO

The disaster and subsequent suspensions of all but two nuclear power plants in the wake of the Fukushima mishap have resulted in renewed environmental concerns such as heightened greenhouse gases (GHG) emissions due to Japanese utilities companies having to ramp up thermal power stations at the maximum load factors to compensate for power supply shortfall. The power sector before the accident had accounted for about 30 per cent of GHG emissions in Japan. With the expected higher emissions from thermal plants, this could see emissions rise to close to 200 million tons annually from higher oil and liquefied natural gas (LNG) consumption. That would be a blow to the pledge by former Prime Minister Yukio Hatoyama in September 2009 to cut Japan's GHG emissions by 25 per cent by 2020. In order to achieve the target, Japan had previously planned to introduce more nuclear power plants and renewable energy power sources. To partially offset the increase in GHG emissions due to the cut in output from nuclear power stations, the government is now seeking ways to improve energy efficiency on both the business and household fronts through the deployment of more efficient facilities. The Research Institute of Innovative Technology for Earth (RITE) has estimated that the marginal abatement cost would be US$476 per ton of carbon oxide to achieve 25 per cent reduction which Mr Hatoyama had pledged (Akimoto, 2010). Abatement cost is higher in Japan compared to other developed countries due to its already high energy efficiency, leaving little room for further improvement as Table 2.1 shows. Because of this, it seems clear that Japan will need to carry out more cost effective projects abroad and make use of the offset crediting mechanism to help with global reduction of GHG emissions. This can be achieved by technology transfer through bilateral agreements with growing economies, especially those in Asia, where there is still much room

Table 2.1: Energy Efficiency of Major Economies.

Country	Total Primary Energy Supply/GDP Ton Oil Equivalent/US$1,000 (2000)
Brazil	0.29
China	0.75
India	0.75
France	0.18
Germany	0.16
Japan	0.10
UK	0.12
USA	0.19

Source: IEA Key World Energy Statistics (2010).

to improve energy efficiency in areas such as power generation and industrial production processes including steel-making. In other words, Japan can still play a leading role in lowering of GHG emissions while partaking in economic growth in the region.

Status of GHG Emissions in Japan

In early 1970s, the knowledge of environmental harm among most Japanese were limited to the notion of acid rain which many believed resulted from emissions from power plants and oil refineries. That perception changed by the advent of the 1980s when the idea of global warming from the greenhouse effect from gases such as methane, carbon dioxide and hydrofluorocarbons (HFCs) started to gain traction. Backed by the Intergovernmental Panel on Climate Change (IPCC) established by the World Meteorological Organisation and the United Nations Environmental Programme to assess climate change and global warming issues in 1988, the 1992 Earth Summit in Rio de Janeiro saw the adoption of the United Nations Framework Convention on Climate Change (UNFCCC) which aimed to make efforts to stabilise GHG concentration in the atmosphere. This was followed by the announcement of Kyoto Protocol in December 1997 to limit global emissions by both developed countries as well as transitional industrialised economies or Annex-I countries. The Kyoto Protocol had called for Annex-I countries to make commitments to limit or reduce emissions of six of the GHGs as the first step.[1] The Japanese government accepted a six per cent GHG reduction target for the 2008–2012 period which was lower than the 8 per cent by the European Union (EU) and 7 per cent by the United States. It was, however, broadly acknowledged that even 6 per cent was tough to achieve despite the introduction of various energy saving measures by Japan following the oil shocks in the 1970s. As a result, it was proposed that the 6 per cent reduction will have to be met partly by forest management and partly by the adoption of the so-called Kyoto mechanism which involves collaboration between Annex-I and Non-Annex-I countries.[2] The Kyoto Protocol allows for several 'flexible mechanisms' such as emissions trading that allow Annex I countries to meet their GHG emission caps by purchasing emission reductions credits from elsewhere through financial exchanges and projects that reduce emissions in non-Annex I countries or from Annex I countries with excess allowances. The concept of emission trading was proposed in 1960s by a Canadian economist and has been utilised mainly in the United States (Portney and Stavins, 2010).

Domestically, the Japanese government introduced measures such as the 'eco-point' system which rewarded consumers who bought low carbon dioxide emission cars or install high efficiency electric appliances in their homes. In business sector, the Federation of Japanese Industries (Keidanren) also set voluntary benchmarks for its members in different industries to work towards the Kyoto target. In Japan, about 34 per cent of GHG emission comes from industrial sector, 21 per cent from the transport sector, 19 per cent from service and other sectors, and 14 per cent from households. Keidanren's voluntary efficiency targets differed from industry to industry. For the power sector, it was based on carbon dioxide emission per kilowatt per hour (kWh) while that of the steel sector was by per ton of steel produced. However, despite the efforts by the private enterprises, Keidanren had no intention to make use of voluntary offset credits to be created in voluntary market (Bayon *et al.*, 2009) to achieve its voluntary target. It was widely recognised that Japan would not be able to meet the Kyoto target due to the high abatement costs for the industrial sector, which means that the Clean Development Mechanism (CDM)[3] proposed by Brazilian representatives under the Kyoto Protocol using carbon offsets (Antholis and Talbott, 2010) would have to play a big part in lowering the country's GHG emissions even for private enterprises. The CDM allows a country with an emission-reduction or emission-limitation commitment under the Kyoto Protocol to implement emission reduction projects in developing countries. Such projects can earn Certified Emission Reduction (CER) credits, each equivalent to one tonne of CO_2, which can be traded and counted towards meeting Kyoto targets (Youngman, 2010). A CDM project activity might involve, for example, a rural electrification project using solar panels, fuel-switching schemes or the installation of more energy-efficient boilers. The mechanism stimulates sustainable development and emission reductions, while giving industrialised countries some flexibility in how they meet their emission reduction or limitation targets. Operational since the beginning of 2006, the mechanism has already registered more than 1,650 projects and expected to produce CERs (or carbon credits) amounting to more than 2.9 billion tonnes of CO_2 equivalent for the first commitment period (2008–2012) under the Kyoto Protocol.

Weaning off Nuclear Power

After the Fukushima Daiichi plant shutdown in the wake of the March 2011 natural disasters, it has become less tenable for the government to continue operations of nuclear power plants due to rising opposition from the public and local governments. Japanese power companies operate 50 nuclear power plants with total installed capacity of about 45,000 megawatts (MW) and account for about 30 per cent of total electricity supply amounting to 300 billion kilowatt-hours (kWh) of power annually. Only two plants have since been allowed to operate to avoid blackouts in the Kansai districts. To replace the supply from the nuclear power plants, Japan's nine regional utility companies will have to run their thermal power plants at their maximum loads. Load factors of thermal power plants for May–August 2012 had in fact rose by 13 per cent to 45 per cent period over the same period the previous year with oil consumption up drastically as Figure 2.1 for utilities in the central region shows.

To replace the power supply from the suspended nuclear power plants, the power companies would have to either burn 60 million tons oil or 39 million tons of liquefied natural gas (LNG) or alternatively 90 million tons of coal. Realistically, however coal is not a viable option due to their high carbon emission loads leaving LNG and oil as the best substitutes though most oil-fired plants tend to be of lower efficiency due to their age. But whichever is used, it will add to Japan's overall emission, not to mention issues of energy security as the fuels will have to be imported. Before the 11 March 2011 earthquake, Japan's power companies accounted for about 30 per cent of total carbon dioxide emissions in Japan with 8 million tons of oil, 43 million tons of LNG and 84 million tons coal consumed annually

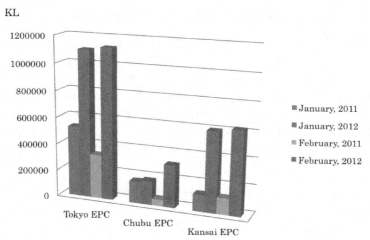

Figure 2.1: Oil Consumption at Central Electric Power Companies.
Source: The Federation of Electric Power Companies.

Table 2.2: Thermal Power Plants in Japan.

Fuel	Units	Installed Capacity(MW)
Coal	69	34,528
Oil	117	45,044
LNG	86	58,773
Total	272	135,804

Source: Ministry of Economy, Trade and Industry (2010).

based on their installed capacities (Table 2.2). If the remaining 48 nuclear power plants in the country stay shut and both LNG and oil-fired plants are used as substitutes for power generation on a 50/50 basis, it will mean that an additional 30 million tons of oil and 19 million tons LNG will be burnt annually.

Further, it means that additional carbon dioxide emission of about 190 million tons will be produced annually. That would see total GHG emissions in Japan increased by 15 per cent. By limiting or abolishing the generation of nuclear power, Japan will have to pursue the increased use of renewable energy such as solar, wind, geothermal, biomass and small hydro power plants more aggressively.

Future Carbon Dioxide Emission under New Energy Policy

While Mr Hatoyama had pledged at United Nations conference in 2009 that Japan would reduce GHG emissions by 25 per cent by 2020 based on 1990 emission levels, it would be impossible to meet this target under current circumstances without the power supply generated by nuclear plants under the new post-Fukushima governmental policy. The new parameters are outlined below on how Tokyo proposed to deal with GHG emissions to tackle climate change:

1. Japan will make efforts to reduce GHG emissions by 80 per cent in 2050 based on 1990 emission levels.
2. Japan will have a target of around 20 per cent GHG reduction by 2030 with the introduction of more renewable energy sources.
3. Japan is unable to cite a specific GHG reduction number by 2020 due to the unclear status of its nuclear power stations, though a range of five to nine per cent in reduction is expected.

At the moment, the most pressing issue facing Japanese policymakers is to ensure there is sufficient means and enough fuel supply to meet the demand of domestic households and the country's industries. They are in no position to adequately address GHG emissions presently due to the uncertainties over the future and status of nuclear power stations. Japan, however, can still certainly contribute to efforts to tackle global warming and climate change issues through GHG reduction projects with other Asian nations under the Kyoto credit offset mechanism.

Use of CDM by Japanese Companies

As noted previously, the Japanese Business Federation or Keidanren has established voluntary GHG emission targets for each industry. Some sectors have taken the path of using emission credits under the Kyoto mechanism to achieve their goals. The power industry for instance has committed to obtaining 260 million tons of credits, mostly from China. While the prices of the credits were not made public, it was believed that the average price would be about 2,000¥ (about US$20) per carbon dioxide ton, which is considerably lower than the estimated US$500 in marginal abatement cost. It has been estimated that the utility companies will spend more than

500 billion ¥ or more than US$5 billion for the purchase of the offset credits. In addition to private sectors, the Japanese government has bought another 100 million tons in credits in case the private sector quota is insufficient to achieve the minus 6 per cent target. It is estimated that both the private and public sectors will spend close to one trillion ¥ for the credits.

The CDM projects undertaken by Japanese companies for credit offsets are, however, not without problems. The process is often tedious and long drawn due to cumbersome, opaque and complicated procedures for methodology approval and MRV (measurement, reporting and verification) and low capability of some DOEs (Designated Operational Entities) (Oko-Institute, 2010). There is also a tendency to concentrate development aid in large projects rather than those at a smaller scale as well as capacity issues including lack of infrastructure, social amenities and regulations as well as human and political resources in some countries (Elsworth and Worthington, 2010). Hence, there seems to be under-representation in certain regions of the world like sub-Saharan Africa whereas more industrialised countries, like China, Brazil and India tend to be the main beneficiaries. As Figure 2.2 shows, China accounts for more than 50 per cent while India has 20 per cent share of CERs or carbon credits issued for CDM projects by host (developing) countries. At some countries, CDM projects were blamed not to reduce GHG emission but to increase overall emission (Bullard *et al.*, 2010) and no real reduction was achievable at some projects in a certain sector (Haya, 2009). Those problems led to opinions for necessity of CDM process reform (Wara and Victor, 2008).

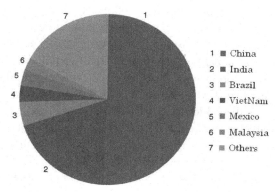

Figure 2.2:
Source: UNFCCC (2012).

Furthermore, in the case of Japan, there is no clear incentive to pursue CDM projects after 2013 due to the fact that Tokyo has not set any specific targets beyond the first commitment period under the Kyoto Protocol. The Japanese government has also said at the 17th session of the Conference of the Parties (COP 17) in South Africa that the Kyoto Protocol has not been proven to be effective as countries with obligations cover only 25 per cent of global emissions — which is why Japan would not set any specific target.

New Approach to International Collaboration

The lack of Japanese commitment to specific targets beyond Kyoto however does not mean that Tokyo will not pursue any actions to lower GHG emissions. In fact, it is encouraging Japanese businesses to look at alternative options. Even in the United States, which did not ratify the Kyoto Protocol, serious arguments on climate change have broken out (Pooley, 2010) and intensity targets instead of absolute reduction numbers have been discussed as an alternative option (Herzog *et al.*, 2006). While EU commission desires to broaden use of CDM credits (EU Commission, 2007), one alternative to the CDM concept is proposed in EU as Sectoral Crediting Mechanism (SCM), which attempts to verify emissions of a broad segment of the economy of a developing country against an agreed baseline. If emissions fall below the baseline, credits would be issued which could be used for compliance with emission reduction targets. In some ways, the SCM is comparable to the CDM except that instead of covering a project-related activity, it would reward sector-wide mitigation efforts (Baron, 2006). According to the proposal, credits would not be directly handed over to the private sector as in the case of CDM but to the government, thereby providing a direct stimulus to implement more climate friendly policies. Under a sectoral mechanism therefore, the host country government would have a more active role than in the CDM and would have to ensure that the emission reductions are actually achieved. The SCM is understood to have some other merits — like for instance, more extensive collaboration is possible as it does not cover one project, but a sector (Aasrud *et al.*, 2009). It can also be applied to the field where CDM project is not approved (Baron and Ellis, 2006). According to one study, it has been estimated that if the SCM is applied to the global steel industry, it would be possible to cut GHG emissions by 340 million tonnes per year (Prins *et al.*, 2009).

In addition to SCM, there is also the bilateral offset crediting mechanism (BOCM) which is actually a Japanese idea. It uses a mechanism to transfer low carbon technologies inclusive of funding through bilateral agreements between a developed and a developing country — like for example Japan and Vietnam — on a number of GHG reducing projects. Both parties would agree on the level and the methodology to achieve the reduction. Credits can be transferred to the developed country when targets are met. The Japanese government is currently in discussions with several Asian countries including India, Indonesia, Thailand and Vietnam to implement BOCM projects in sectors ranging from power, steel, electronics to cement, buildings and construction.

Conclusion

Due to the situation with the country's nuclear plants, it is rather difficult to forecast future GHG emissions in Japan or specify any 2020 target for the reduction of GHG emission. Japan can however play its role in contributions to tackling climate change and global warming issues. The use of the bilateral offset crediting mechanism could be one of the ways it can assist in the sustainable development of developing countries through technology transfer and funding. The issues at the moment would be one of determining the credits volume needed and price levels for transfer to Japan. Developed countries have to make every effort to reduce GHG emissions domestically as well as assist developing countries achieve growth through more effective energy use and introducing ways to cut back on emissions. The ways that Japan can help to reduce the impact of global warming can be summarised below:

- Encourage conservation of energy among domestic households and industries
- Enhance further energy efficiency in industrial output
- Reduce costs in the deployment of renewable energy sources
- Introduce energy efficient facilities to developing countries
- Facilitate software and technology transfer in plant operations to more developing countries
- Establish methodology for BOCM agreements
- Facilitate further discussions with Asian countries on areas for technology transfer

52   *Environmental Policies in Asia*

Endnotes

[1] Article 3 of the Kyoto Protocol defines the details of the first commitments period.

[2] Under the plan, 3.9 per cent of reduction is to be achieved through forest management and 1.6 per cent via the Kyoto offset mechanism.

[3] CDM is defined in Article 12, and JI is in Article 6 of the Kyoto Protocol.

References

Aasrud, André and Richard Baron, Barbara Buchner and Kevin McCall. *Sectoral Market Mechanisms-Issued for Negotiation and Domestic Implementation.* Paris: OECD/IEA, 2009.

Akimoto, Keigo. "Analyses on GHG Mitigation Costs and Measures and their Implications." International Conference on Post-Kyoto Climate Change Mitigation Modelling, Seoul, 2010. Available online at http://www.rite.or.jp/ Japanese/labo/sysken/papers/shiryo/Seoul_Symposium-Akimoto20100617. pdf. Last accessed on 7 August, 2013.

Antholis, William and Strobe Talbott. *Fast Forward.* Washington, DC: Brookings Institution Press, 2010.

Baron, Richard. *Sectoral Approaches to GHG Mitigation: Scenarios for Integration.* Paris: OECD/IEA, 2006.

Baron, Richard and Jane Ellis. *Sectoral Crediting Mechanisms for Greenhouse Gas Mitigation: Institutional and Operational Issues.* Paris: OECD/IEA, 2006.

Bayon, Ricardo, Amanda Hawn and Katherine Hamilton. *Voluntary Carbon Markets.* London: Earthscan, 2009.

Bullard, Nicola (ed.). "The Clean Development Mechanism Projects in the Philippines: Costly Dirty Money-Making Schemes." Focus on the Global South, 2010. Available online at http://focusweb.org/sites/www.focusweb. org/files/CDM%20Web%20version%20lowres.pdf. Last accessed on 19 August, 2013.

Elsworth, Rob and Bryony Worthington. *International Offsets and the EU 2009.* London: Sandbag, 2010.

EU Commission. *Limiting Global Climate Change to 2 Degrees Celsius, 2007 The Way Ahead for 2020 and Beyond.* Brussels: EU Commission, 2007.

Haya, Barbara. *Measuring Emissions Against an Alternative Future: Fundamental Flaws in the Structure of the Kyoto Protocol's Clean Development Mechanism.* Berkeley, CA: University of California Berkeley, 2009.

Herzog, Timothy, Kevin Baumert and Jonathan Pershing. *Intensity An analysis of Greenhouse Gas Intensity Target.* Washington, DC: World Resources Institute, 2006.

IEA (International Energy Agency). *2010 Key World Energy Statistics*. Paris: International Energy Agency, 2010.

Ministry of Economy, Trade and Industry, Government of Japan. *Denryoku-jukyuno Giyou (Outline of Power Supply and Demand) 2009 (in Japanese)*. Tokyo: METI, 2010.

Oko-Institute. *Rating of Designated Operational Entities (DOEs) accredited under the Clean Development Mechanism (CDM)*. Berlin: Oko-Institute, 2010.

Pooley, Eric. *The Climate War*. New York: Hyperion, 2010.

Portney, Paul R. and Robert N. Stavins. *Public Policies for Environmental Protection*. 2nd ed. Washington, DC: Resources for the Future, 2010.

Prins, Gwyn. *The Hartwell Paper New Direction for Climate Policy after the Crash of 2009*. Oxford: Institute for Science, Innovation and Society, University of Oxford, 2009.

The Federation of Electric Power Companies of Japan. "Data of power generation" (in Japanese). N.d. Available online at http://www.fepc.or.jp/library/data/hatsujuden/index.html. Last accessed on 19 August, 2013. UNFCCC (United Nations Framework Convention on Climate Change). "Clean Development Mechanism." 2012. Available online at http://cdm.unfccc.int. Last accessed on 28 September, 2012.

Wara, Michal W. and David G. Victor. "A Realistic Policy on International Carbon Offsets." Working Paper No.74, Stanford University, 2008. Available online at http://pesd.stanford.edu/publications/a_realistic_policy_on_ international_carbon_offsets. Last accessed on 19 August, 2013.

Youngman, Rob. "A Comparison of Greenhouse Gas Emissions Offsets Project Development and Approval Processes." *Background paper for the EPRI Green House Gas Emissions Offset Policy Dialogue* No.8, EPRI, 2010. Available online at http://eea.epri.com/pdf/ghg-offset-policy-dialogue/ workshop08/EPRI_Offsets_Wrkshp8_Background-Paper_Offset-Dvlpmnt-Approval-Processes_Final2_063010.pdf. Last accessed on 19 August, 2013.

ENVIRONMENTAL IMPACTS OF 'FAST DEVELOPMENT' IN ASIA

3. Policies for Environmentally Sustainable Development: Perspectives from Vietnam

NGUYEN Huu Ninh

Vietnam is one of the fast-growing economies in Asia and it is going through wide ranging transformation: from an inward-looking state planned economy to one that is becoming increasingly market-oriented and linked to global markets (World Bank, 2012a). The country has made huge strides in its economic development raising living standards for millions while drastically reducing poverty among its population. Indeed, this Southeast Asian nation has risen from an extremely impoverished to a low middle-income country in an astonishing span of less than two decades. The economy grew on average by about 7.5 per cent per annum in the past decade though the rate did slip to 6.3 per cent since 2008. This is still rather commendable given the extent of the global slowdown. It achieved its middle income status nation — as defined by the World Bank as countries with a per capita income of US$1,000 — in 2008 and now harbours hopes of emulating some of its Asian neighbours with the ambition of joining the ranks of industrialised nations by 2020. Not surprisingly, Vietnam is now increasingly attracting foreign direct investment (FDI) and Official Development Assistance (ODA) from donors such as the World Bank, Asian Development Bank, Japan and the European Union. However, it is still a relatively poor country with an estimated 10.7 per cent of the population living in poverty in 2010, despite a marked improvement from 58.1 per cent in 1993. Much of its economic development had largely relied on the country's own natural resources, particularly agriculture, fisheries, and forestry. Such dependence inevitably puts stress on the environment due to the knock-on effects of deforestation, land degradation, overfishing, and pollution. In fact, it also seems to be experiencing the effects from climate change judging by the higher frequency and intensity of droughts, floods, tropical cyclones as well as threats from rising sea-levels, particularly in the Mekong and Red river deltas (Nguyen Huu Ninh, 2007; Nguyen Huu Ninh *et al.*, 2014). There is certainly a need for Vietnam to devote greater attention to more robust policies aimed at environmental protection and sustainable development. In order to integrate into the UN's framework, the Strategic Orientation for Sustainable Development in Vietnam (Agenda Vietnam 21) was issued by the government in 2004. The Green Growth Strategy (2011–2020) with a vision toward 2050 is being prepared by the Ministry of Planning and Investment (MPI) to be submitted to the government. With these efforts, Vietnam hopes to make greater inroads in achieving the goals of developing a greener economy in the coming decades.

Geographical and Socio-Economic Context

With a coastline of 3,260 km and territorial sea surface of more than 1 million sq km, Vietnam is one of 16 countries with the richest biodiversity in the world (MARD, 2002). It is still largely dominated by an agrarian economy and more than half of the country's population of 87 million derives its livelihood from the fertile Red River and Mekong River deltas. The country is the world's second largest rice exporter with seven million tons shipped abroad in 2011. In addition to rice production, fisheries and aquaculture also contribute significantly to the economy with agriculture alone accounting for 20 per cent of gross domestic product (GDP) in 2010. Although agriculture remains a vital part of Vietnam's economy, its percentage of total national economic output is decreasing in the face of rapid national industrialisation (Index Mundi, 2011).

The Mekong River Delta in southern Vietnam is the "rice stomach" of the country. With an area of 40,000 sq km, the low-level plains are usually not more than three metres above sea level. About 10,000 sq km of the delta are reserved for rice cultivation, making it as one of the major rice-growing regions of the world. The Mekong River is one of the 12 great rivers of the world, 4,200 km long with a catchment area of 795,000 sq km. It is home to 18 million people spread across 13 provinces and cities with a population density of 435 people per square kilometre. It has been estimated that approximately 80 per cent of the delta's population or four out of five denizens are dependent on agriculture. The region accounts for 90 per cent of national rice exports and nearly 60 per cent of the country's exports of fishery products.

With the adoption of the economic policy of *doi moi* (renovation or new changes) since the mid-1980s, Vietnam has made impressive progress in its shift from a centrally planned economy to a more open market-oriented economic system. Its economic growth is in fact only second to China in Asia. In 1986–1987, Vietnam spelled out the following goals of *doi moi* which was to:

- Replace a centrally planned economy with a market economy that has a socialist orientation;
- Build a democratic legalistic society in which the state belongs to the people, is elected by the people and works for the people;
- Carry out an open-door economic policy, promoting cooperation and relations with all countries for the common benefits of development.

The US economic embargo against Vietnam was finally lifted in 1994 prompting the doors of economic reforms to swing even wider and leading to greater inflows of ODA and FDI as Vietnam rebuilt relations anew with international sponsors and financial organisations. Further integration with global markets followed with membership into the Association of Southeast Asian Nations (ASEAN) and ASEAN Free Trade Area (AFTA) in 1995 and accession to the World Trade Organisation (WTO) in 2007.

The key features of Vietnam from the World Bank's annual country reports (World Bank, 2012b; UNDP, 2010) are found in Tables 3.1 and 3.2 below.

The government of Vietnam has rolled out regular five-year socio-economic plans. The average GDP growth rate of the latest 5–year period from 2006 to 2010 was approximately 7 per cent per year with the GDP per capita in 2010 weighing in at about US$1,160. The increased exposure to the global economy however has its drawbacks. The consumer price index (CPI), for instance, rose by 18.13 per cent in 2011, which was a new high for the country's inflation rate. The upshot was that the central bank of Vietnam had to take the drastic action of sharply depreciating the Vietnamese currency on 11 February, 2011 by 7 per cent, the most since 1993. It was also the fourth such devaluation in 15 months which was aimed at curbing the trade deficit as well as narrowing the gap between official and black market currency exchange rates (Bloomberg News, 2011). Vietnam's GDP growth in 2011 was 5.9 per cent, down from 6.8 per cent in 2010. The Central Bank began to lower key lending rates in July 2012 after inflation retreated to a lower rate of 12 per cent. Despite experiencing slower growth

Table 3.1: Basic National Statistics (Data for the Year(s) Indicated).

	Vietnam	Lao PDR	Cambodia
Land area (square kilometres)	331,114	236,800	181,035
Population (millions) (2009)	87.2	6.3	14.8
Urban population (%) (2009)	28	32	22
Annual population growth (%) (2009)	1.2	1.8	1.7
Population below national poverty line (%) (2008)	14.5	27.6	30.1 (2009)
Population below $2 a day (PPP) at 2005 international prices (%) (2008)	38.5	66.0	56.5 (2007)
Gross National Income per capita, Atlas Method (US$) (2009)	1000	880	650
Growth in Gross Domestic Product (GDP) (%) (2008/9)	6.3/5.3	7.3/6.4	6.7/−1.9
Role of agriculture (value added, % of GDP) (2009)	21	35 (2008)	35
Role of industry (value added, % of GDP) (2009)	40	28 (2008)	23

Source: World Bank (2012a).

in 2011–2012, Vietnam remains on track as an emerging growth nation in the medium to long term.

In terms of its economic development, there is however a gap between theory and practice when it comes to issues of managing environmental protection in the country amid the fevered pace of GDP growth. While Vietnam has made progress in the areas of policy development and implementation, it still needs to have better and proper managing tools in environmental protection policymaking. Loopholes in institutional, state management and supervisory frameworks have often given rise to opportunities for corruption, which has direct impact on sustainable development, especially when the country shares its water and aquaculture resources with several neighbouring countries.

State Policies on Environment and Sustainable Development

The Law on Environmental Protection was passed on 27 December, 1993 by the National Assembly and came into effect on 10 January, 1994 with the aim of providing environmental protection while sustaining the pace of

Table 3.2: Key Development Indicators of the Lower Mekong Nations and Other Selected Nations in Southeast Asia.

Indicators	Cambodia	Lao PDR	Vietnam	Thailand	Myanmar
Human Development Index Rank (2010)	124	122	113	92	132
Human Development Index value (2010)	0.494	0.497	0.572	0.654	0.451
Gender Inequality Index (updated) Rank (2008)	124	122	113	92	n/a
Gender Inequality Index (updated) Value (2008)	0.641	0.644	0.464	0.536	n/a
Ratio of income share of richest 10% to poorest 10% (2007)	11.5	7.3	9.7	13.1	n/a
Education index (2007)	0.704	0.68	0.81	0.88	0.78
Education index rank (2007)	137	133	116	87	138
Life expectancy at birth (years) (2010)	62.2	65.9	74.5	69.3	62.7
Population using an improved drinking water source (%) (2008)	61	57	94	98	71
People living with HIV, ages 15–49 (%) (2007)	0.80	0.20	0.50	1.40	0.70

Sources: Compiled by author with data from UNDP (2012), MDGI (2012), World Bank (2012a).

economic development of the country (National Assembly of S.R. Vietnam, 1994). It is estimated that economic losses arising from environmental damage account for 1.5–3.0 per cent of GDP. This does not include the knock-on effects estimated at hundreds of millions of dollars in health care related burdens foisted upon the larger community. Consequently, environmental problems must be identified and solutions put forward in the next five years in order to mobilise the resources needed to fulfil the goals set in the "national strategy for environmental protection to 2010 with a vision to 2020" (MONRE, 2010a).

In 2003, the government kick started the national strategy for environmental protection with the launch of 36 programmes, projects and schemes aimed at pollution control, prevention and improvement of the environment. In 2004, the Vietnam Communist Party issued the Politburo Resolution No. 41-NQ/TW on Environmental Protection taking into account the country's accelerated pace of industrialisation and modernisation. In late November 2005, its lawmakers passed a revised Law on Environmental Protection (National Assembly of S.R. Vietnam, 2005) with updates and significant changes made to the initial framework established in 1993. The Prime Minister's Office also stepped into the fray and issued a National Action Program in 2005 providing more detailed and specific legal guidance in areas such as pollution control, waste management, strategic environmental assessment (SEA) and environmental impact assessment (EIA). They also covered in greater detail how to deal with management of river basin areas and marine biodiversity, environmental monitoring, financial support and incentives, technology development and setting of environmental technical standards among other measures. Steps were also taken to expand the scope of environmental protection planning, monitoring, and development process from the central government to provincial and city levels. The Strategic Orientation for Sustainable Development in Vietnam was approved by the state in 2004, and is a framework which defines strategic direction as well as provides a legal foundation that enabled ministries, local authorities, organisations and individuals to coordinate and carry out measures to ensure sustainable development into the 21st century (S.R. Vietnam, 2004) in the following areas:

1. Sustainable development in accordance with Vietnam's projected growth
2. Identify key economic areas for sustainable development
3. Identify key social areas for sustainable development
4. Prioritisation of areas in utilisation of natural resources, environment protection, and pollution control for sustainable development
5. Implementation of sustainable development programmes

Giving the new stance towards future sustainability, priority should be placed with regards to natural resource utilisation, environment protection, and pollution control from the following perspectives:

1. Institutional and legal
2. Economic
3. Science, technology, and environmental
4. Social and public awareness

These steps are necessary if Vietnam is to realise its drive for greener growth. This would require the need to restructure its economy with an aim of raising economic efficiencies and competitiveness, while effectively reducing greenhouse gas in response to climate changes.

Climate Change Predictions

The Fourth Assessment Report of the Intergovernmental Panel on Climate Change (IPCC) had indicated that climate change will seriously affect developing countries. Vietnam was cited as one of the countries that is most vulnerable to the adverse impact of climate change (IPCC, 2007; Dasgupta *et al.*, 2007). The Ministry of Natural Resources and Environment (MONRE) has since been assigned to oversee the issues and challenges facing Vietnam as spelt out by the United Nations Framework Convention on Climate Change (UNFCCC). According to the UNFCCC, these are some of the possible impact of climate change and scenarios facing Vietnam (MONRE 2003, 2010b):

- The average temperature in the medium term may increase by 2.4–2.6°C by the end of 21st century. Inland average temperature mainly in the northern highlands will rise by 2.8°C. These temperature increases will create drought leading to heavy losses in agricultural crops and an increase in the occurrence of epidemic diseases in most parts of the country.
- By 2100, the annual rainfall in the Northern Zone is projected to increase by 7.3 to 7.9 per cent. The increase in the South Central Zone will be smaller, averaging 1.0 to 3.2 per cent. Rainfall is projected to decline during the dry season in almost every zone, but particularly in the south. Overall rainfall is likely to rise in all parts of the country during the rainy season. Hence total annual rainfall is set to increase throughout the country.
- Annual river flows in the northern parts of the North Central Coast are set to increase. In contrast, the flows in the South Central Coast are expected to decrease. Flood flows in most rivers will increase while flows during dry season are expected to decline.
- The evapotranspiration rate or loss of water from the soil by evaporation and transpiration from plants will also rise by 7–10 per cent for 2050, and 12–16 per cent for 2100 due to shifts in temperatures. As rainfall is concentrated during the rainy season, rainfall during the dry season will decrease by 2100 in the central regions and droughts will be more frequent.
- Sea levels may rise by 28–33 cm come 2050 and 100 cm by 2100 compared to the corresponding 1980–1999 base levels. The World Bank (2007) has indicated that with a coastline of 3,260 km and with two of the largest river deltas in the world, Vietnam will be one of top

ten countries in the world that will bear the brunt of damages brought about by climate change. With rising sea levels, the annual flood-ridden areas will expand with the impact will be most likely to be felt in the Mekong River Delta where 90 per cent of the flood plains are located. The rise in sea levels may also lead to higher risks of saltwater intrusion of rivers and underground water resources, causing serious social and economic losses. If the sea level rises by 100 cm, it would potentially lead to a land loss of over 5 per cent and displacement of 11 per cent of Vietnam's population. As a consequence of climate change, Vietnam is one of the most disaster-prone countries in the world. According to MONRE (2009), about six to eight storms and tropical depressions hit Vietnam each year over the period between 1960 and 2005. The runoff from rains, when added to rivers already swollen by monsoon rains threatens to devastate millions of households with water inundation. Disasters in Vietnam occur in all geographical areas and economic zones with most severe damage caused by tropical storms, water inundation, drought, salt water intrusion, storm surge, landslides and flash floods (Table 3.3). Between 1989 and 2008, Vietnam lost at least 1 per cent of its annual GDP to natural disasters.

Perspectives on Green Economy

The world enters the 21st century with many new challenges such as population, poverty, environmental degradation, climate change and economic crises. The Rio+20 Policy focused mainly on transitions to from pollution-producing or 'brown' economies to green economies and institutional frameworks for sustainable development (Rio+20, 2012).

The green economy is important because the balance of nature may become irreversible if the degradation of the Earth's environment reaches a critical threshold where human existence is threatened. With the green economy in place, local ecosystem services can be preserved, and not overwhelmed by the aggregate destruction caused by the brown economy. By scaling up the green economy in global communities while lessening the negative impact of brown economic activities, it is possible to achieve sustainability for communities and societies living within their carrying capacities.

There is a need to shift away from the old mind-set of using gross domestic product (GDP) per capita as a primary gauge of economic progress. This

Table 3.3: Disasters in Different Geographic Areas and Economic Zones.

Disaster	Geographic Areas and Economic Zones							
	North East and North West	Red River Delta	North Central Coast	South Central Coast	Central Highlands	Southern East	Mekong River Delta	Coastal Economic Zone
Storm	***	****	****	****	**	***	***	****
Flood	—	****	****	***	***	***	*****	****
Flash flood	***	—	***	***	***	***	*	***
Whirlwind	**	**	**	**	*	**	**	**
Drought	***	*	**	***	**	***	*	***
Desertification	—	—	*	**	**	**	*	**
Saline intrusion	—	*	**	**	*	**	***	**
Inundation	**	***	**	**	—	**	***	***
Landslide	—	**	**	**	*	**	***	**
Storm surge	—	**	**	**	**	**	***	**
Fire	**	*	**	***	—	***	***	***
Industrial and environmental hazard	—	**	**	**	***	***	**	***

Key: Very severe (****), Severe (***), Medium (**), Light (*), None (—)
Source: Ministry of Agriculture and Rural Development and CCFSC (2005).

needs to be done by taking into account natural, ecological, social, human and produced capital, and not just economic output. This approach as seen in the Human Security Index can only be met by taking initial steps to restructure economic activities and infrastructure by investing in natural and human resources in order to lower greenhouse gas emission, use less natural resources, generate less waste and reduce social inequality.

The Green Growth Strategy is by the Ministry of Planning and Investment (MPI) integrated into both the Socioeconomic Development Strategy 2011–2020 and Strategic Orientation for Sustainable Development. The necessity of Vietnam's green economy is based on the following facts:

- Low productivity, efficiency and economic competiveness;
- Growth in a brown economy is often characterised by reliance on cheap labour, low efficiency in the exploitation and depletion of non-renewable natural resources while polluting the environment with attendant risks to the community;
- Environmentally sound economic sectors have yet to be fully developed;
- Energy needs are currently mostly met by fossil-derived sources which has lower efficiency;
- Climate change impact especially in Mekong River and Red River deltas;
- Threat of decline in exports in times of financial recession on global scale.

Given the necessity of shifting away from the unsustainable, brown economic model, the objectives of green economy require a strategy incorporating the following actions:

- Incentivise and encourage economic activities to use natural resources more efficiently while phasing out the sectors that are wasteful or contribute to a higher degree of environmental pollution;
- Upgrading of technology with the aim to better deploy natural resources and reduce greenhouse gas emission in response to the threats of climate change; and
- Improving livelihoods by generating employment in green industries and establishing ecologically sound environs and communal lifestyles.

The various ways how green growth can be attained is shown in Figure 3.1.

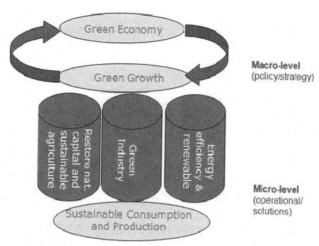

Figure 3.1: Green Growth is Driven by Sector-Strategy Realisation of Green Growth and Green Economy in Related Sectors.
Source: MPI, 2012.

There are three key strategic directions for Vietnam to take towards achieving a green economy — reducing greenhouse gas emission; having greener production output; and encouraging greener lifestyles and consumption habits. These will be challenges, but at the same time also opportunities for enterprises to take steps to comply with regulations on environmental practices and look into areas where they can contribute to corporate social responsibility. These efforts towards a greener economy will not only mitigate the impact of climate change but also reap other benefits such as enabling Vietnamese businesses to compete with leading foreign enterprises in offering eco-friendly products and services (Figure 3.2) in global markets.

The Vietnam Green Label initiative by the Ministry of Natural Resources and Environment for example is designed to help enterprises compete both locally and globally. According to the quantitative indexes and targets set up by Ministry of Planning and Investment (MPI), the average GDP per capita will double over the 2010 level by 2020 while energy consumption per capita reduced by 2.5–3.0 per cent per year and greenhouse gas emission lowered by 10–15 per cent under the proposed green strategic roadmap for Vietnam. With a modern and efficient economic structure, the value of hi-tech products and services will account for about 42–45 per cent of total GDP with the aggregate productivity of this sector contributing to about 35 per cent of Vietnam's economic growth over this period. By

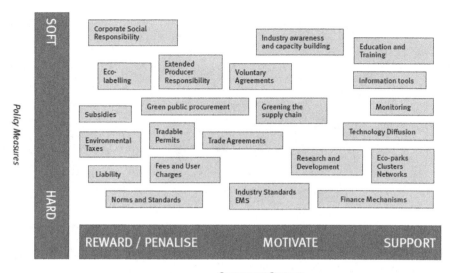

Government Strategy

Figure 3.2: Green Policy Matrix for Greening of Sectors.
Source: MPI, 2012.

2030, Vietnam will achieve middle-income country status; develop sufficient and appropriate material, technical, human, and institutional bases for a widespread implementation of green growth economic and social activities. Annual total greenhouse gas emission will be lowered by 2–3 per cent each year with the aggregate productivity of the green sectors contributing to at least 50 per cent of national growth. By 2050, green energy and technologies are expected to be widely used. The state is meanwhile developing a green gross domestic product (GDP) index expected to be ready for use in 2014 to track progress in the coming decades.

The roadmap to a green economy will however need the co-operation of top-tier companies to form a core group for its initial implementation, followed by the necessity to facilitate the transfer of green technology to small and medium enterprises (SME) which make up 98 per cent of Vietnam's businesses and contribute to a sizable proportion of national economic growth. According to the MPI, about 544,394 enterprises were registered during the first half of 2010. These included more than 39,500 new businesses with a total registered capital of VND230.2 trillion ($11.2 billion) (Business-in-Asia.com, 2011). However, I would suggest the relation between climate change, business and growth will have to be taken

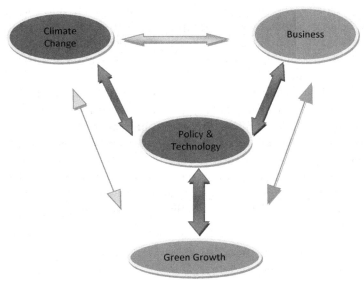

Figure 3.3: The Relevance between Climate Change, Business and Green Growth.

into consideration in medium and long-term planning that will need innovations in technology and policymaking to play key roles in efforts towards a greener economy (Figure 3.3).

Conclusion

Sustainable development which ensures equitable economic growth while taking into account issues pertaining to health, security and socioeconomic wellbeing will require limits being placed on societies in order to protect natural ecosystems in the face of vulnerability to the impact of human population growth (Adger *et al.* 2001).

There are still questions on how Vietnam will be able to direct its national policy towards a sustainable green oriented strategy for the future even as it shows its commitment to tackle climate change by following a "green roadmap." A number of emerging issues will have to be confronted in order to achieve a balance between economic and social values. There are three areas of priority to address with regards to Vietnam's development path in coming decades.

First, there are the challenges relating to globalisation and the impact of climate change which include risks pertaining to regulation, reputation and litigation. Vietnam, as a latecomer to the open global market should learn from international experiences to seek improvement on how to manage its own development.

Second, Vietnam must follow an economic path that is aligned with global greening efforts, while at the same time ensuring efforts are been made to take into consideration the equity and wellbeing of its citizens, particularly those in rural areas where 70 per cent of its population are still dependent on agriculture for their livelihood.

Third, the legal system and socioeconomic restructure should be re-engineered to become more flexible in order to address the many local, regional, and global challenges and realise the diverse opportunities emanating from a greener economy in the coming decades.

References

Adger, Neil W., Mick Kelly and Nguyen Huu Ninh. *Living with Environmental Change: Social Vulnerability, Adaptation and Resilience in Vietnam.* London: Routledge, 2001.

Bloomberg News. "Vietnam Must Tackle Inflation After Dong Devaluation, IMF, City Group Says." February 12, 2011. Available online at http://www.bloomberg.com/news/2011-02-11/vietnam-s-record-devaluation-adds-urgency-for-action-on-prices-imf-says.html. Last accessed on 12 August, 2013.

Business-in-Asia.com. "Small Medium Enterprise (SME) in Vietnam." 2011. Available online at http://www.business-in-asia.com/vietnam/sme_in_vietnam.html. Last accessed on 12 August, 2012.

CCFSC (Central Committee for Flood and Storm Control) and MARD (Ministry of Agriculture and Rural Development), Government of Vietnam. "National Report on Disasters in Vietnam, Vietnam Central Committee for Flood and Storm Control." Working paper for the World Conference on Disaster Reduction. Kobe-Hyogo, Japan, 2005. Available online at http://www.unisdr.org/2005/mdgs-drr/national-reports/Vietnam-report.pdf. Last accessed on 13 August, 2013.

Dasgupta, Susmita and others. "The Impact of Sea Level Rise on Developing Countries: a Comparative Analysis." World Bank Policy Research Working Paper No. 4136, 2007. Available online at http://econ.worldbank.org/external/default/main?pagePK=64165259&theSitePK=469372&piPK=64165421&menuPK=64166093&entityID=000016406_20070209161430. Last accessed on 12 August, 2013.

Index Mundi. "Vietnam Economy Profile." 2011. Available online at http://www. indexmundi.com/vietnam/economy_profile.html. Last accessed on 12 July, 2011.

IPCC (Intergovernmental Panel on Climate Change). *Fourth Assessment Report of Climate Change*. Cambridge, U.K.: Cambridge University Press. 2007.

MARD (Ministry of Agriculture and Rural Development), Government of Vietnam. "National Strategies on Managing Reserves of Vietnam 2002–2010." 2002. Available online at http://asia.ifad.org/web/vietnam/ resources?p_p_id=1_WAR_resource_libraryportlet&_1_WAR_resource_library portlet_jspPage = %2Fhtml%2Fresource_library%2Fentry_detail.jsp&_1_ WAR_resource_libraryportlet_entryId=1077. Last accessed on 10 September, 2012.

MDG (Millennium Development Goals). "Millennium Development Goals Indicators." 2012. Available online at http://unstats.un.org/unsd/mdg/Default. aspx. Last accessed on 13 August, 2013.

MONRE (Ministry of Natural Resources and Environment), Government of Vietnam. "Initial National Communication under the United Nations Framework Convention on Climate Change." 2003. Available online at http:// unfccc.int/resource/docs/natc/vnmnc01.pdf. Last accessed on 12 August, 2012.

MONRE (Ministry of Natural Resources and Environment), Government of Vietnam. "Vietnam Climate Change, Sea-level Rise Scenarios." 2009. Available online at http://www.preventionweb.net/files/11348_ClimateChange SeaLevelScenariosforVi.pdf. Last accessed on 13 August, 2013.

MONRE (Ministry of Natural Resources and Environment), Government of Vietnam. "Report on National Environment Status." 2010a. Available online at http://www.theredddesk.org/sites/default/files/national_env_strategy_1. pdf. Last accessed on 13 August, 2013.

MONRE (Ministry of Natural Resources and Environment), Government of Vietnam. "Second National Communication under the United Nations Framework Convention on Climate Change." 2010b. Available online at http://unfccc.int/resource/docs/natc/vnmnc02.pdf. Last accessed on 21 August, 2013.

MPI (Ministry of Planning and Investment), Government of Vietnam. "Vietnam's Green Growth Strategy." 2012. Available online at http://www.greengrowth-elearning.org/pdf/VietNam-GreenGrowth-Strategy.pdf. Last accessed on 13 August, 2012.

National Assembly of S.R.Vietnam. "Environmental Protection Law." Vietnam, 1994.

National Assembly of S.R.Vietnam. "Environmental Protection Law (Revised)." Vietnam, 2005.

Nguyen Huu Ninh. "Flooding in Mekong River Delta, Vietnam." *UNDP Human Development Report 2007/2008* 53 (2007).

Nguyen Huu Ninh and others. "Socio vulnerability to climate change in Cambodia, Lao PDR and Vietnam." In *Sustainable Development: Asia-Pacific Perspectives,* edited by Pak Sum Low. Cambridge University Press, 2014 (forthcoming).

Rio+20 Policy Brief. "Interconnected Risks and Solutions for a Planet Under Pressure." *Rio+20 Policy Brief* 5, 2012. Available online at http://www.planetunderpressure2012.net/pdf/policy_interconissues.pdf. Last accessed on 19 July, 2012.

Socialist Republic of *Vietnam. The Strategic Orientation for Sustainable Development in Vietnam.* Hanoi, Vietnam, 2004. Available online at http://va21.gov.vn/Images/Upload/file/VN%20A21_EN.pdf. Last accessed on 7 August, 2012.

UNDP (United Nations Development Programme). "Human Development Report: The Real Wealth of Nations: Pathways to Human Development." 2010. Available online at http://hdr.undp.org/en/reports/global/hdr2010/chapters/. Last accessed on 12 August, 2013.

UNDP (United Nations Development Programme). "International Human Development Indicators." 2012. Available online at http://hdr.undp.org/en/statistics/. Last accessed on 13 August, 2013.

World Bank. "World Development Indicators." 2012a. Available online at http://data.worldbank.org/indicator. Last accessed on 16 July, 2012.

World Bank. "Vietnam Overview". 2012b. Available online at http://www.worldbank.org/en/country/vietnam/overview. Last accessed on 16 July, 2012.

4. Resource-Environmental Foundation for Green and Low-Carbon Development in China

ZHU Shou-xian

Global warming induced by anthropogenic greenhouse gas (GHG) emissions has become a growing focus of global attention. Green and low-carbon development has emerged and evolved as a new concept. This is noticeable from the United Nations Framework Convention on Climate Change (UNFCCC) to the Kyoto Protocol, to the contentious post-Kyoto negotiations to escalating discussions on development and emission rights. It is imperative for China to make the necessary transition from reliance on high-carbon emitting conventional fossil fuels to a low-carbon template for its future development.

As the world's largest emitter and the largest developing country, China has to cope with the challenge of balancing its consumption of natural resources while maintaining stability in ways that may not be comparable to other countries. This is especially so in the light of its growing population who aspire higher standards of living in the coming decades. To be sure, mounting pressures will emerge, to arrest the erosion or even destruction of an already fragile ecosystem. This is indeed inevitable, given the rampant consumption of the nation's natural resources, especially if the state continues to adhere to its well-worn path of a headlong rush into untrammelled economic growth which was characteristic of the past decades. There is hence a serious need to rethink and reshape the country's development plans towards a greener and lower carbon blueprint. This ought to be implemented by carefully balancing the deployment of natural resources, making genuine improvements to the management and sustainability of its environment landscape. At the same time, it needs to pace with its economic development. However, more in-depth research and studies will be needed if China wants to attain this future roadmap towards a lower carbon path to national economic development.

International Comparative Study on Resource Environmental Foundation for Green and Low Carbon Development in China

Opinions currently vary widely as to how to achieve green and low-carbon developmental paths due to the lack of veritable international yardsticks. Britain was the first to raise the concept of low-carbon economy with the goal of building a low-carbon economy by 2050. Japan followed suit when it also announced its ambition to attain the same goal by 2050. These notions of low-carbon economies in both countries assume that there will be corresponding efforts by the international community to also reduce greenhouse gas emissions. It has also become vogue for big cities such as London and New York to put forward similar development blueprints as evident by the formation of the low-carbon city alliance or "C40 Cities" (C40, 2013). In 2010, China made similar pronouncements with the launch of an experimental, national low-carbon project (NDRC, 2010). One that will be implemented in five provinces — Guangdong, Liaoning, Hubei, Shaanxi and Yunnan and eight cities, namely Tianjin, Chongqing, Shenzhen, Xiamen, Hangzhou, Nanchang, Guiyang and Baoding. Officials in these provinces and cities have promised to commit to the research and development of low-carbon plans, accelerate the establishment of lower-carbon emitting industrial hubs and proactively promote low-carbon lifestyles and consumption habits to help tackle global climate changes.

To evaluate the green and low-carbon development of a country or an economic entity, a holistic approach should be adopted instead of merely measuring emissions but ignoring links to the global community from both import and export channels. The Copenhagen Declaration for Low Carbon City Development Indicators for example (CCDLCCDI, 2008), points out those indicators should include not only internal emissions, but also take into consideration the carbon footprints arising from trade related linkages. Regarding green and low-carbon development as a development form in which both carbon productivity and human development can advance (Pan, 2012), this chapter proposes the following seven indicators as guides to evaluate efforts by a country or an economic entity to a achieve green and low-carbon course of development:

1. Per capita carbon emission
2. Carbon productivity
3. Technical standards
4. Energy structure
5. Carbon emission elasticity
6. Impact of imports & exports
7. Environmental carrying capacity.

Per Capita Carbon Emission

Per capita carbon emission is not only closely correlated to a discrete phase of economic development, but production and consumption patterns. According to Carbon Dioxide Information Analysis Center (CDIAC, 2013), a unit of the US Department of Energy (DOE), the per capita emission of CO_2 in China in 2010 was 6.1 tonnes; India 1.7 tonnes; Indonesia 2.0 tonnes; Japan 8.9 tonnes; Malaysia 7.02 tonnes; Singapore 7.04 tonnes; Vietnam 1.8 tonnes with the world average weighing in at 4.9 tonnes (World Bank, 2013). Research shows that per capita GHG emission and per capita GDP has a relation similar to a misshapen, reversed U curve, with developing countries including China still on side of the rising arc (Zhuang, 2008). Developing countries are still in the process of industrialisation, urbanisation and modernisation, which is often characterised by a huge appetite for energy. Hence, they have to confront the challenging tasks of economic and social development.[1]

But as pointed out in the "Stern Review", the positive correlation between per capita income growth and per capita emission will often become protracted if there is insufficient policy intervention globally to mitigate such trends (Stern, 2007). Consequently, per capita carbon emission is an important indicator for the evaluation of green and low-carbon development (see Figure 4.1).

Carbon Productivity

Carbon productivity refers to GDP output per equivalent tonne of carbon emission. It has a reciprocal relationship to carbon emission per GDP, and is usually used to measure economic efficiency. It is directly

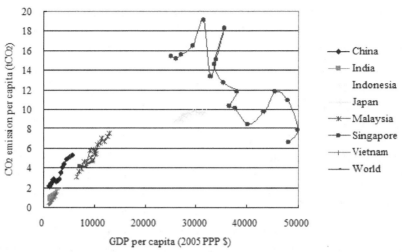

Figure 4.1: Per Capita GDP and Per Capita Carbon Emissions in 7 Countries (1990–2008) (World Bank, 2013).

correlated to per capita carbon emission and per capita GDP, but not with income levels. According to World Resources Institute (WRI), Sweden had the highest carbon productivity of $6684 per tonne of CO_2 in 2008 among developed countries, with Singapore weighing in at $5241/tCO_2$ and Japan at $3380/tCO_2$. The corresponding figures for developing countries saw India coming in at $2088/tCO_2$, Indonesia $2046/tCO_2$, Malaysia $1842/tCO_2$, Vietnam $1814/tCO_2$, China $1050/tCO_2$. Interestingly, some highly underdeveloped countries had very high carbon productivity ratings in the survey. These include Afghanistan with the highest ranking of $35,087/tCO_2$ followed by Chad and Mali in second and third placing. As an indicator for low-carbon development, carbon productivity is the best indicator to evaluate countries at comparable levels of economic development. Among 30 OECD countries, Turkey for example, is the only country with a Human Development Index (HDI) score of less than 0.74 which places it in the high HDI category. The carbon productivity levels of OECD countries generally fall between $1368\sim6685/tCO_2$ with the average coming in at $3468/tCO_2$. The HDI of 20 African countries are less than 0.5 while the average carbon productivity is as high as $6113/tCO_2$ (see Figure 4.2), which is much higher than the average for OECD countries.

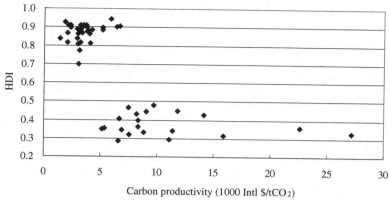

Figure 4.2: Carbon Productivity and HDI in Different Countries (IEA, n.d.; UNDP, n.d.).

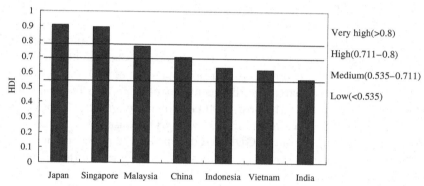

Figure 4.3: HDI in Different Countries (UNDP, n.d.).

Technical standards

Technical standards can refer to physical standards (such as emission per ton steel, per kilometre, per unit electricity) or specific technology (such as super-critical units), as well as policy standards (such as those relating to mileage, tail pipe gas emission, building energy efficiency). Take the example of a coal-fired power plant: The average coal consumption for power generation in China in 2005 was 374g/kWh, far behind advanced international levels such as 320g/kWh for Japan's Tokyo Electricity Co; 331.6g/kWh for France's Electricity Co. or 332.1g/kWh for Bavaria Electricity Co. in Germany in 1999. This meant that the coal efficiency for electric power generation for the sector in China as a whole in 2005 was about 50g/kWh lower than the level in aforementioned countries a few years earlier (Zhang, 2006). A closer look reveals that large units in China have similar efficiency with those of their international peers. The average efficiency, however, is much lower due to the large number of smaller power plants operating in the country. Another example is tail pipe gas standards. The EU had adopted Level IV standards in 2006, while Level III wasn't adopted in Beijing until 2005 and the rest of China until 2007. The EU mandated Level V standards in 2011, while China only adopted Level IV in 2010. Due to disparity in economic development, the gap in the timeline for the adoption of such technical standards can sometimes lead to the emergence of technology or trade barriers. The transformation to a low-carbon economy would not be possible without technology advancement. Technical innovation is one of the core driving forces, and hence an integral indicator of the state of progress in a low-carbon economy. Table 4.1 shows the comparison of energy consumption data in key sectors in China versus advanced international norms.

Figure 4.4 demonstrates the consistency of three trends and in particular the close correlation between energy consumption and CO2 emissions. Figure 4.5 shows that energy consumption per unit of GDP is declining due to technological progress. A divergent pattern can also be seen from Figure 4.1 with respect to the post-2000 GDP performance of China *vis-à-vis* its energy consumption in conjunction with CO2 emissions. The nation's energy consumption per unit of GDP had dropped by 72 per cent from 1978 to 2010 (at 1978 constant prices). It is reasonable to attribute this trend to the advances achieved by improved energy efficiencies due to better utilisation of technology.

Energy structure

Carbon emission is largely caused by fossil energy consumption — with that of oil lower than coal but higher than natural gas. Green plants are carbon-neutral, while renewable energy, such as solar, hydro, wind and nuclear energy, is considered clean zero-carbon energy forms (Zhang, 2003). Greenhouse gas (GHG) as identified in the Kyoto Protocol, includes the following six gases: CO_2, CH_4, N2O, SF_6, HFCs and PFCs. CO_2 accounts for 80 per cent of all GHG emissions. Energy structures can be evaluated by two indicators: energy carbon intensity (carbon emission per unit energy) which reflects the national energy consumption structure (see Figure 4.6); and the proportion of zero-carbon energy (from renewable energy sources). Both are

Table 4.1: Comparison of Primary Energy Consumption Levels Between China and Advanced International Yardsticks.

Energy Consumption by Industry (kgce refers to kilogram of coal equivalent)	China			International Advanced level	Gap (2007)	
	2000	2005	2007		Per unit	+%
Coal Consumption for Thermal Power Supply/ gce/kWh	392	370	356	312	44	14.1
Comparable Energy Consumption of Steel/kgce/t (Large and Medium-Sized Enterprises)	784	714	668	610	58	9.5
AC Electrolytic Aluminum Consumption/ kWh/t	15, 480	14, 680	14, 488	14, 100	388	2.8
Overall Energy Consumption of Copper Smelting/kgce/t	1, 277	780	610	500	110	22.0
Overall Energy Consumption of Cement/kgce/t	181	167	158	127	31	24.4
Overall Energy Consumption Flat Glass/ kgce/weight box	25	22	17	15	2	13.3
Overall Energy Consumption of Crude Oil Processing/ kgce/t	118	114	110	73	37	50.7
Overall Energy Consumption of Ethylene/kgce/t	1, 125	1, 073	984	629	355	56.4

(Continued)

Table 4.1: (*Continued*)

Energy Consumption by Industry (kgce refers to kilogram of coal equivalent)	China			International Advanced level	Gap (2007)	
	2000	2005	2007		Per unit	+%
Overall Energy Consumption of Ammonia/kgce/t	1,699	1,650	1,553	1,000	553	55.3
Overall Energy Consumption of Caustic Soda/ kgce/t	1,435	1,297	1,203	910	293	32.2
Overall Energy Consumption of Sodium Carbonate/ kgce/t	406	396	363	310	53	17.1
Power Consumption of Calcium Carbide/kWh/t		3,450	3,418	3,030	388	12.8

Source: 2050 China Energy and CO_2 Emissions Report, 2009.

factored into total primary energy consumption figures. With regards to the first indicator, IEA data shows that in 2009, North Korea had the highest energy carbon intensity of 3.44 tCO2/toe (carbon dioxide emitted per ton of oil equivalent). Among developed countries, Singapore weighed in at 2.43tCO2/toe and Japan at 2.32tCO2/toe while the figure for developing countries such as India was 2.35tCO2/toe and China 3.03tCO2/toe. As to the second indicator, China had previously set targets of renewable energy accounting for 10 per cent by 2010 and 15 per cent by 2020 in its developmental plans compared to the EU's target of 20 per cent by 2020 (Zhuang, 2008).

Carbon emission elasticity

Carbon emission elasticity refers to the rate of carbon emissions relative to the rate of increase in GDP. The goal of green and low-carbon development is to achieve high economic growth with a low-carbon rate

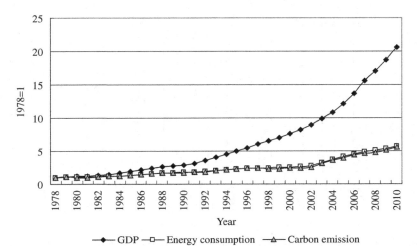

Figure 4.4: GDP, Energy Consumption and CO₂ Emission of China (1978–2010) (At 1978 Constant Price).

Source: China Statistical Yearbook, 2011.

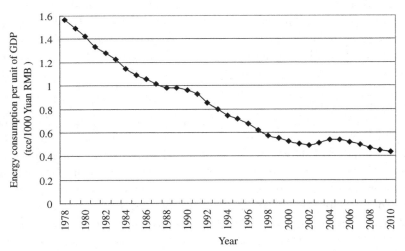

Figure 4.5: China's energy consumption per unit of GDP (1978–2010) (At 1978 constant price).

Source: China Statistical Yearbook, 2011.

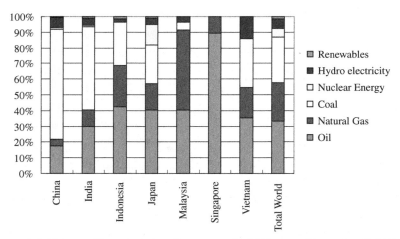

Figure 4.6: Energy Consumption Structure in Different Countries (2010).
Source: BP (2011).

increase. Low-carbon development can be categorised into "absolute low-carbon development" and "relative low-carbon development" based on carbon emission elasticity (Tapio, 2005). Absolute low-carbon development is defined as carbon emission elasticity lower than 0; while relative low-carbon development is defined as carbon emission elasticity between 0 and 0.8 (Lei and Zhuang, 2011). Based on the Climate Analysis Indicators Tool's (CAIT) database and analyses of the carbon emission elasticity of the world's 20 largest emitter countries through six 5-year periods (1975–1980; 1980–1985; 1985–1990; 1990–1995; 1995–2000 and 2000–2005, it was found that developed countries including the US, Britain, Germany, Canada, Australia, Italy, Spain, France, Japan and Russia each underwent at least one episode of decoupling (that is when the carbon emission elasticity fell below 0) during the periods surveyed. Though some developing countries experienced negative readings for their carbon emission elasticity, it was observed that those episodes had stemmed mainly from negative economic growth. Most showed carbon emission elasticity readings in the 0–0.8 range for the survey. An ideal transition towards low-carbon state of economic development would be one that demonstrates declining carbon emission elasticity amid positive economic growth. Thus, carbon emission elasticity is a helpful tool to evaluate the status of low-carbon economy development from a macroeconomic perspective, though the validity can be skewed by economic fluctuations. However, there is still widespread debate over the use of this indicator as merely focusing on the decoupling of carbon emission and economic performance by itself cannot be a guarantee of signs of GHG improvement or stabilisation.

Import and export linkages

Globalisation has enhanced the integration of the world's economy leading to a deepening correlation between trade development and economic growth as well as a continuous increase of the ratio of international trade to global GDP. In this context, China has become the main production and manufacturing base with its economy becoming increasingly dependent on international trade. Its total imports and exports have both experienced growth rates of more than 20 per cent each year since 2001. In 2011, China's trade with the rest of the world amounted to US$3.6 trillion. Its imports comprised a fair proportion of high value-added products while exports include a high percentage of low value-added energy intensive products. The country's "biological trade deficit" is also expanding due to net exports with research showing that roughly a quarter of the total primary energy consumed in China is used for the production of exports (Chen *et al.*, 2008). There is, however, widespread contention over how embedded energy or carbon can be factored into the calculus of achieving a low-carbon economy as the trade data is not easily available. As a result, this chapter will not include it in the indicators being used.

Environmental carrying capacity

The study of environmental carrying capacity is significant in that it helps to determine what triggers our economic behaviour and hence how it can be channelled into the development of a low-carbon living environment. There are already huge pressures exerted on China's ecosystems from the discharge of water and solid waste as well as gas emissions that have led to high social costs. The annual cost of economic losses and environmental damage exceeded 1.4 trillion Yuan RMB ($220 billion) in 2009, up 9.2 per cent from the year before, according to the Chinese Environmental and Economic Accounting Report (Wang, 2009). China has only 1.2 per cent of global crude oil proven reserves and 70 per cent of its energy demand is met by the burning of coal which has led to severe air pollution from the emission of CO_2, SO_2, NOX. The 12th Five-Year-Plan was the first to look into the issue of economic development based on a greener and low-carbon blueprint. To build a resource-conserving and environmentally friendly society is of significance given the country's resource constraints and increasing risks to its environment. These could be encouraged through the introduction of a carrot and stick approach using both incentives and disincentives to promote conservation of natural resources as well as green consumption and production habits.

Conclusion

In order to mitigate the depletion of its resources, degradation of its environment and decline in the quality of life for its citizens, China should first take concrete steps via its policy making mechanisms as well as technology innovations to speed up the pace of its transition to a green and low-carbon society. The leadership has to make efforts to de-carbonise segments of its economic structure and improve the overall energy mix. Based on regional differences, China can re-adjust inter-provincial industrial structures through the gradual transfer of technology and optimisation of their industrial configurations. From the standpoint of energy security and low carbon development, it is imperative to cut back on coal consumption and dependence on oil imports by developing more low-carbon and zero carbon energy sources. Under the 12th Five-Year-Plan's "comprehensive scheme on energy saving and emission reduction", concerted efforts would be made to optimise industrial structure, promote technological advancement, eliminate backward production capacity, facilitate upgrading of traditional industries and make adjustments to energy structures. The scheme also calls for the need to develop hydropower without impairment to the ecological environment, as well as encourage the use of natural gas and renewable energy sources such as wind power, solar power, biomass and geothermal energy.

Secondly, advanced technology will play an important role in lowering energy and carbon emissions, so it is necessary to carry out technology research and development, transfer, and deployment. Current research and development capabilities in the areas of low-carbon technology are relatively insufficient. It is particularly important to enhance international cooperation in technology transfer and make use of the successful experience of other countries for reference. Compared with other developed regions, there is still much room to reduce energy intensity in China. There is a wide gap in energy efficiency per unit product in major sectors between China and advanced international yardsticks. Improvements in energy efficiency can achieve multiple objectives such as energy security, low carbon emissions and enhancing competitiveness.

Thirdly, there is the need to develop CO_2 inventories and a toolbox for low-carbon management that could assist the policymakers in their development of management policies. According to the low-carbon development matrix, the toolbox should consist of three database or software — a list of emission sources to enable the collection, monitoring and forecast of emissions by different sectors and fields; a list that shows the consumption levels of various buildings or configurations and a list of the emission factors from different means of transportation.

Fourthly, there must be concerted efforts to carry out low-carbon development planning and ensure the strengthening of low-carbon management. China is in a critical phase of social and economic development, so it is vital to integrate low carbon development goals into the context of local social and economic development planning. It should combine its own emission reduction targets based on the low carbon development experience of different areas to map out practical road maps in order to come up with an integrated solution for low-carbon development. At the same time, the government should formulate relevant policies to strengthen low-carbon management, pay more attention to key areas such as low-carbon buildings and development of clean energy vehicle technology while encouraging and advocating low-carbon consumption. The State Council has designated a National Low-Carbon Day from 2013 onwards with the aim of promoting greater public awareness about climate change and encouraging wider public participation in order to reinforce the country's commitment to low-carbon development policies.

Appendix

Table 4A: Environmental Sustainability in Different Countries.

HDI Rank	Countries	Adjusted Net Savings (% of GNI) 2005–2009	Ecological Footprint (Hectares Per Capita) 2007	Environmental Performance Index (Value 1–100) 2010	Share of Fossil Fuels (% of Total) 2007	Share of Renewables (% of Total) 2007	Per Capita (Tonnes) 2008	Growth (Average Annual % Growth) 1970/2008
		Composite Measures of Sustainability			Primary Energy Supply		Carbon Dioxide Emissions	
12	Japan	12.11	4.73	72.50	82.99	3.44	9.50	0.67
26	Singapore	32.95	5.34	69.60	100.00	0.00	7.00	−0.59
61	Malaysia	15.45	4.86	65.00	95.08	4.97	7.70	4.70
101	China	39.69	2.21	49.00	86.91	12.30	5.24	4.62
124	Indonesia	11.01	1.21	44.60	65.65	34.35	1.80	4.77
128	Vietnam	16.55	1.40	59.00	53.98	45.55	1.47	2.13
134	India	24.09	0.91	48.30	71.12	28.14	1.47	3.80
	Very High Human Development	6.56	5.88	68.18	81.90	7.22	11.34	0.31
	High Human Development	5.02	3.14	63.51	81.19	15.90	5.95	1.81
	Medium Human Development	27.24	1.59	50.32	77.28	22.22	3.18	3.94
	Low Human Development	—	1.17	46.25	—	—	0.38	0.58
	World	18.3	2.4	54.4	72.3	25.1	4.4	2.5

Table 4A: (*Continued*)

HDI Rank	Countries	Pollution		Natural Resource Depletion and Biodiversity				
		Greenhouse Gas Emissions Per Capita (Tonnes) 2005	Urban Pollution (Micrograms Per Cubic Metre) 2008	Natural Resource Depletion (% of GNI) 2009	Fresh Water Withdrawals (% of Total Renewable Water Resources) 2003–2010b	Forest Area (% of Land Area) 2008	Change in Forest Area (%) 1990–2008	Endangered Species (% of All Species) 2010
12	Japan	0.99	27.14	0.00	—	68.48	0.05	15.09
26	Singapore	1.37	30.81	—	—	3.29	0.00	16.59
61	Malaysia	2.44	19.95	7.88	—	62.79	−7.80	17.75
101	China	1.49	65.61	3.15	19.51	21.59	28.12	12.19
124	Indonesia	1.52	72.35	6.50	—	52.88	−19.19	16.15
128	Vietnam	1.28	52.71	7.21	9.28	43.57	44.28	12.03
134	India	0.74	59.23	4.17	40.05	22.92	6.58	13.42
	Very High Human Development	2.66	23.80	0.77	—	5.77	1.18	14.13
	High Human Development	2.85	29.93	8.75	—	10.19	−3.41	10.78
	Medium Human Development	1.20	61.38	4.41	—	2.91	8.30	12.89
	Low Human Development	—	69.45	8.72	—	1.58	−13.91	7.55
	World	1.7	52	2.4	—	1.7	−1.2	12

Source: UNDP (2011).

References

BP (British Petroleum). "BP Statistical Review of World Energy June 2011." 2011. Available online at http://www.bp.com/assets/bp_internet/ globalbp/globalbp_uk_english/reports_and_publications/statistical_energy_ review_2011/STAGING/local_assets/pdf/statistical_review_of_world_energy_ full_report_2011.pdf. Last accessed on 26 August, 2013.

C40 (C40 CITIES, Climate Leadership Group). "Home." 2013. Available online at http://www.c40cities.org/. Last accessed on 13 August, 2013.

CCDLCCDI (Copenhagen Declaration for Low Carbon City Development Indicators). "Copenhagen Declaration for Low Carbon City Development Indicators." September 3, 2008. Available online at http://www.pamlin.net/ new/?p=503. Last accessed on 26 August, 2013.

CDIAC (Carbon Dioxide Information Analysis Center). "Fossil-Fuel CO2 Emissions." 2013. Available online at http://cdiac.ornl.gov/trends/emis/meth_ reg.html. Last accessed on 13 August, 2013.

Chen, Ying, Pan Jiahua and Xie Laihui. "Embedded Energy in China's Importing and Exporting Products and Its Policy Implications." *Economy Researches* 7 (2008): 11–25.

Lei Hongpeng and Zhuang Guiyang. *Low-Carbon City: Why and How [in Chinese]*. Beijing: China Environmental Science Press, 2011, pp. 19–23.

National Bureau of Statistics of China. *China Statistical Yearbook 2011*. Beijing: China Statistics Press, 2012.

NDRC (National Development and Reform Commission), the Peoples' Republic of China. "Notice Regarding Low-Carbon Provinces and Low-Carbon City Pilot Studies [in Chinese]." 2010. Available online at http://www. gov.cn/zwgk/2010-08/10/content_1675733.htm. Last accessed on 13 August, 2013.

IEA (International Energy Agency). "Statistics and Balances." Available online at http://www.iea.org/stats/index.asp. Last accessed on 15 August, 2013.

Pan Jiahua, Zhuang Guiyang and Zhu Shouxian. *Low Carbon Cities: Economic Analysis and Development Indicators with Case Studies [in Chinese]*. Beijing: Social Sciences Academic Press, 2012, pp. 28–29.

Stern, Nicholas. *The Economics of Climate Change: The Stern Review*. Cambridge, UK: Cambridge University Press, 2007.

Tapio, Petri. "Towards a Theory of Decoupling: Degrees of Decoupling in the EU and the Case of Road Traffic in Finland Between 1970 and 2001." *Journal of Transport Policy* 12, 2 (2005): 137–151.

The Task Force for 2050 China Energy and CO$_2$ Emissions Report. *2050 China Energy and CO2 Emissions Report [in Chinese]*. Beijing: Science Press, 2009.

UNDP (United Nations Development Programme). "Human Development Report." 2011. Available online at http://hdr.undp.org/en/media/HDR_ 2011_Statistical_Tables.xls. Last accessed on 27 August, 2013.

UNDP (United Nations Development Programme). "Human Development Reports: Human Development Index." Available online at http://hdr.undp. org/en/statistics/hdi/. Last accessed on 15 August, 2013.

Wang, Jinnan. *Chinese Environmental and Economic Accounting Report 2009 [in Chinese]*. Beijing: China Environmental Science Press, 2009.

World Bank. "Data Catalog." 2013. Available online at http://data.worldbank. org/data-catalog. Last accessed on 13 August, 2013.

Zhang, Anhua. "Variables of Energy Efficiency in China's Electricity Sector." *Demand Side Management in Electricity Sector* 8, 6 (2006): 1–4.

Zhang, Lei. "Economic Development and Its Bearing on CO_2 Emissions." *Acta Geographica Sinica* 58, 4 (2003): 629–637.

Zhuang, Guiyang. "How will China Move towards Becoming a Low Carbon Economy?" *Journal of China & World Economy* 16, 3 (2008): 93–105.

5. China's Environmental Governance: Evolution and Limitations

WU Fuzuo

It has been widely acknowledged that China, one of the world's fastest growing and most populous countries, has been facing some serious environmental challenges since the 1950s. This has led to environmental degradation especially since its opening-up and reform policy in the late 1970s (Smil, 1980; Boxer, 1989; Sanders, 1999; Ross, 1998; Zhang *et al.*, 1999; Ho, 2003). This policy has driven its continuously phenomenal economic growth, transforming it into the second largest economy in the world. As a result, China was ranked 116th among 132 countries assessed for environmental sustainability in 2012 (Emerson *et al.*, 2012). To address the environmental challenges, China has begun to create a comprehensive domestic framework, institutionally and legislatively, since the 1970s. Hence, it has already established its environmental governance which "comprises the rules, practices, policies and institutions that shape how humans interact with the environment" (UNEP, 2009). However, this does not follow that China's environmental challenges have been tackled successfully and effectively and that China's environmental situation has been improved greatly. In reality, the scale and seriousness of its environmental problems persisted even in the 2000s.

The main purpose of this article is to explore the evolution and limitations of China's environmental governance. For this purpose, it has been divided into four sections: The first examines the status of China's environmental governance by assessing the development of its environment-related institutions, legislation and national development plans. The next analyses the practical result of this governance and how China lags far behind despite its great efforts. The third section discusses the inherent limitations in China's environmental governance that has led to the discrepancy between its efforts and results. In the final section, a brief conclusion has been drawn.

The Evolution of China's Environmental Governance

The origin of China's environmental governance can be traced back to the 1970s and early 1980s when it became increasingly aware of the need to address environmental problems after its participation in the United Nations Conference on the Human Environment in Stockholm, in June 1972. Since then, China has embarked on multi-dimensional efforts to govern its environment. Among others targets, the evolution of its environmental institutions, legislation and national development plans are indeed, most significant.

Institutionally, China has evolved from a country with no governmental institutions to address the environmental issues, to one with multiple-level governmental bodies in charge of environmental protection (Zhang *et al.*, 1999). More specifically, at the national level, China had no administrative agency for environmental affairs until 1974 when the Environmental Protection Bureau (EPB) was established. Its staff comprised of only 20 persons and it had no authority over the provincial and local environmental management. In the early 1980s, EPB lost its independence by being incorporated into the Ministry of Urban and Rural Construction and Environmental Protection. It had not regained its independent status until after the governmental reorganisations that occurred twice — in the mid and late 1980s — when EPB's authority and staff members increased (Yale Center for Environmental Law and Policy *et al.*, 2011). In 1998, the status of EPB was elevated to the ministerial level and renamed as the State Environmental Protection Agency (SEPA). Although SEPA did not have a permanent seat in the State Council as its counterparts then, it reported directly to the Vice Premier for environmental protection and its staff members increased to nearly 2,000 (Ho and Vermeer, 2006). In March 2008, SEPA was further elevated to full ministry status, becoming the Ministry of Environmental Protection (MEP). It had a permanent seat in the State Council, which demonstrated China's strong political will to tackle environmental challenges. Hence, it empowered the Ministry, which had the administrative authority to make decisions and had access to resources (Qiu and Liu, 2009). Since the mid-1980s, China has created EPBs at all local levels, including provincial, municipal and county, to directly manage local environmental issues. It hence established a four-tier management system, from national to local levels, to vertically govern its environment (Mol and Carter, 2006). According to official statistics, there are 12,849 environmental-protection administration departments at different levels all over China. These have 193,911 people engaging in environmental administration, monitoring, scientific research, publicity and education. They exist in addition to 5,655 environmental supervision and environmental law enforcement organs with nearly 120,000 staff members (MEP, 2012).

In parallel with its institutional efforts, legislatively, China has created a comprehensive legal system to protect its environment. It not only includes laws promulgated by the National People's Congress (NPC) and its Standing Committee, but also a variety of administrative regulations, standards and measures issued by the State Council on all major environmental sectors (State Council, 2006). At the national level, so far China has some 20 environmental laws adopted by the NPC, around 140 executive regulations issued by the State Council, and a series of sector regulations and environmental standards set by the SEPA (Mol and Carter, 2006). Therefore, some scholars commented, "Currently China is in the unique position of enacting extensive environmental legislation alongside considerable economic development" (Zeng and Eastin, 2007). One characteristic of this process is that China's environmental legislation has evolved from general to specific and from an ambiguous, weak and loose status to a clearer and tighter status. For instance, China promulgated its first environmental law entitled the *Environmental Protection Law* (EPL) in 1979, but it was only "trial" or provisional. Later, China strengthened it by changing it to a permanent law in 1989. The later version expanded the specific responsibilities for environmental protection at all levels of government. It created Five New Systems for pollution control and added strong sanctions to help improve enforcement, which was regarded as a significant improvement (Muldavin, 2000). This law is currently under revision in order to adjust the environmental regulatory framework in light of China's fast economic development (OECD, 2006). In addition, since the 1980s, China has issued some specific laws, such as the Water Pollution Protection and Control Law, the Ambient Pollution Protection and Control Law, and the Ocean and Sea Environmental Protection Law to govern some specific subjects that are addressed more generally in the EPL.

The second characteristic in the evolution of China's legislation is that it has become more enforceable. Although China has promulgated many laws to protect its environment, most of them remained largely unenforceable due to lack of regulations on sanctions for violations. This had not changed until the 2000s when China further amended previously issued or amended laws. For instance, the amended *Law on Air Pollution Prevention and Control* in the 1990s did not contain details on how to impose fines. In contrast, in the 2000 *Law on the Prevention and Control of Atmospheric Pollution*, some detailed rules on minimum and maximum sanction levels were added in Articles 46–65 (Order of the President of the People's Republic of China, 2000). The same is true with the 2003 *Cleaner Production Promotion Law*, amended on 29th February, 2012, which provides clear definitions by issuing the list of activities and also sets fine limits between 50,000 and 500,000 Yuan (Standing Committee of NPC, 2012).

Another significant aspect in the evolution of China's environmental governance is that environmental protection has been gradually raised from a low-status issue to a high-status one in China's national development strategy. This can be illustrated by China's National Economic and Social Development Five-Year Plans (FYPs). So far, China has issued 12 FYPs. Amongst these, the issue of environmental protection had not even been briefly touched upon, until the guidelines for each of the 6th (1981–1985), 7th (1986–1990), and 8th (1991–1995) FYPs were formed, which contained sections on environmental improvement for those five years. They provided policy direction for all the above-mentioned governmental institutions to implement environmental legislation and policies (Chan *et al.*, 1995: 334). At the same time however, when compared with the priorities given to the economic development, the environmental issue was regarded as low-status one. However, it is important to note that this situation has begun to shift since the 9th FYP (1996–2000). It has done so by emphasising on more balanced growth at the national and local levels rather than solely concentrating on the goal of maximising gross domestic product. In fact, it was during the 9th FYP that the serious deterioration of the environment was acknowledged for the first time. It called for the establishment of environmental management and legislative systems to implement its strategy for sustainable development and set forth concrete distant targets for environmental sectors to be achieved in the year of 2000 (NPC, 1996). This shift was strengthened in the 10th (2001–2005) FYP, with concrete targets being set for the year of 2005. Based on a notion passed by Chinese President Hu Jintao in March 2005 (Xinhuanet, 2005), both 11th (2006–2010) and 12th (2011–2015) FYPs not only set some concrete quantitative targets in some environmental sectors, but also assigned specific characteristics for compliance to those targets. This was done by dividing them into two categories, namely either "expected" or "compulsory" (NPC, 2006) (see Table 5.1). Expected targets are those that are anticipated to be achieved through the workings of market forces, with the government providing overall macroeconomic stability and the necessary regulatory institutions. Compulsory ones are those that are imposed by the central government, where the responsibility of enforcement remains with central government agencies and local governments. Furthermore, both Plans even set the green index, namely, a reduction in energy consumption per unit of GDP by 20 per cent and 16 per cent respectively over the two periods.

In line with these FYPs, the Chinese environmental authorities have developed Five-Year Environment Plans (FYEPs). These are further broken down into sectoral five-year plans, in areas such as water management in key rivers and lakes, air pollution reduction, hazardous waste management, and nature conservation. At the sub-national level, local governments develop their own five-year environmental plans based on the national FYEPs (OECD, 2006).

In sum, to govern its environment, China has not only established both institutional agencies and a comprehensive environmental legislation but also incorporated the environmental protection into its FYPs. As a result, Vaclav Smil, a leading expert on China's environment pointed out that "The [Chinese] government pays more attention to the environment than was the norm in virtually all western countries at comparable stages of their economic development" (Smil, 1998). Even so, however, the evolution of China's efforts to govern its environment does not necessarily guarantee that its environmental problems have been addressed successfully and effectively. Put differently, China's environmental governance so far has not proved to be up to the task of maintaining and improving, its overall environmental quality.

The State of China's Environment

The state of China's environment is the most useful indicator to evaluate the result of China's environmental governance. This section is devoted to investigating China's current environmental situation, focusing on its SO_2 and CO_2 emissions and pollution levels — especially water and air pollution — during the period between 1995 and 2010 (see Table 5.2) for statistics' convenience.

Table 5.1: Some Environmental Targets in the 11th and 12th FYPs.

Sectors	11th FYP				12th FYP			
	2005	2010	Annual Growth (%)	Characteristics	2010	2015	Annual Growth (%)	Characteristics
Farmland (million acres)	122	120	−0.3	Compulsory	181.8	181.8	[0]	Compulsory
Reduction of water consumption per unit industry added value (%)			[30]	Compulsory			[30]	Compulsory
Efficiency rate of agricultural irrigation water	0.45	0.5	[0.05]	Expected	0.5	0.53	[0.03]	Expected
Reduction of energy consumption per unit GDP (%)			[20]	Compulsory			[16]	Compulsory
Reduction of CO_2 per unit GDP (%)							[17]	Compulsory
Total reduction of main pollutants discharge (%)			[10]	Compulsory			[8]	Compulsory
Comprehensive use rate of industrial solid waste (%)	55.8	60	[4.2]	Expected				
Forest Coverage (%)	18.2	20	[1.8]	Compulsory	20.36	21.66	[1.3]	Compulsory
Accumulation (billion cm^3)					1.37	1.43	[6]	Compulsory

Note: Numbers with [ ] are aggregate numbers for the five years.
Sources: NPC, 2006; 2011.

Table 5.2: The State of China's Environment (1995–2010): Take SO_2 and CO_2 Emissions and Pollution Accidents as Examples.

	SO_2 Emissions (10,000 Tons)	CO_2 Emissions (Mt of CO_2)	Total Number of Accidents	Total Costs (10,000 Yuan)	Number of Water Pollution	Number of Air Pollution
				Pollution Accidents		
1995	1,891	3,320	1,966	–	–	–
1996	–	3,463	1,446	–	677	585
1997	1,852	3,469	1,992	8366.1	986	752
1998	2,090	3,324	1,442	19843.7	788	464
1999	1857.5	3,318	1,614	5710.6	888	582
2000	1995.1	3,405	2,411	17807.9	1138	864
2001	1947.8	3,487	1,842	12272.4	1096	576
2002	1926.6	3,694	1,921	4640.9	1097	597
2003	2158.7	4,525	1,843	3374.9	1042	654
2004	2254.9	4,769	1,441	36365.7	753	569
2005	2549.3	5,101	1,406	10515.0 (not including the cost incurred by Songhua River accident)	693	538
2006	2588.8	5,648	842	13471.1	482	323
2007	2468.1	6,071	462	3016.0	178	134
2008	2321.2	6,550	474	18185.6	198	141
2009	2214.4	6,877	418	43354.4	116	130
2010	2185.1	–	420	2256.9	135	157

Note: – represents the data is not available.

Sources: MEP, 1995–2010; *People's Republic of China Year Book*, 1995–2000; The World Bank, 2010; International Energy Agency (IEA) 2006–2011.

In terms of SO_2, according to certain research findings, China has contributed about one-fourth of the global emissions and more than 90 per cent of East Asian emissions since the 1990s (Lu *et al.*, 2010). The Chinese government set a target of reducing its SO_2 emissions during its 10th FYP by 10 per cent by 2005 based on the 2000 levels. However, it turned out that rather than reaching the target, China's SO_2 emissions in 2005 were in fact 78 per cent higher than the level of 2000. In other words, China failed to reach the target. The main reason was attributed to "the massive increase in fossil-fuel consumption resulting from rapid economic growth, the lag of the introduction of desulphurisation equipment, and the low efficiency of the installed desulphurisation devices" (*Ibid.* p. 6312). In contrast, during the 11th FYP, China succeeded in reducing its SO_2 emissions by 14.29 per cent compared to the 2006 levels, which was 4.29 per cent higher than the originally self-imposed 10 per cent target (*People's Daily*, 2011). Even so, the current SO_2 emissions are still so high that it continues to result in nearly half of China's cities suffering from acid rain problems.

As far as CO_2 is concerned, China's emissions have been growing so fast that it surpassed the US as the largest emitter in the world in 2006, according to the Netherlands Environmental Assessment Agency (2007). Till the time of writing, China's CO_2 emissions have accounted for nearly $1/4$ of the world's total CO_2 emissions (IEA, 2011). Recent research states that, China's CO_2 emissions won't peak until 2030 or so (Zhou *et al.*, 2011). This means that China's CO_2 emissions will continue to rise at least in next 20 years or so, which in turn will have negative impacts on climate change.

As Table 5.2 shows, China has made much progress in addressing pollution, especially air and water pollution over the past decade, which is reflected by the reduction of the number of pollution accidents and costs. However, in practice, air and water pollution still persists. According to the World Bank issued World Development Indicator 2011, based on the criteria of PM 10 (particulate matter with an aerodynamic diameter smaller than 10 micrometers), 24 of the 74 most polluted cities in the world are located in China (World Bank, 2011). According to the *2010 Environmental Performance Index* (EPI), China scored 40.1 on a range of 0–100 for the human impact of air pollution policy category, far below the average scores for countries in its income and regional peer groups (63.4 and 58.6 respectively) (Emerson *et al.*, 2010). Empirically, in the final quarter of 2011, due to air pollution, some Chinese cities and regions including Beijing experienced the worst fog in history. It led to a shutdown of highways and hundreds of flights across the country either being cancelled or delayed due to low visibility. In this context, addressing air pollution has been listed as a top priority in China's 12th FYP (Sun, 2012). Specifically, on February 29th, 2012, the MEP and General Administration of Quality Supervision, Inspection and Quarantine jointly issued the revised *Ambient Air Quality Standards* by using PM 2.5, a stricter standard, to replace its existing PM 10 to evaluate air quality, in addition to the ozone-8-hour standard (MEP and General Administration of Quality Supervision, Inspection and Quarantine, 2012).

With regard to water pollution, the quality of China's surface water and groundwater has deteriorated significantly under the pressure of rapid industrial development, continuing population growth, and increased use of chemical fertilisers and pesticides. According to *Report on the State of the Environment in China* (SOE), an annual official document issued by MEP, the overall situation of China's water pollution remains serious. In 2009, for instance, China's seven big rivers (the Yangtze River, Yellow River, Pearl River, Songhua River, Huaihe River, Haihe River and Liaohe River) were slightly polluted. However, Haihe River remained heavy polluted, more than 40 per cent of its water was only applicable to irrigation. Among the 408 sections of 203 rivers under national monitoring, sections with water quality ranged from Grade I to III, Grade IV to V, and inferior to Grade V accounted for 57.3 per cent, 24.3 per cent and 18.4 per cent respectively (MEP, 2009).[1] In addition, among the 26 key lakes (reservoir) under the national monitoring program, 19.2 per cent only met Grade V, the minimum water quality standard, and 34.9 per cent inferior to this grade (*Ibid.*). This meant that more than half of the water in China's lakes was so polluted that they could only be applicable to irrigation or be too polluted for human use. This deterioration, in turn, has led to a serious problem for urban and rural drinking water. According to SOE in 2009, 27 per cent of city water sources were below the drinking standard (*Ibid.*). The direct result of water pollution, according to the World Bank, is that the polluted water has entered into China's food supply chain to have already had some negative implications on its food security, which might pose direct health problems for its citizens (World Bank, 2007; Freeman and Lu, 2008).

In addition to those economic costs incurred by pollution accidents in Table 5.2, China's environmental degradation has already caused some other economic and social costs. For instance, China Metrological Administration (CMA) has directly attributed the 2001 floods to climate change. The disaster caused 1000 plus deaths and US $3.6 billion in damages (Szymanski, 2002). In addition, at a seminar on *Special Report on Managing the Risks of Extreme Events and Disasters to Advance Climate Change Adaptation (SREX)* in April last year, Zheng Guoguang, Administrator of CMA, pointed out that China is one of the countries that has been most severely affected by meteorological disasters (Liu, 2012). Furthermore, pollution has become a major cause of various health disorders. For instance, according to the World Bank, as much as 13 per cent of all urban deaths may be premature due to air pollution (World Bank, 2007). By 2020, the World Bank estimates that China will have to spend US$390 billion annually, or 13 per cent of its national GDP, to treat diseases caused by pollution (Lam, 2008).

In short, China's on-going environmental degradation, especially its SO_2 and CO_2 emissions and its water and air pollution, is sufficient enough to attest to the low efficiency, even if not a failure, of its environmental governance.

The Limitations of China's Environmental Governance

The low efficiency of China's environmental governance stems rightly from some inherent defects of the governance itself. The greater prioritisation of economic development over environmental degradation and other institutional and legislative limitations are key limitations. In addition, there is insufficient participation on the part of its NGOs and individuals.

On paper, environmental protection is firmly established as a high priority in China's national development strategy, as discussed above. In practice, however, whenever a perceived conflict between environmental protection and economic development emerges, the former usually gives way to the latter. The short-lived Green GDP is a good case in point. The concept of "Green GDP" was first put forth by Chinese President Hu Jintao in a speech at a symposium on population, resources and environment held by the Central Government in March 2004 (Xinhuanet, 2004). In that same year, the process of calculation of green GDP was initiated. After two years' work, the result, called *China Green National Accounting Study Report 2004*, was publically issued in 2006. Even though the resulting "Green GDP" estimates were highly conservative, they still served as a wake-up call for China's leadership by proving that the annual costs incurred by its environmental pollution were US$51 billion (at the official exchange rate at the time of the study in 2004), equalling 3.05 per cent of China's GDP in 2004 (SEPA, 2006). The Green GDP was rejected and therefore blocked so strongly by the local governments that it has been postponed indefinitely since 2006 (Zhang, 2006). Accordingly, Pan Yuan, China's Vice Minister of MEP, had to admit that the wide-spread ideology of "development first, environmental protection later or pollute first, then clean up" is a root cause of the low ranking environmental sustainability in China's development process (Pan, 2007).

Admittedly, as mentioned above, China has largely overcome the institutional weakness of its environmental bureaucracy at the national level in terms of status and personnel. However, at the various sub-national levels, there are still some obvious defects in this regard. For instance, EPBs at sub-national levels still face both financial and administrative constraints that hinder them from fully enforcing their role in environmental protection. In terms of the former, with a decentralised administrative system in China, most EPBs' resources usually come directly from the local governments whose primary concerns are economic. Thus, EPBs are vulnerable to the local governments' leverage to protect some local firms from being put under the environmental regulation. In some provinces, in contrast, EPBs entirely rely on levies and fees collected from polluting factories under their jurisdiction, which puts them in a quandary, since their efforts to lower pollution output will erode into their main source of revenue (Anonymous Netizen, 2010; Qin, 2007).[2] Under these circumstances, EPBs lack incentives to strictly implement the environmental laws and regulations. It is hence no surprise that pollution continues to exist in China. At the same time, administratively, most local EPBs' personnel appointments depend on the local governments themselves. Thus, the EPBs' capabilities to take independent actions to implement environmental laws are largely constrained (Qin, 2007). Moreover, although local officials' environmental performance has been incorporated into the cadre evaluation system, receives much less weight as compared to their economic performance. This has created an incentive for officials to disregard the environmental costs of economic growth (Zhang, 2008).

When it comes to the legislative limitations in China's environmental governance, the problem lies not in that it does not have a comprehensive environmental legal framework, but that the environmental laws themselves are not clear on crucial issues such as penalties for non-compliance. Even if there are, the bar is usually too low to be meaningful and effective. Take the accident of Songhua River in Northern China in November 2005 as an example. This incident had not only brought some serious negative impacts on China's environment, economy and society at the domestic level, but also negatively influenced China's neighbouring countries, especially Russia. Even so, the maximum fine charged by China's current environmental laws is just 1 million Yuan, which was actually imposed 1 year after that accident. Moreover, the fine is only allowed to be imposed once. Against this backdrop, "this low and one-off penalty is hardly a deterrent to environmental offenders" (Zhang, p. 3909). In fact, some violators tend to prefer paying token fines to complying with the law. As a result, it has been argued that in China there are both too many environmental laws and not enough (Lam, 2008).

Another obvious defect in China's environmental governance is the weak public involvement from environmental NGOs and the local citizens. With regards to the former, it is true that environmental NGOs have sprung up and played a role in China's environmental governance since the mid-1990s (Yang, 2005; Schwartz, 2004). However, most of those NGOs in China in practice are not truly independent of the state. More specifically, research states that not only government-organised NGOs (GONGOs) but also student groups, community organisations and even international NGOs with offices in China have a unique relationship with the Chinese government. This is because all these groups are largely dependent on the government's political permission and support and therefore require adhering to the government's policies (Lam, 2008; Schwartz, 2004). With regard to the latter, according to the EPL, every citizen has been granted the right to make formal complaints about any environmental damages. In reality, however, two situations usually make local citizens refrain from using legal rights to protect the local environment. First, local citizens who have no other means of living but relying on pollution-related income are unlikely to take any actions to bring down the local pollution-producing industry (Rooij, 2006). Second, even if local pollution victims use the legal right to sue for damages to their health or economic livelihood, they have seldom won their cases due to the fact that China's court system is not only too weak but also too inexperienced to handle any pollution-related cases. The main reason for this is that local courts treat economic development rather environmental protection as their top priority. Furthermore, they lack of standard guidelines on evidence collection, pollution victims' rights, and the assessment of causality and damages in those cases on the other (Lam, 2008).

In sum, this section has highlighted the main factors that have hindered improvement in China's environmental governance. These factors include, the greater prioritisation of economic development over environmental protection, institutional limitations especially those faced by the local EPBs the cadre evaluation system, legislative limitations in terms of penalty for noncompliance and weak public involvement.

Conclusion

Over the past three decades, China has gradually established its environmental governance to address the negative impacts caused by its fast economic development. On the one hand, China has not only built up a comprehensive institutional and legislative framework to govern its environment, but also incorporated the environmental protection into its national development strategy. Despite this, China's environment is under constant strain. For instance, China's SO_2 emissions continue to be high while its CO_2 emissions continue to grow. In addition, its pollution-related problems continue to be severe especially in terms of water and air pollution. This embarrassing environmental situation reflects that China's environmental governance is weak. This can be attributed largely to some inherent limitations of its governance itself. Most importantly, China's local governments still maintain the traditional ideological perception that economic development ought to be given greater prioritisation over environmental protection. As a result, China's local EPBs face both financial and administrative constraints which hinder them from performing their role of fully and effectively protecting the environment. Furthermore, China's environmental legislation has some inherent defects. For instance, it possesses weak regulations on non-compliance and its bar for penalties is set fairly low. In addition, the extent of China's public involvement in the governance process is rather limited. Thus, it can be safely concluded that the evolution of China's environmental governance cannot guarantee the effective environmental protection, at its current state. Only when those inherent limitations are overcome will such governance be able to make a real difference.

Endnotes

1 According to China's Environmental Quality Standards for Surface Water, various surface water bodies within its territory are divided into five classes based on functions: Class I is mainly applicable to the water from sources, and the national nature reserves; Class II is mainly applicable to the first class of protected areas for centralized sources of drinking water, the protected areas for rare fishes, and the spawning fields of fishes and shrimps; Class III is mainly applicable to second class of protected areas for centralized sources of drinking water, protected areas for the common fishes and swimming areas; Class IV is mainly applicable to the water areas for industrial use and entertainment which is not directly touched by human bodies; Class V is mainly applicable to the water bodies for agricultural use and landscape requirement (MEP, 1997; 2009).

2 For instance, one anonymous netizen asked the Secretary of Hebei Provincial Party committee why the wages of the local EPBs' employees cannot be

incorporated into the local finance (Anonymous Netizen, 2010). For another instance, one county EPB in Anhui Province could barely pay the wages of its employees through the fees charged from pollution discharge and therefore cannot afford to obtain any advanced equipment to carry out inspections, see Qin (2007).

References

Anonymous Netizen. "Why the Wages of the Local EPBs' Employees Cannot Be Incorporated into the Local Finance? [in Chinese]." 2010. Available online at http://liuyan.people.com.cn/redirect.php?fid = 543&tid=591566&goto= nextnewset. Last accessed on 25 April, 2012.

Boxer, Baruch. "China's Environmental Prospects." *Asian Survey* 29, 7 (1989): 669–686.

Chan, Hon S., Koon-Kwai Wong, K. C. Cheung and Jack Man-kueng Lo. "The Implementation Gap in Environmental Management in China: The Case of Guangzhou, Zhengzhou, and Nanjing." *Public Administration Review* 55, 4 (1995): 333–340.

Emerson, Jay, Daniel C. Etsy, Christine Kim, Tanja Srebotnjak, Marc A. Levy, Valentina Mara, Alex de Sherbinin and Malanding Jaiteh. *2010 Environmental Performance Index.* New Haven: Yale Center for Environmental Law and Policy, 2010.

Freeman III, Charles W. and Xiaoqing Lu. *Assessing Chinese Government Response to the Challenge of Environment and Health.* Washington, DC: Center for Strategic and International Studies, 2008.

Ho, Peter. "Mao's War against Nature? The Environmental Impact of the Grain-First Campaign in China." *The China Journal* 50 (2003): 37–59.

Ho, Peter and Eduard B. Vermeer. "China's Limits to Growth? The Difference between Absolute, Relative and Precautionary Limits." *Development and Change* 37, 1 (2006): 255–271.

IEA (International Energy Agency). *Key World Energy Statistics,* 2006–2011. Available online at http://www.iea.org/publications/free_all.asp. Last accessed 24 April, 2012.

IEA (International Energy Agency). *Key World Energy Statistics 2011.* 2012. Available online at http://www.iea.org/textbase/nppdf/free/2011/key_world_energy_stats.pdf. Last accessed on 25 April, 2012.

Lam, Debra. "The Reality of Environmental Sustainability in China." *City* 12, 2 (2008): 245–254.

Liu, Yi. "Economic Damages Caused by Extreme Weather Events will Increase [in Chinese]." *People's Daily,* April 27, 2012, p.3.

Lu, Zifeng D. G. Streets, Qiang Zhang, Siwen Wang, Gregory R. Carmichael, Yafang Cheng, Chao Wei, Mian Chin, Thomas Diehl and Qian Tan. "Sulfur Dioxide Emissions in China and Sulfur Trends in East Asia since 2000." *Atmospheric Chemistry and Physics* 10 (2010): 6311–6331.

MEP (Ministry of Environmental Protection of the People's Republic of China). "The National Standards of the People's Republic of China Environmental Quality Standards for Surface Water." 1997. Available online at http://english.sepa.gov.cn/SOE/soechina1997/water/waters.htm. Last accessed on 25 April, 2012.

MEP (Ministry of Environmental Protection of the People's Republic of China). "Report On the State of the Environment In China 2009." 2009. Available online at http://english.sepa.gov.cn/standards_reports/soe/soe2009/201104/t20110411_208976.htm. Last accessed on 25 April, 2012.

MEP (Ministry of Environmental Protection of the People's Republic of China). "Bulletin of National Environmental Statistics (2010) [in Chinese]." 2012. Available online at http://zls.mep.gov.cn/hjtj/qghjtjgb/201201/t20120118_222703.htm. Last accessed on 25 April, 2012.

MEP (Ministry of Environmental Protection of the People's Republic of China). "Bulletin of National Environmental Statistics [in Chinese]." 1995–2010. Available online at http://www.mep.gov.cn/zwgk/hjtj/qghjtjgb/. Last accessed on 24 April, 2012.

MEP and General Administration of Quality Supervision, Inspection and Quarantine of the People's Republic of China. "Ambient Air Quality Standards [in Chinese]." 2012. Available online at http://kjs.mep.gov.cn/pv_obj_cache/pv_obj_id_A2091821785E1F0CAD9E86D0D1A83F5E328B0400/filename/W020120410330232398521.pdf. Last accessed on 16th August, 2013.

Mol, Arthur P. J. and Neil T. Carter. "China's Environmental Governance in Transition." *Environmental Politics* 15, 2 (2006): 149–170.

Muldavin, Joshua. "The Paradoxes of Environmental Policy and Resource Management in Reform-Era China." *Economic Geography* 76, 3 (2000): 244–271.

Netherlands Environmental Assessment Agency. "China Now no. 1 in CO$_2$ Emissions; USA in Second Position." 2007. Available online at http://www.pbl.nl/en/news/pressreleases/2007/20070619Chinanowno1inCO2emissionsUSAinsecondposition. Last accessed on 15 April, 2012.

NPC (National People's Congress). "The Outline of the 9th Five-Year Plan for National Economic and Social Development and the Distant Targets for the Year of 2000 [in Chinese]." 1996. Available online at http://www.sdpc.gov.cn/fzgh/ghwb/gjjh/P020070912638573307712.pdf. Last accessed on 16 April, 2012.

NPC (National People's Congress). "The Outline of the 11th Five-Year Plan for National Economic and Social Development [in Chinese]." 2006. Available online at http://ghs.ndrc.gov.cn/ghjd/115gyxj/001a.htm. Last accessed on 16 April, 2012.

NPC (National People's Congress). "The Outline of the 12th Five-Year Plan for National Economic and Social Development [in Chinese]." 2011. Available online at http://www.sdpc.gov.cn/fzgh/ghwb/gjjh/P0201109195 92208575015.pdf. Last accessed on 16 April 2012.

OECD (Organisation for Economic Co-operation and Development). "Environmental Compliance and Enforcement in China." 2006. Available online at http://www.oecd.org/dataoecd/33/5/37867511.pdf. Last accessed on 15 April, 2012.

Order of the President of the People's Republic of China (No. 32). "Law of the People's Republic of China on the Prevention and Control of Atmospheric Pollution." 2000. Available online at http://www.fdi.gov.cn/pub/FDI_EN/Laws/GeneralLawsandRegulations/BasicLaws/t20060620_50974. jsp. Last accessed on 15 April, 2012.

Pan, Yue. "Thoughts on China's Environmental Issues." *China Environmental News*, February 9, 2007. Available online at http://www.cenews.com. cn / historynews / 06_07 / 200712 / t20071229_34287.html. Last accessed on 15 April, 2012.

People's Daily. "The Situation of the Realization of Main Targets during the 11th Five-Year Plan [in Chinese]." March 17, 2011, p. 1.

People's Republic of China Year Book 1995–2000. Beijing: China Statistics Press, 1995–2000.

Qin, Peihua. "Anhui Lingbi: EPB's Personnel is Too Many, and the Pollution Discharge Fees are not Enough for Eating [in Chinese]." *People's Daily*, July 31, 2007. Available online at http://news.xinhuanet.com/newscenter/2007– 07/31/content_6453425.htm. Last accessed on 15 April, 2012.

Qiu, Xin and Honglin Liu. "China's Environmental Super Ministry Reform: Background, Challenges and the Future." *Environmental Law Reporter* 39, 2 (2009): 10152–10163. http:www.epa.gov/ogc/china/xin.pdf. Accessed on 16 August, 2013.

Rooij, Benjamin van. "Implementation of Chinese Environmental Law: Regular Enforcement and Political Campaigns." *Development and Change* 37, 1 (2006): 57–74.

Ross, Lester. "China: Environmental Protection, Domestic Policy Trends, Patterns of Participation in Regimes and Compliance with International Norms." *The China Quarterly* 156 (1998): 809–835.

Sanders, Richard. "The Political Economy of Chinese Environmental Protection: Lessons of the Mao and Deng Years." *Third World Quarterly* 20, 6 (1999): 1201–1214.

Schwartz, Jonathan. "Environmental NGOs in China: Roles and Limits." *Pacific Affairs* 77, 1 (2004): 28–49.

SEPA (State Environmental Protection Administration). *China Green National Accounting Study Report*. Beijing: State Environmental Protection Administration of China and the National Bureau of Statistics of China, 2006.

Smil, Vaclav. "Environmental Degradation in China." *Asian Survey* 20, 8 (1980): 777–788.

Smil, Vaclav. *The Environment Outlook for China*, unpublished manuscript, 1998. In Jonathan Schwartz, "The Impact of State Capacity on Enforcement of Environmental Policies: The Case of China." *Journal of Environment & Development* 12, 1 (2003): 50–81.

Standing Committee of NPC. "Cleaner Production Promotion Law of the People's Republic of China (2012 Amendment) [in Chinese]." *People's Daily*, April 19, 2012, p. 16.

State Council. "Environmental Protection in China (1996–2005)." 2006. Available online at http://www.china.org.cn/english/MATERIAL/170257.htm. Last accessed on 16 August, 2013.

Sun, Xiuyan. "Tackling Air Pollution as a Top Priority during the 12th Five-Year Plan [in Chinese]." *People's Daily*, April 27, 2012, p. 13.

Szymanski, Tauna. "The Clean Development Mechanism in China." *The China Business Review* 29, 6 (2002). Available online at https://www.chinabusinessreview.com/public/0211/szymanski.html. Last accessed on 15 April, 2012.

UNEP (United Nations Environment Programme). "Environmental governance." 2009. Available online at http://www.unep.org/pdf/brochures/EnvironmentalGovernance.pdf. Last accessed on 19 August, 2013.

World Bank. *Cost of Pollution in China: Economic Estimates of Physical Damages*. Washington, DC: the World Bank, 2007.

World Bank. "CO_2 Emissions (kt)." 2010. Available online at http://data.worldbank.org/indicator/EN.ATM.CO2E. KT?page=1. Last accessed on 24 April, 2012.

World Bank. *World Development Indicators 2011*. Washington, DC: the World Bank, 2011.

Xinhuanet. "Hu Jintao: Speech at the Symposium on Population, Resources and Environment Held by the Central Government (Full Text) (March 10, 2004) [in Chinese]." *Xinhua Agency*, April 4, 2004. Available online at http://news.xinhuanet.com/newscenter/2004-04/04/content_1400092_1.htm. Last accessed on 15 April, 2012.

Xinhuanet. "Hu Jintao Emphasizes to Implement Environmental and Resources Work and Put Social and Economic Development in a Benign Circle." *Xinhua Agency*, March 13, 2005. Available online at http://news.xinhuanet.com/newscenter/2005-03/13/content_2689920.htm. Last accessed on 15 April, 2012.

Yale Center for Environmental Law and Policy, Center for International Earth Science Information Network, Chinese Academy for Environmental Planning and City University of Hong Kong. "Towards a China Environmental Performance Index." 2011. Available online at http://environment.yale.edu / envirocenter /files / China - EPI - Report.pdf. Last accessed on 15 April, 2012.

Yale Center for Environmental Law and Policy, Center for International Earth Science Information Network, World Economic Forum and Joint Research Centre and European Commission. "2012 Environmental Performance Index and Pilot Trend Environmental Performance Index." 2012. Available online at http://sedac.ciesin.columbia.edu/data/set/epi-environmental-performance-index-pilot-trend-2012. Last accessed on 18 February, 2014.

Yang, Guobin. "Environmental NGOs and Institutional Dynamics in China." *The China Quarterly* 181 (2005): 46–66.

Zeng, Ka and Josh Eastin. "International Economic Integration and Environmental Protection: The Case of China." *International Studies Quarterly* l51, 4 (2007): 971–995.

Zhang, Li. "Special Planning: The Embarrassing Situation of Green GDP, Why Unpopular [in Chinese]." *People's Daily Online*, December 11, 2006. Available online at http://env.people.com.cn/GB/5151908.html. Last accessed on 20 April, 2012.

Zhang, Weijiong and others. "Can China Be a Clean Tiger?: Growth Strategies and Environmental Realities." *Pacific Affairs* 72, 1 (1999): 23–37.

Zhang, Zhong Xiang. "Asian Energy and Environmental Policy: Promoting Growth While Preserving the Environment." *Energy Policy* 36, 10 (2008): 3905–3922.

Zhou, Nan and others. "Peak CO_2? China's Emissions Trajectories to 2050." Lawrence Berkeley National Laboratory, 2011. Available online at http://china.lbl.gov/sites/china.lbl.gov/files/ECEEE_2050_Study.pdf. Last accessed on 12 April, 2012.

6. Fragmentation to Integration: Environmental and Sustainable Development Challenges in Malaysia

CHEE Yoke Ling and LIM Li Ching

The topic of sustainable development drew renewed vigour at the Rio+20 Summit in June 2012 in Rio de Janeiro, two decades after the historic United Nations Summit on Environment and Development in the same Brazilian city in 1992. There were several noteworthy achievements in the 1990s from the relatively swift negotiation to the quick adoption of the UN treaties in areas relating to climate change, biological diversity and bio-safety. The current global economic malaise in developed countries and social inequalities between and within countries has highlighted the failure of living up to the commitment made by many countries towards the paradigm shift towards more sustainable economic models in terms of production and consumption patterns. More worrying, Rio+20 actually witnessed many developed countries retreating from their responsibility of providing the means for developing countries to fulfil the sustainable development agenda.[1]

Malaysia was one of the leading actors at the 1992 Rio Summit and has continued to make efforts to achieve balance and integration in sustainability on the environmental, social and economic fronts. Like many other developing countries, it was prompted to set up a national environmental agency, the Department of Environment in Malaysia, following the UN Conference on the Human Environment in Stockholm as far back as 1972. The first major environmental law — the Environmental Quality Act — was passed in 1974 to curb pollution by effluents from the country's rubber and palm oil sectors, while older regulations such as those related to forestry, land use and soil conservation were updated by both federal and state governments.

More policies and laws have since been enacted to manage the exploitation of natural resources and environmental protection as well as to comply with Malaysia's treaty obligations or to deal with new, emerging issues. However, such efforts have been compromised to some extent due to a host of factors relating to (i) the fragmentation of governance within the federal system of government; (ii) insufficient coordination at all levels of government (iii) inadequate capacity for effective implementation and enforcement of environmental policies and laws as well as (iv) the lack of access to information and meaningful public participation.

In the meantime, a new threat to sustainable development has since emerged in the guise of the bilateral trade and investment agreements signed between Malaysia and developed countries. An area of contention in these agreements is that of the right of foreign investors to take a host government to private arbitration, which can sometimes impinge on interpretation of environmental laws and how they may be enforced.

Malaysia in the Global Economic Context

Before the 1997 Asian financial crisis, there was a moment when it had seemed that the admixture of strong economic growth and the country's rich natural resource base could set Malaysia on a more sustainable pathway of economic development. The chief minister of the state of Penang, Dr. Koh Tsu Koon, even suggested foregoing a few points in GDP growth in return for a higher quality of life. The onset of the financial crisis, however, saw the economic imperative taking precedent as Malaysia found itself increasingly dependent on foreign markets, especially its commodity exports such as palm oil, rubber, timber and petroleum to keep its economy afloat. The former chief economist of United Nations Conference on Trade and Development (UNCTAD) and advisor to the Group of 24[2] developing countries at the IMF, Dr. Yilmaz Akyuz (2012) in his analysis of whether growth in the developing world had decoupled from that of developed OECD countries, made the following observation:

> *"The unprecedented acceleration of growth in the developing world in the new millennium in comparison with advanced economies is due not so much to improvements in underlying fundamentals as to exceptionally favourable global economic conditions, shaped mainly by unsustainable policies in advanced economies. The only developing economy which has had a major impact on global conditions, notably on commodity prices, is China. However, growth in China has been driven first by a rapid expansion of exports to advanced economies and more recently, after the global crisis, by an investment boom,*

neither of which is replicable or sustainable over the longer term. To maintain a rapid growth, export-led Asian economies need to reduce their dependence on foreign markets."

Akyuz noted that some 60 per cent of growth in Korea, Taiwan and Thailand and even a greater proportion of growth in Malaysia, Singapore and Vietnam during 2003–2007 had come from exports. Most of the exports eventually ended in advanced economies either directly or through China via component parts or finished goods. An examination of eight Asian countries in a four-year study undertaken by Akyuz (2011) also uncovered several systemic and structural weaknesses in these export-driven economies, including a high degree of vulnerability to trade shocks. It has been estimated that a third to 40 per cent of every US$100 worth of Chinese exports to the US and the European Union (EU), are accrued to East and Southeast Asia. In fact, Asian economies have actually been affected to a greater extent by the recent financial turmoil in the developed countries compared to the 1997 Asian financial crisis (Akyuz, 2011). In 2009, the Malaysian economy contracted 6.2 per cent in the first quarter. The average annual GDP growth rate since then was 4.6 per cent which compares poorly to the 1990s when Malaysia often carded annual growth rates of up to 8 per cent (UNDP, 2012). It is not surprising, then, that the economic imperative remains dominant in the absence of other indicators of well-being and a re-orientation of the economy.

According to government data, Malaysia is said to be on the way towards achieving all its eight Millennium Development Goals (MDGs) established under the 10th Malaysia Plan (2011–2015). The development trajectory has however been driven primarily by a combination of low wages and high revenue for petroleum, palm oil and rubber commodities as well as foreign direct investment in the manufacturing sector (UNDP, 2012). In other words, very little of the profits in the form of oil royalties, for example, have been channelled towards the development of the states that produce the bulk of the exports and also happen to be the poorest in Malaysia.

Since Prime Minister Najib Razak took office in 2009, the main narrative of his New Economic Model (NEM) has been driven by what are perceived to be the more pressing problems facing the economy — that of governance and efficiency, issues of transparency, accountability and institutional streamlining on the one hand, and the purported need to escape the 'middle income trap' and to become a 'high-income' (pegged at a per capita income of RM 48,000) nation by 2020 on the other.[3] Malaysia's inadequate financial, technological and market infrastructure and human capital have been pinpointed as reasons why it cannot compete in economically higher-value-added products and services. The next stage of Malaysia's development trajectory under "The Economic Transformation Programme" is aimed at moving out of the purported middle income trap towards a high-income goal by 2020.[4]

The notion that Malaysians are 'trapped' with a 'middle income' bracket has been questioned. Malaysians on average earned less than RM2,400 per month in 2011.[5] When the government distributed RM500 in 2012 in aid to families that earned less than RM3,000 per month, four million households qualified for the programme (Najib, 2012). Although Malaysia has narrowed the rural-urban poverty gap, the rural poor still accounted for two-thirds of poor households in 2009. The Gini coefficient for 2009 was 0.441, not much different from the previous 20 years. Malaysia has, in fact, the highest inequality in Southeast Asia (Bangura, 2010). The 10th Malaysia Plan admits that there are 2.4 million vulnerable households which make up the bottom 40 per cent of the population (UNDP, 2012).

The government have claimed a certain measure of success in lowering poverty rates from 16 per cent in 1990 to 3.8 per cent in 2009 (NTS, 2012). Its poverty yardstick was however based on the World Bank's minimum standard of US$2 per capita per day, and does not take into account the gulf in costs of living between urban and rural areas or the effects of inflation (UNDP, 2011). Instead of 'absolute' poverty, many NGOs have called for the use of 'relative' poverty which considers the criteria for poverty as earning amounting to less than 50 per cent of the monthly household median income. Since the national household median income is RM2,841 a month, the poverty line would be set at RM1,500 per household, which would have put 21.6 per cent of total households under the threshold (Vinod, 2012).

What does this mean for sustainable development prospects for Malaysia and other developing countries? Among the policy options forwarded by various experts are those that call for the need for more investment in renewable energy, sustainable/ecological/organic agriculture, health and education, environmental remediation, among others. At the same time, wages should be increased to lift domestic consumption in line with sustainability principles, while exports should be of value-added quality products. Intra-regional trade and South-South Trade and Development Cooperation have also gained impetus. All these would need a greater degree of transformation in the country's institutional framework and policymaking process if the sustainable socioeconomic goals are to be realised.

Overview of Selected Policy Frameworks, Gaps and Challenges, and Governance Issues

The constitutional set-up of Malaysia itself poses major challenges to how it can respond to the scale of the global environmental crisis — from resource depletion to climate change — as well as its own domestic socio-political and economic realities. As a federation of states, Malaysia provides for a division of legislative power between the federal and state governments. The handling of external affairs is covered in the Federal List in the 9th Schedule of the Constitution and includes jurisdiction over treaties, agreements and conventions signed with other countries. Maritime and estuarine fishing and fisheries, for instance, are found in the Federal List while river fishing is on the State List.

Apart from the federal territories of Kuala Lumpur and Labuan, land management matters such as land tenure, land improvement and soil conservation, mining, compulsory land acquisition are on the State List. Agriculture and forestry/forests are also within the purview of the states' legislative power. The Constitution further provides for a Concurrent List where both the federal and state legislatures have overlapping or joint jurisdiction over protection of wild animals and wild birds, national parks, town and country planning, drainage and irrigation as well as rehabilitation of mining land. The east Malaysian states of Sarawak and Sabah have more autonomous authority over several matters, including land and natural resources (except for petroleum resources). Article 76 in the Constitution enables Parliament to enact laws with respect to State matters (a) for the purpose of implementing any treaty, agreement or convention with any other country, or any decision of an international organisation of which the Federation is a member; (b) for the purpose of promoting uniformity of the laws of two or more States; or (c) if so requested by the Legislative Assembly of any State. Federal-state mechanisms exist to formulate national policies but the consent of the States is either legally or politically required. A review of environmental laws in 1991–1992 by the Ministry of Science, Technology and the Environment with participation of the state governments and NGOs did recommend that the Constitution be amended to explicitly make environment a federal matter. This however did not gain much political support.

In practice, the federation structure has created obstacles for the development of comprehensive and coherent policies in environmental and natural resource management. Much of the failure of integration of environmental dimension into development planning stems from the overriding preoccupation with economic growth and the use of GDP and per capita income as a measure of well-being. Meanwhile, the focus on environmental issues that marked the immediate post-Rio 1992 five-year plans seemed to have faded considerably into the background in subsequent plans. The influence of the Environment and Natural Resources Section within the Economic Planning Unit (EPU) of the Prime Minister's Office remains weak compared to that of the Macro Economics Section responsible for the formulation of the national plans. So it would appear that integration within the EPU itself remains wanting, let alone among various ministries and agencies across the government.

Despite these shortcomings, the Ministry of Natural Resources and Environment has not been indifferent or inactive. It has in fact introduced numerous policies, laws and regulations aimed at grafting environment concerns into national development planning. Climate-resilient growth strategies have been incorporated in the 10th Malaysia Plan (2011–2015). Rules, regulations and policies notwithstanding, serious problems have however continued to blemish Malaysia's environmental track record due to issues with legal implementation, enforcement and coherence in the absence of a comprehensive legislative framework. Loopholes remain in older laws which have yet to catch up with many new issues. There is also limited administrative and technical capacity to carry out proper coordination, monitoring and evaluation, as well as inadequate science-policy interface among institutions involved in environmental conservation and management. The division of powers between the federal government and the states with respect to natural resource management and land ownership have also resulted in implementation problems (UNDP, 2012). The next section provides a brief overview of selected policies that relate to environmental and natural resource management in Malaysia.

Selected Policies

1. *Biological diversity*

Policy framework

As a party to the Convention on Biological Diversity (CBD), Malaysia is obliged to conserve and sustain biological diversity, as well as to ensure the fair and equitable sharing of benefits arising from the utilisation of genetic resources. The conservation of Malaysia's biological diversity received a boost with the formulation of the National Policy on Biological Diversity in 1998. For the first time, there was a move away from sectoral policies to address biological diversity as a whole. To curb poaching and related crimes, wildlife conservation was strengthened with the replacement of the Protection of Wildlife Act 1972 with the more up-to-date Wildlife Conservation Act 2010. Other policies, laws and regulations enacted to protect biodiversity include the National Wetland Policy 2002, Biosafety Act 2007, International Trade in Endangered Species Act 2008 and the National Tiger Conservation Action Plan 2009. In 2009, the Common Vision on Biodiversity was articulated to take on the implementation of existing policies and programmes on biological diversity further by managing biodiversity in a holistic manner and incorporating it into the planning and development process.

Gaps and challenges

Habitat loss and fragmentation however continues to be a threat to biodiversity resources. There is no single comprehensive legislation in Malaysia that is geared towards biological diversity conservation and management as a whole. Much of the legislation still remains sector-based such as the Fisheries Act 1985, deals mainly with the conservation and management of fisheries resources while and the Forestry Act 1984 focuses on forest management. Most of these sectoral laws were enacted without specific consideration given to the issue of conservation and management of biological diversity as a whole. Although laws to regulate the exploitation of natural resources and protection of the environment exist and have been updated to deal with new and emerging issues, implementation and enforcement remain serious challenges. Issues of sustainable forest management and the threat of the integrity of rainforests from logging remain. The process towards establishing a national legal framework on access and benefit-sharing has been slow. One of the main challenges is the fact that land use and allocation of most natural resources remain in state jurisdiction.

Governance issues

A key weakness in the governance of biological diversity matters in Malaysia lies in the distinct separation of powers between the federal and state governments over resources such as land, forest and water. While most biodiversity-related policies such as the National Biodiversity Policy, the National Forestry Policy and the National Land Policy have been established at the federal level, their adoption has remained weak at state levels, where effective implementation is most needed. To address this challenge, the Malaysian government established in 1998 the highest decision-making body on biodiversity conservation, the National Biodiversity Council which is chaired by the Prime Minister. Efforts have been made to incorporate biological diversity into sectoral policies and the development planning process. A recent example would be the formulation of the National Strategies and Action Plans on Agricultural Biodiversity Conservation and Sustainable Utilisation, which outlines the actions needed to protect the country's agricultural biodiversity. Nonetheless, one of the biggest challenges facing Malaysia today is that of empowering of people with knowledge of their rights and access to information as well as creation of mechanisms for genuine public participation so that national policymaking and development project decisions can truly be aligned with the needs of the economy, society and the environment, which are the three key pillars for sustainable development.

2. *Forest*

Malaysia rainforests are some of the oldest in the world, covering 59 per cent (19.42 million ha) of its total land area. Of these, 5.88 million ha is found in the main peninsula and 4.30 million ha in Sabah and 9.24 million ha in Sarawak in Borneo. As one of the 12 most bio-diverse countries in the world, Malaysia also boasts of several categories of forest — dipterocarp and montane forests, wetland forests such as peat swamp, mangrove and freshwater swamp forests, heath forest as well as vegetative covers on limestone and quartz ridges. Timber-based products are significant contributors to the economy with raw logs and sawn timber making up the bulk of timber exports before it was banned in favour of the development of downstream industrial activities. There are long standing disputes over native customary rights in the state of Sarawak where most of the country's remaining forests are found (Suhakam, 2008).

Policy framework

Under the federal system, land and forest come under the jurisdiction of the state. The National Forestry Council was set up in 1972 to harmonise policies between federal and state governments. The deputy prime minister chairs the council whose members include chief ministers of the 13 states. The National Forestry Policy (NFP) was introduced in 1978 to consolidate the policies of forestry of the states. In 1992, the NFP was revised following complaints over the country's forestry practices in particular those relating to deforestation in the state of Sarawak. The National Forestry Act was enacted in 1984, replacing the Forest Enactment of 1934, to promote further uniformity of states' laws with respect to the administration, management and conservation of forests in line with the revised NFP.

Of the total 19.663 million ha of forest land, 72.73 per cent or 14.301 million ha are gazetted as a Permanent Forest Reserve (PFR) (FAO 2010). Another 1.946 million ha outside the PFR area are gazetted as protected areas under the National Parks Act 1990. Within the PFRs, 2.694 million ha (18.84 per cent) are designated as protected forest while the remaining 11.607 million ha (81.16 per cent) are production forest where commercial harvesting is permitted which enables the state to earn revenue from logging licences in the form of royalty and cess. In Sarawak, forest matters are separately regulated by the Forest Ordinance 1954 but managed by the Sarawak Forestry Corporation while in Sabah, the Sabah Forest Enactment 1968 was enacted to regulate and control activities related to the removal of forest products.

Gaps and challenges

The accuracy of official forestry data has been found to be wanting when comparing figures from different government sources at both state and national levels. The de-gazetting of PFR is lacking in transparency and often carried out with little consultation. The expansion of oil palm plantations in particular, has cast serious doubts on the high forest cover percentage claim. Despite its claim of practising sustainable forest management for the last two decades, the decline in Malaysia's timber yield suggests otherwise. It is evident that the forestry sector can no longer rely on natural forest production. It is estimated that about 2.8 million ha of land area are available for reforestation. A total of 375,000 ha will be planted with fast growing species with a planned planting rate of 25,000 ha annually for the next 15 years, based on the projection of a 12–15 year rotational cycle. From the 25,000 ha, it is projected that 5 million cubic metres of wood can be harvested every year.[6]

Criticism has been directed at the government's preference for monoculture plantation instead of genuine rehabilitation of highly degraded forests as well as the lack of enforcement of harvesting rules. There have also been reports of persistent violations of the rights of indigenous peoples of Sabah and Sarawak over their ancestral land by commercial loggers and plantation concessions parcelled out by state governments, often without consultation or fair and adequate compensation.

It is important to note that Malaysia is a signatory to the United Nations Declaration of the Rights of Indigenous Peoples, of which free, prior, informed consent is a key principle. Over the years there have been suggestions that the federal government[7] compensates state governments if the latter were to refrain from deforestation activities. This however requires resources that are not available and certainly insufficient for long-term conservation purposes. Related to this is the lack of commitments by developed countries under the relevant UN treaties in funds to developing countries to ensure sustainable development pathways that are not detrimental to the world's forests.

3. *Biosafety*

Malaysia, like many Asian countries has identified biotechnology as a major sector for investment. This is reflected in its National Biotechnology Policy 2005, which focuses on the agriculture sector, health related natural products and bio-generic drugs, bio-processing and bio-manufacturing. However, the government is also aware of the need to balance biotechnology with appropriate biosafety policy, laws and measures to ensure that the risks associated with genetically modified organisms (GMOs) are appropriately addressed. Malaysia was the first country to raise the biosafety issue at the Convention on Biological Diversity especially those pertaining to the need for handling, safe transfer and use of any modified living organism. This eventually led to the Cartagena Protocol on Biosafety, the only international law to specifically regulate genetic engineering and GMOs. Malaysia became a party to the Cartagena Protocol on 3rd December, 2003.

Policy framework

The National Policy on Biological Diversity 1998 set the scene for the biosafety policy and regulatory framework in Malaysia. Developing a national biosafety law however took many years and in the meantime several interim measures were put in place to provide guidance on GMOs matters. The 'Guideline on the Release of GMOs to the Environment' was developed in 1997 and the Genetic Modification Advisory Committee (GMAC) established to advise the Ministry of Natural Resources and Environment on GMOs imported for food, feed or processing. The Biosafety Act was finally passed in 2007 after a difficult process that necessitated a lot of inter-ministerial consultations in order to achieve balance between Malaysia's biotechnology aspirations and concern for biosafety. It is a law that allows for the regulation of release, import, export and contained use of living modified organisms (LMOs) and the release of their products. The Biosafety Act is an attempt to reflect Malaysia's international commitments and to ensure that biotechnology in Malaysia is carried out in a manner that does not pose risks to human, plant and animal health as well as the environment or biological diversity. It is also crucial that socio-economic, religious, ethical and moral issues are taken into account.

The Biosafety Act is consistent with the Cartagena Protocol saw the set-up of administrative structures to oversee biosafety in the country. These include the National Biosafety Board (NBB), which is the inter-ministerial, supreme body on biosafety that makes decisions on applications; the Genetic Modification Advisory Committee (GMAC) which advises the NBB on scientific, technical and other relevant issues and the Director-General of Biosafety, which is responsible for the implementation and enforcement under the Act.

Gaps and challenges

The implementation of the Biosafety Act 2007 is just beginning and much capacity building and training are still needed, particularly in areas such as risk assessment and management, monitoring, inspection and enforcement, sampling and detection. Education and the raising of biosafety awareness among government agencies, consumers, farmers and the general public are also necessary. One obvious gap in the Act is the lack of provisions for liability and redress including compensation in the event of LMO misuse or mishap. International negotiations have in the meantime been completed with regards to the Nagoya-Kuala Lumpur Supplementary Protocol on Liability and Redress to the Cartagena Protocol on Biosafety adopted in 2010. The Supplementary Protocol sets the minimum standards and would be evaluated and incorporated as appropriate into Malaysia's biosafety legal framework. As science evolves and as new evidence or early warnings come to light, biosafety policy and laws should also be flexible to accommodate these findings.

Governance issues

The GMAC plays a key role as the advisory body to the government that evaluates the risks assessments provided by applicants. It needs to have diversity of multi-disciplinary expertise and operate independently while taking into account minority or dissenting views. Acknowledgement of the uncertainties surrounding genetic engineering and the gaps in knowledge would also allow honest evaluation of GMOs and their products. The issue of public consultation and participation in decision-making is also critical. Decisions of the NBB related to approvals and notifications must be made available to the public. Regrettably, this provision is not mandatory at the moment. In addition, the Biosafety Act contains a provision on the mandatory identification and labelling of all LMOs and associated products containing or derived from LMOs. The Food (Amendment) Regulations 2010 allow for the labelling of GM food, which is regulated by the Ministry of Health so that consumers can make informed choices regarding GM food.

4. *Climate change*

Malaysia is not immune to rising temperatures and sea levels as well as changes in the intensity and frequency of weather related phenomena due to global climate change. The bleaching of coral reefs with potential adverse effects for marine life, higher risk of flooding in coastal areas, the possibility of more malaria and dengue outbreaks, adverse impact on agriculture and consequently food security are areas of serious concerns. Malaysia has already experienced an increase in temperature of 0.18°C per decade since 1951 and that there has been an average annual rise in sea level by approximately 1.3 mm at two coastal sites in Peninsular Malaysia since 1986. Modelling results estimate that the weather may become warmer with an estimated temperature rise of 2°C by 2041–2050. More extreme hydrological conditions are expected (Kavvas, *et al.*, 2006). A substantial increase in monthly rainfall over the northeast coastal region and decrease in monthly rainfall in the west coast of Peninsular Malaysia have been projected. Significant changes in annual rainfall patterns are also expected in the western regions of Sabah and Sarawak by the end of the century.

Policy framework

Malaysia ratified the UN Framework Convention on Climate Change (UNFCCC) in 1994 and the subsequent Kyoto Protocol in 2002. The National Steering Committee on Climate Change was set up in 1994 to guide national responses to climate change. The National Policy on Climate Change 2009 was established to ensure that climate change measures are incorporated into development plans. The policy provides the framework to mobilise and guide government agencies, industry, communities as well as other stakeholders in addressing the challenges of climate change in a holistic manner that can help navigate the nation towards sustainability. Malaysia has also pledged to voluntarily reduce its emissions intensity from 2005 levels by up to 40 per cent by 2020.[8] This is conditional on receiving the appropriate technology transfer and financing from developed countries. A National Energy Efficiency Master Plan is currently being developed. The federal government is also moving towards greater integration in the management of water resources and supply services through the introduction of the National Water Resources Policy.

Gaps and challenges

The inclusion of climate change in development planning in all sectors of the economy remains a huge challenge. It requires the integration of climate change responses in national development and sectoral planning and implementation. There is also a need to ensure more coherence in the policymaking process and better coordination across agencies. Particularly crucial is the need to develop climate resilience in agriculture, given the potentially devastating effects from climate changes and to ensure disaster preparedness. The means of implementation via financing, appropriate technology and capacity building will need to be better mobilised at both national and international levels. In addition to efforts at overcoming barriers with regards to technology. transfer, Malaysia will also have to invest more in research and development including areas such as climate modelling and early warning systems.

5. *Green technology*

Green technology refers to the development and deployment of products, equipment and systems used in the conservation of natural environment and resources while minimising the negative impact of human activities. These products, equipment and systems should be able to retard or minimise environment degradation; have zero or low greenhouse gas (GHG) emissions; promote healthy environments for all forms of life; conserve the use of energy and natural resources and promote the use of renewable resources. The sectors that have been targeted include energy, water and waste management, buildings, transportation, manufacturing, and information and communications technology (ICT).

Policy framework

The National Green Technology Policy was launched in 2009 to provide guidance and create new opportunities for businesses and industries in the area of environment friendly technology. Its aims include the need to: reduce energy usage; facilitate growth of the green technology sector; increase national capability and capacity for innovation in green technology; develop and enhance Malaysia's global competitiveness in green technology; ensure sustainable development and conserve the environment for future generations as well as raise public awareness. Some of the initiatives for Malaysia's green technology framework include:

- Promotion of renewable energy: The 10th Malaysia Plan sets a renewable energy target of 985 MW or 5.5 per cent of total electricity generation by 2015. Capacity is expected to increase to 2,065 MW in 2020 and grow to about 3,484 MW by 2030, according to the National Renewable Energy Policy and Action Plan (2009).[9] The Renewable Energy Policy and Action Plans were approved in 2010. This was followed by the enactment of the Renewable Energy Act 2011, which provides for the establishment of a special feed-in-tariff system to catalyse the adoption of renewable energy under the newly established Sustainable Energy Development Authority. A Renewable Energy Fund has also been established to support the development of renewable energy.

  The Malaysian government is currently in the final stages of developing the National Energy Efficiency Master Plan which aims to achieve cumulative energy savings of 4,000 kilo tonnes of oil equivalent across all sectors by 2015. The plan also seeks to lower electricity consumption by 10 per cent by 2020. Some important pieces of legislation currently being developed include the Energy Efficiency Act,

Low Carbon Green Growth Act and the Low Carbon Cities Framework (Economic Planning Unit (2012), personal communication).

- The Green Technology Financing Scheme is a soft loan initiative aimed at improving the supply and utilisation of green technology through companies that are producers, innovators or users of green technology. As an incentive, the Malaysian governments would bear 2 per cent of the total interest/profit rate while providing a guarantee of 60 per cent for financing. Up to 140 companies are expected to benefit from the scheme.[10]

- The Low Carbon Cities Framework aims to reduce the carbon emissions of cities and townships, and guide them towards greener solutions. The towns of Putrajaya and Cyberjaya are being developed to showcase green technology. The Green Building Index has been developed to promote sustainability in the built environment.

- The Malaysian Green Labelling Program focuses on standards and green labels. Policies and instruments have been initiated at the institutional level, while green procurement manuals, procedures and standards are currently being developed by the Ministry of Finance in collaboration with the Ministry of Energy, Green Technology and Water, and Malaysia's research and standards development agency, SIRIM.

- The Ministry of Energy, Green Technology and Water is working with the Ministry of Transport and the Ministry of International Trade and Industry to develop the infrastructure roadmap for the use of electric vehicles in Malaysia.

Gaps and challenges

In terms of the energy sector, a major challenge for Malaysia would be to progressively wean the country off its dependence on fossil fuels, namely oil, gas and coal. One consideration is to decouple economic growth and carbon emissions, which requires policy, institutional commitment and coherence at all levels. There is a need to promote and implement energy efficiency and renewable energy so that any shortfall can be bridged. Public awareness needs to be enhanced while the right incentives will have to be put in place. In addition, appropriate research and innovation in green technology are also required as there is still no comprehensive understanding in areas relating to technology assessment.

Governance issues

The Ministry of Energy, Green Technology and Water was established in April 2009 after a cabinet reshuffle replacing the Ministry of Energy, Water and Communications. The setting up of a ministry dedicated in large part to green technology was followed quickly by the establishment of the National Green Technology Council in 2010 (later to become the National Green Technology and Climate Change Council) and the restructuring of an existing agency to become the Malaysian Green Technology Corporation (GreenTech Malaysia). The council, which is chaired by the Prime Minister, aims to coordinate policy and action at the national level. Its working committees are focused on various aspects relevant to climate change in areas such as industry, transportation, human capital, research and innovation, promotion and awareness and adaptation. In addition, there is a need to ensure integration of policies and decision-making across sectors as climate change is a cross-cutting issue. There are various councils which address issues of importance and related to climate change such as the National Forestry Council which was set up in 1972 to better harmonise policies among federal and state governments while the National Water Resources Council was set up in 1998 to pursue more effective water management.

6. *Environmental quality*

The introduction of the Environmental Quality Act (EQA) in 1974 was an attempt to come up with a comprehensive law in dealing with environmental matters. It was with this Act that an agency responsible for the environment was first established — the Department of Environment (DOE), which is now under the Ministry of Natural Resources and Environment. The DOE primarily deals with matters involving air and water quality, industrial wastes, noise levels and environmental impact assessments. The use of Environmental Impact Assessment (EIA) was introduced during the 1980s to address environmental concerns during planning stages of industrial projects.

Policy framework

The EQA was the beginning of an organised and committed effort of the government as regards the environment in general. It contains sections directly related to air pollution, noise pollution, pollution of inland waters, oil pollution, crude palm oil, raw natural rubber and others. Environmental reporting procedures became a requirement for certain prescribed activities when the EIA regulations were tagged on later. Significantly, unlike other resource-related legislation, the EQA is applicable to the whole of Malaysia. The Environmental Quality Order 1987 also made it mandatory for 19 categories of activities to have environmental impact assessment reports (EIAs) submitted and approved by the Department of Environment before any activity can be carried out.

Gaps and challenges

Many environmentalists and concerned citizens have, however, expressed their frustrations with the EIA process, while many developers view EIAs as mere a 'formality' to be complied with. Approval for EIAs comes from the inadequately staffed and budget-strapped DOE. Furthermore, the go-ahead given to a number of controversial projects has given rise to the public perception that there had been undue influence from high-level officials in the approval process involving large-scale private sector projects. Furthermore, there had been loopholes in the EIA procedures such as:

- Over-generous 50-ha limitation for construction of resorts, hotels and hillside infrastructure
- Developers parcelling out projects into less than 50-ha portions in order to circumvent EIA requirements
- Logging sites can avoid EIA scrutiny if the area is less than 500 ha
- The quality and independence of EIA reports have also come under scrutiny due to the associated costs and relationships between EIA consultants and their paymasters.
- Environmental planning requires forethought and conscientious efforts to avoid damage to natural surroundings and communities. Unfortunately, all too often bulldozers move in before the final EIA has properly addressed preventive measures, often without public input.

Governance issues

The DOE primarily deals with matters involving air and water quality, industrial wastes, noise levels and environmental impact assessments or in short oversight of environmental quality. The issue of natural resources management is, however, not within its purview and rests largely with the individual states, especially with regards to forests, wetlands, land, rivers and mineral resources. It is only through the EIA process that the DOE has some supervisory role. There has been much criticism that inadequate attention had be given to environmental concerns at state levels.

Public participation is the key to an EIA process. Two examples of widespread public participation were sparked off by the proposed mammoth development project at Penang Hill and the Sungai Selangor dam. Both these sprung from initiatives by local NGOs. However, apart from these notable exceptions, there has been a distinct lack of effective participation in the review process. This is not a result of a lack of interest on the part of the public, but due to poor sharing of information and inadequate notification on the part of the DOE. Furthermore, in many instances, projects have been approved by the DOE on the basis of preliminary EIAs.

The handling of environmental policies can certainly be improved not only through a more supportive institutional framework but also through sufficient financial and technological back-up that are in symmetry with the economic and social dimensions of sustainable economic development for any genuine transformation to take place.

Emergence of the "Green Movement"

Perhaps the most surprising development on the environmental front was the rise in 2012 of Malaysia's own Green Movement. While activism against logging, oil palm plantations and pollution and unsustainable exploitation of water and other resources had in the past intermittently received civil society backing, 2012 saw an unprecedented upsurge of citizens rallying in unseen-before numbers and the formation of a grassroots green movement that challenged the government's policies. Five issues, in particular have served as rallying points:

Nuclear plans: The government had in December 2010 announced plans to build two nuclear power plants to meet rising energy demand by 2021. A civil campaign was launched to press the government into abandoning these plans out of concerns that they would be disastrous for public health, safety and the environment in Malaysia. Plans for a proposed plant have since been put on hold following Japan's problems with its nuclear plants after the March 2011 earthquake.

Mega-dams in Sarawak: Indigenous communities and activists have for years resisted moves by both the state and federal governments to build mammoth hydroelectric projects.[11] A plan is underway to build 12 mega-dams under the Sarawak Corridor of Renewable Energy (SCORE) to transform Sarawak into a "developed state" by 2020. The 944 MW Murum Dam would require the resettlement of 1,400 people from the Penan and Kenyah communities while the 1,000 MW Baram Dam will displace some 20,000 indigenous peoples and submerge 412 sq. km of forests. There have been protests over the loss of native customary land, homes, livelihoods and natural biodiversity that such projects would cause. The Save Sarawak Rivers Network was set up in February 2012 to oppose the dam construction (ENS, 2012) and considerable efforts have since been made to inform and mobilise people against the plan (Ling, 2013).

Raub gold-mining: It was discovered in the middle of the last decade that operations by a gold-mining company in Raub in Pahang had not comply with international standards and could cause long-term harm to local residents and the environment. The facility, only 200–300 meters away from the nearest village, uses the 'carbon-in-leach' method and consumes 400 tonnes of sodium cyanide a year. Booklets to raise awareness were printed by local residents and a massive rally took place in October 2011 in Kuantan as a result (Netto, 2012).

Pengerang Integrated Petroleum Complex (PIPC): An ambitious project to develop this complex in Johor has caused an uproar amongst several fishing villages that make up a significant proportion of the local population. Critics argue that the plant will cause large-scale social and economic dislocation. It is expected that about 600 families from seven villages would have to be relocated without adequate compensation. In addition, there have also been questions related to public health concerns and the demands placed on land, water, energy resources and loss of livelihood. Local NGOs were consequently formed and several protests were organised in 2012, including one on 30 September 2012 that saw more than 3,000 participants (Fann, 2012; Chong, 2013).

Lynas Rare Earth Refinery: There has been strong opposition and numerous rallies from residents of Gebeng in Pahang and activists against a controversial rare earth refinery operated by Australian company Lynas. Rare earth minerals are often found in ores which contain small amounts of radioactive elements such as uranium and thorium, so extracting them raises a number of health and safety issues (MITI, 2011). Some of the protests have seen some 20,000 'green shirts' joined a mammoth rally calling for electoral reform (Netto, 2012). The historic scale of the green movement has demonstrated that environmental issues can no longer be dismissed by invoking 'Malaysia's development' aspirations.

Threat from Bilateral Free Trade Agreements

The proliferation of bilateral free trade agreements (FTAs) between developed and developing countries has become a source of concern due to provision for foreign investors to sue a government directly via an investor-to-state dispute settlement (ISDS) mechanism under private international arbitration tribunals to rule on any act, policy or law — including those put in place to protect the environment or public health. The precursor of the right for investor-to-state dispute under a trade agreement is the North American Free Trade Agreement (NAFTA). Total claims filed under NAFTA-style deals as of August 2013 numbered 80 with 20 cases dismissed and 13 cases won by investors with compensation totalling US$405.4 million. A few cases were withdrawn and many are still pending (Public Citizen, 2013).[12] Of note is that a fair number of cases involved issues relating to environmental regulations.

Conclusion

The scale of the ecological challenge — from depleting forests and degraded soils to climate change — demands fundamental rethinking of development approaches. There is a need to re-orientate, and truly integrate, the three dimensions of sustainable development. At the same time, economic and social well-being are also priorities and despite its achievements so far, Malaysia is still a long way from attaining sustainability on the environmental front due to the current shortcomings. Furthermore, it will have to safeguard itself against new threats such as surrendering its policy space and sovereignty via FTAs and bilateral investment agreements. No country can rise to the sustainable development challenge on its own especially amid the current atmosphere of fragmented international cooperation. Countries in Asia, including Malaysia will have to step up to the plate to forge common interests and take the lead.

Endnotes

[1] See TWN (2012).

[2] The Intergovernmental Group of Twenty-Four on International Monetary Affairs and Development (Group of 24) is a chapter of the Group of 77,

established in 1971 to coordinate the positions of developing countries on international monetary and development finance issues and to ensure that their interests were adequately represented in negotiations on international monetary matters.

3 On 1 December 2009, Second Minister of Finance Ahmad Husni Hanadzlah said in a speech at the "National Economic Outlook Conference 2010–2011" that among the top economic concerns in Malaysia were the state of education, corruption, government over-reach in economic affairs, public institutions, the brain-drain, and low domestic investments. See also Wong Chun Wai, "From the Heart and Refreshing", *The Sunday Star*, 13 December, 2009.

4 See ETP (2011).

5 It was RM1,916 in 2009. See Prime Minister Najib Abdul Razak's 2012 Budget Speech (2011); see also Economic Transformation Programme (2010).

6 See MTIB (2013).

7 See FEM (2013).

8 Government of Malaysia. The Rt. Hon. Prime Minister's Speech. 17–18 December 2009. Copenhagen Congress Center (Bella Center) Copenhagen, Denmark.

9 See SEDA (2009).

10 See the GTS (2013).

11 The most controversial was the 2,400MW Bakun Dam where 695 km^2 (equivalent to the size of Singapore) was to be flooded. Critics pointed out that in both East Malaysia and Peninsular Malaysia there is an over-supply of electricity, which made the hydroelectric project unnecessary. After two failed starts, the privatisation of the project to a logging company with no experience in dam construction, two postponed completion targets; eventual takeover by the government with "compensation" to the logging company, which had completed only 50 per cent of the engineering work, the flooding process was initiated on 13 October, 2010. Vast tropical rainforests and its biodiversity, as well as 15 indigenous communities, suffered as a result. There was much discontent among the local population, along with unresolved compensation claims, loss of livelihood and other social problems.

12 See Public Citizen (2013).

References

Akyuz, Yilmaz. "The Staggering Rise of the South?" *South Centre Research* 44 (2012). Available online at http://www.southcentre.org/index.php?option= com_content&view=article&id=1691%3Athe-staggering-rise-of-the-south& Itemid=335&lang=en. Last accessed on 14 August, 2013.

Akyuz, Yilmaz, ed. *The Financial Crisis and Asian Developing Countries*. Penang: Third World Network, 2011.

Bangura, Yusuf. *Combating Poverty and Inequality: Structural Change, Social Policy and Politics.* Geneva: United Nations Research Institute for Social Development, 2010.

Chong, Debra. "Questions over New Year Deaths of Pengerang Family." *The Malaysian Insider,* January 2, 2013. Available online at http://www.the malaysianinsider.com/malaysia/article/questions-over-new-year-deaths-of-pengerang-family. Last accessed on 14 August, 2013.

ENS (Environment News Service). "Hydro Tasmania to Withdraw From Sarawak Dam-Building Program." December 5, 2012. Available online at http://ens-newswire.com/2012/12/05/hydro-tasmania-to-withdraw-from-sarawak-dam-building-program/. Last accessed on 14 August, 2013.

ETP (Economic Transformation Programme). 2010. "About ETP". Available online at http://etp.pemandu.gov.my/About_ETP-@-Overview_of_ETP.aspx. Last accessed on 3 October, 2013.

ETP (Economic Transformation Programme). "A Roadmap for Malaysia: A Special Report." 2011. Available online at http://etp.pemandu.gov.my/upload/ETP_TheEdge_Pull_out.pdf. Last accessed on 14 August, 2013.

FAO (Food and Agriculture Organization of the United Nations). Global Forest Resources Assessment 2010: Country Report — Malaysia. Available online at http://www.fao.org/docrep/013/al558e/al558e.pdf. Last accessed on 3 October 2013.

Fann, Thomas. "10 Big Questions about Pengerang." *Harakah Daily,* September 25, 2012. Available online at http://en.harakahdaily.net/index.php/articles/analysis-a-opinion/5844-10-big-questions-about-pengerang.html. Last accessed on 14 August, 2013.

FEM (Friends of the Earth Malaysia). "Sahabat Alam Malaysia — SAM." Available online at https://www.facebook.com/pages/Sahabat-Alam-Malaysia-SAM/374958359261992. Last accessed on 3 October, 2013.

Gimbad, Elizabeth. "Rethinking Poverty in Sabah." *The Malaysian Insider,* December 13, 2012. Available online at http://www.themalaysianinsider.com/sideviews/article/rethinking-poverty-in-sabah-elizabeth-gimbad. Last accessed on 14 August, 2013.

GTS (Green Technology Financing Scheme). The Green Technology Financing Scheme Website. Available online at http://www.gtfs.my/news/green-technology-financing-scheme-website. Last accessed on 3 October, 2013.

Kavvas, M. Levent, Z. Q. Richard Chen and Norika Ohara. "Impact of climate change on the hydrologic regime and water resources of Peninsular Malaysia." NAHRIM. 2006. Available online at http://www.nahrim.gov.my/download/pksa/RegHCM_PM_Report_9_21_06_Ex%20v1.pdf. Last accessed on 3 October, 2013.

Ling, Gan Pei. "Environmental Hot Potatoes in 2013." *The Nut Graph*, January 28, 2013. Available online at http://www. thenutgraph.com/environmental-hot-potatoes-in-2013/. Last accessed on 14 August, 2013.

MITI (Ministry of International Trade and Industry), Government of Malaysia. "The Lynas Fact Sheet." 2011. Available online at http://www.miti.gov.my/cms/content.jsp?id=com.tms.cms.article.Article_4008ad57-c0a81573-7a607a 60-19ec542e. Last accessed on 14 August, 2013.

MTIB (Malaysian Timber International Board). "Forest Plantation". 2013. Available online at http://www.mtib.gov.my/index.php?option=com_content& view=article&id=94. Last accessed on 3 October, 2013.

Netto, Anil. "Malaysia's Green Movement Goes Political." *Inter Press Service*, July 21, 2012. Available online at http://www.ipsnews.net/2012/07/ malaysias-green-movement-goes-political/. Last accessed on 14 August, 2013.

NTS (New Straits Times). "No Poverty in Malaysia by 2015." November 3, 2012. Available online at http://www.nst.com.my/nation/general/no-poverty-in-malaysia-by-2015-1.165803. Last accessed on 14 August, 2013.

Prime Minister Najib Abdul Razak. "The 2012 Budget Speech: Introducing the Supply Bill (2012)." Speech, Dewan Rakayat, Kuala Lumpur, October 7, 2011. Available online at http://www.sabah.gov.my/main/Content/budget/National/BajetNasional12.pdf. Last accessed on 14 August, 2013.

——— "Transformation: A Journey." Speech, *New Straits Times*. April 2, 2012. Available online at http://www.nst.com.my/top-news/a-better-malaysia-1.69956#ixzz2JugxGzZa. Last accessed on 14 August, 2013.

Public Citizen. "Table of Foreign Investor-State Cases and Claims under NAFTA and Other U.S. Trade Deals." 2013. Available online at http://www.citizen.org/documents/investor-state-chart.pdf. Last accessed on 10 September, 2013.

SEDA (Sustainable Energy Development Authority of Malaysia). "National Renewable Energy Policy and Action Plan." Available online at http://seda.gov.my/?omaneg=00010100000001010101000100001000000000000000 00000&s=31. Last accessed on 3 October, 2013.

Suhakam (Human Rights Commission of Malaysia). Legal Perspectives on Native Customary Land Rights in Sarawak. 2008. Available online at http://www.suhakam.org.my/c/document_library/get_file?p_l_id=30217&folderId= 26470&name=DLFE-711.pdf. Last accessed on 11 September, 2013.

TWN (Third World Network). TWN Update on Sustainable Development Conference. 2012. Available online at http://www.twn.my/sdc2012.htm. Last accessed on 14 August 2013.

UNDP (United Nations Development Programme). "Malaysia: The Millennium Goals at 2010." 2011. Available online at http://www.undp.org.my/files/editor_files/files/Malaysia%20MDGs%20report%20clean%200419.pdf. Last accessed on 14 August, 2013.

UNDP (United Nations Development Programme). "Country Programme for Malaysia, 2013–2015." 2012. Available online at http://www.undp.org. my/files/editor_files/files/CP_MAL_2013-2015.pdf. Last accessed on 14 August, 2013.

Vinod, G. "Review Unrealistic Poverty Benchmark." *Free Malaysia Today*, August 22, 2012. Available online at http://www.freemalaysiatoday.com/ category/nation/2012/08/22/review%20unrealistic%20poverty%20bench mark/. Last accessed on 14 August, 2013.

ENVIRONMENTAL POLICY IMPLEMENTATION: ACHIEVEMENTS AND CHALLENGES

7. Governing the Common Firm: The Evolution of Environmental Policy for Small Businesses in India

Sudhir Chella RAJAN

Small firms present a conundrum for policymakers in many developing countries. On the one hand, their low capital requirements, relatively high labour productivity and high employment make them a very attractive proposition, especially in those contexts where they can serve as a major source of export earnings (Beck and Demirguc-Kunt, 2006). On the other hand, the very flexibility and informal character of their structure and operations generate challenges when it comes to regulating them, especially in countries where other governance challenges abound, which often end up with greater incentives for many small enterprises to stay hidden in the shadow economy. From an environmental standpoint to the extent that small firms are associated with manufacturing, packaging or other forms of material processing, they are significant multi-point sources of pollution that are often difficult to track, license or regulate (Blackman, 2000).

A variety of approaches have been proposed for managing environmental problems associated with small firms, and recent studies have indicated that many require specific prevailing conditions in order to be successful. These may cover a wide swath of areas to deal with, including issues such as voluntary standards, public disclosure and reviews, financial penalties, various degrees of mandatory regulations, targeted enforcement, taxes, subsidies, grants and fees, education and advice, environmental audits and reviews, pressure from NGOs or local communities as well as keeping up with new technologies for monitoring and ensuring enforcement (Dasgupta *et al.*, 2000; Parker *et al.*, 2009).

A survey by Parker *et al.* (2009) that covers interventions in a large number of OECD countries to incentivise small and medium enterprises (SMEs) to reduce their environmental footprint, suggests that because business conditions are diverse and vary by sector, no single one-size-fits-all policy can produce all the desired outcomes. For instance, the particular character and motivations of the firm and the extent to which they are driven by business performance versus their environmental commitment and 'green' profile will determine the degree of success of the different modes of intervention. If no single framework of policy strategies, no matter how broad, can be effective in controlling pollution even in advanced industrialised countries, with otherwise more effective institutions and well-established rule of law, what are the chances of success in emerging economies where both are lacking?

This question forms the broader motivation for this chapter in the context of India, although I cannot, given the scope of this study, attempt to provide reasonable answers. Rather, I review the policy environment concerning the so-called micro, small and medium enterprise (MSME) segment in India and try to assess the limited success stories of three case studies against the larger challenges that still need to be resolved. Unfortunately, these cases themselves demonstrate the complexities of the problems involving collective action, even when there are strong industry associations that can address some of the problems associated with scale. More typically, small firms are spatially dispersed and poorly organised, which suggests that there are no silver bullets available. The best options, it appears, may be to design macro-policies that encourage technology innovation and training directed towards small firms, especially in sectors where motives of self-interest, such as cost reduction and improved workplace safety, may be easy to identify, and to develop guild-like networks to help technology transfer as well as provide financing and other support mechanisms.

Policy Context in India

The Indian government has long had a strong motivation to promote the growth of small firms. Alongside the strong emphasis on the public sector and heavy industry, the Industrial Policy Resolution of 1948 pledged to develop a framework to integrate cottage and small-scale industries with their larger counterparts, for example, the handloom sector with textile mills. In 1954, a government agency, the Small Industries Development

Organisation (SIDO) was set up to provide resources for cottage and small-scale industries in the form of subsidies, credit facilities, training for business and skills development and a degree of security through government procurement programmes. In the decades that followed, the industrial policies in India remained bifurcated between a strong commitment to traditional sectors such as iron and steel, chemicals and minerals and an interest in promoting SMEs. At various points, the federal government seemed to have diverted its focus to the latter, recognising their potential for job creation and earnings from exports. In 1977, for instance, the brief change in government replacing the Congress Party prompted a strongly-worded, though perhaps somewhat unfair assertion by the Janata Alliance in its Industrial Policy statement:

> "The emphasis of industrial policy so far has been mainly on large industries neglecting cottage industries completely relegating small industries to a minor role. It is the firm policy of this Government to change this approach." [1]

By 1991, even as liberalization policies were being put in place by SIDO, nearly 1,000 products had been reserved for exclusive manufacturing by small and medium firms in order to help SMEs modernize and upgrade their technology. The 1990s was also a period when environmental laws in the country began to acquire some level of maturity. However, most SMEs were either too small or given special exemption, which placed them largely outside the orbit of regulatory scrutiny (Divan and Rosencranz, 2002).

In the next three decades, a series of developments will put SMEs at the forefront of the country's reform efforts. The most important of these was the Micro, Small and Medium Enterprises Development Act of 2006, which designated the category of 'micro' to include manufacturing firms with capital investments under US$50,000; small enterprises with investments up to about a US$1 million; and a medium-size category for the rest with capital outlays under US$2 million. Firms in the service sector have even lower ceilings for the respective classes. The Act liberalised the sector, allowing domestic and unrestricted foreign equity participation in an MSME and easier access to bank credit while creating new facilities such as technology development centres and training institutes. These efforts led to a significant increase in the output of such firms (see Figure 7.1; note that the jump in 2006–2007 is due to changes in classification, but the growth thereafter is substantial).

In policy discourse, MSMEs as a group have turned into a sort of poster child for the new economy in its quest for 'inclusive growth', a point that is

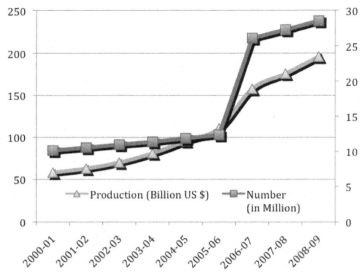

Figure 7.1: Growth in Production and Number of Micro, Small and Medium Sized Enterprises in India.

Source: MSME, 2012.

highlighted to some extent by the Ministry's figures, which indicates that 95 per cent of MSMEs are micro-enterprises (MSME, 2012). Particularly impressive has been the growth of family businesses in rural areas. The fourth annual census of MSMEs reveals a growth in rural output of 255 per cent over a six-year period, which was mostly associated with rising exports of spices, food products and rural crafts. Following the liberalising provisions of the MSME Act, various government agencies and industry associations have also been working vigorously to promote the export orientation of such small firms through the organization of trade fairs, export credit facilities. Much of these efforts have been focused on specific sectors, especially leather and textiles.

It is estimated that MSMEs currently make up nearly half of manufacturing output or about 9 per cent of gross domestic product (GDP), employing about 70 million and account for more than a third of India's export earnings. There are more than 30 million such firms, of which one in four are likely to be involved with some sort of processing or generation of hazardous materials associated with plastics, textile dyes, metal-working and chemicals (see Figure 7.2 and Figure 7.3). There are also a very large

Share by gross output

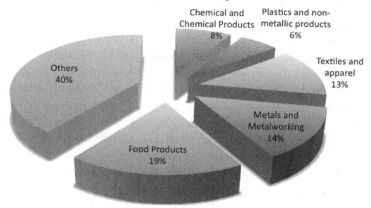

Figure 7.2: Sector Composition of MSMEs by Share of Gross Output.
Source: MSME, 2012.

Share by number of enterprises

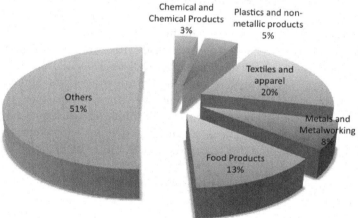

Figure 7.3: Sectoral Share of MSMEs by Number of Enterprises.
Source: MSME, 2012.

number of tiny 'firms', comprising individuals working singly or in partnership with others, largely making up an informal if not shadow economy — a significant though unquantified fraction of which involves waste processing and recycling, primarily in urban areas. Here again, workplace exposure to toxins can be extremely high, particularly for those sorting industrial and commercial waste from electronic parts, battery components and heavy metals from chemical effluents. These entrepreneurs are usually not included in MSME registries and also do not benefit from any of the incentives provided by the government though some form of assistance might come forth from NGOs or self-help groups working within urban slums.

Environmental policy in India has traditionally operated through a system of licensing, applied primarily to large firms in traditional sectors such as cement, chemicals, and iron and steel. Although MSMEs were not all automatically exempt from air and water pollution regulations, state and federal pollution control boards were far less likely to enforce such rules stringently in the case of smaller firms. Since the 1990s, however, environmental challenges associated with the sector have received attention from policymakers, especially within specific categories and clusters where problems have been egregious. Starting in 1994, the Ministry of Environment and Forests (MoEF) began developing 'Clean Technology' initiatives and 'Waste Minimisation Circles' to target the use of new technologies at specific units or clusters within various industrial areas of the country. These were largely part of efforts to provide a sense of 'win-win' opportunities within some industries where the government would provide technical assistance and financing aimed at pollution reduction. Over 100 such 'circles' were established with varying degrees of success in reducing water and energy use as well as a decline in pollutants in electroplating, textile dyeing and food processing units among others around the country. The government has since set up more special funds for modernising tanneries and textile units and instituted special awards to recognise innovation in technology in order to encourage competitiveness while encouraging waste reduction and better use of material resources.

Unfortunately, given the vast number and diversity of small firms in the country, these approaches can best be seen as ad hoc in nature and of little impact, except in those sectors where active industry associations, prompted largely by concerns relating to international competitiveness, have resulted in structural changes and technology upgrades. This can be seen, to some extent, in the leather and textile industries, although it would be unwise to claim that all or even the majority of units in these domains have improved as a result of these efforts. In the case of brick kilns, a concerted attempt by government agencies, bilateral and multilateral donors and voluntary groups to reduce energy use has yielded co-benefits across the industry in the reduction of air pollution. Similar efforts made more recently in the electronic waste sector have not, however, met with the same degree of success, at least as far as small firms are concerned. The government recently issued the e-waste Management & Handling Rules in 2011, which aimed at reducing the use of hazardous substances in electrical and electronic equipment by specifying the thresholds for use of heavy metals such as lead, mercury and cadmium. These rules apply to every producer, consumer or bulk consumer, collection centre, dismantler and recycler of e-waste involved in the manufacture, sale, purchase and processing of electrical and electronic equipment or components, but are explicit in exempting micro and small enterprises.

In the next section, I will review three case studies that have encountered various degrees of success when dealing with small firms in the context of environmental regulatory intervention. They demonstrate the importance of an external impetus — either in the form of judicial intervention, government fiat or international competitive pressure in getting some initial action going. The examples also show that an entire ecosystem of support structures in the form of technology innovation centres, financing mechanisms and political commitment will be necessary to ensure sustainability. Even then, unless the majority of small producers perceive and actually obtain personal benefits from their collective action, it will not be possible to keep a coalition together in the longer run. The common thread in these case studies is spatial clustering within the sector, which brings with it the business and economic advantages of agglomeration that may not extend to all sectors. Nevertheless, some of the lessons learned from these instances may still be valuable if new technologies to build networks are successfully applied and if other conditions also prevail.

Case Studies

a) *Apparel production in Tirupur*

Tirupur is an industrial town in Tamil Nadu, with a population of about half a million people and responsible for nearly 90 per cent of India's knitted garment exports, earning it the title of Banian (Vest or T-shirt) City. There are over 5,000 units in the city, many of which started as household enterprises involved in knitting, bleaching, dyeing, calendaring, finishing and printing processes. Very few are vertically integrated and tend to be small units with relatively few employees. Cumulatively, the city's apparel industry rakes in some US\$3 billion from exports to brand marketers mostly in Europe and North America.[2]

Tirupur is a model of the new regime of 'flexible production'. It can deliver customised pieces within 12 hours and supply up to half a million pieces in a few days (Rangarajan, 2005). There are 15 textile industry associations that provide a variety of technical, financial and marketing assistance and services to their members. Most dyers and bleachers fall into the 'micro' or 'small' end of the MSME spectrum. Although the enterprise owners have highly specialised traditional skills, they are apt to keeping technical know-how within family circles and are resistant to the adoption of new technologies (Swaminathan and Jeyaranjan, 1994).

The entire textile cluster is a major consumer of groundwater, typically at rates that exceed international norms (Erkman and Ramaswamy, 2003). Most of the 800 dyeing and bleaching units in the city are located along the Noyyal or Nallar rivers in which effluents were discharged directly until 1997. The dyeing operations alone were responsible for over 13,000 tonnes of chemical waste annually. As a result of both excessive groundwater withdrawal and the discharge of these effluents — which include caustic soda, hydrochloric acid, sodium hydro-sulphate, sodium hypochlorite and peroxides — groundwater quality in the entire region became unfit for consumption by other domestic, agricultural or industrial users.

In 1989, the government began to provide up to 50 per cent subsidies for the set-up of common effluent treatment plants (CETP), which could be shared by multiple units. Only one such plant was set up by 1997 when, following a complaint from a farmer downstream, the Madras High Court issued an order which threatened to shut down all bleaching and dyeing units unless they complied with regulations. By 2003, a large number of individual effluent treatment plants were set up along with about a dozen CETPs receiving subsidies. The Tirupur Dyers Association was the principal body behind the building of eight such treatment plants with the help of an infusion of government subsidies and contributions from its own members. In addition, the government also started to beef up the infrastructure for power and water as well as a special purpose vehicle for directing investments to the cluster.

Crow and Batz (2006) argue that the equity shares of the Tirupur Dyers' Association had helped to defray the capital costs of compliance with environmental regulation as well as improved productivity levels that led to a greater degree of vertical integration. It appears that the collective action strategies were critical in keeping the industry afloat. One of the main factors that helped to maintain the strength of the coalition was that the industry was mainly dependent on jobs from external clients. The industry association's political clout and legal representation not only contributed to the resources for maintaining a united front, but at the same time provided technical assistance and worked with the regulatory agency to ensure proper enforcement. The local industry eventually developed the reputation of being a responsible cluster while maintaining its international competitive edge.

On reflection, the initial court action and investments by the association in conjunction with the government provided a viable ecosystem for effective collective action. Most critical, of course, was the importance of exports for the cluster which prompted a variety of donor groups, NGOs and the government to pay close attention to the region and its challenges. Nevertheless, the story is neither entirely rosy nor complete. Pollution levels in the region continue to be high and as recently as January 2011, the Chennai High Court ordered all dyeing units to be closed. The problem was that water quality had not improved substantially despite the installation of the treatment facilities. The outcome has been devastating for the industry, which is already facing stiff competition from places like Bangladesh and China. Many enterprises have since relocated to other parts of the country, including Karnataka, Gujarat and Rajasthan, often without the knowledge of pollution control agencies in these states (Preetha, 2012; Reddy, 2012).

b) *Leather tanneries in Palar, Tamil Nadu*

In the case of leather, much like apparel, outside intervention urged the industry to curb polluting practices. Germany, India's largest importer of leather, imposed court orders and a ban on the use of toxic chemicals in leather production process. This effort enjoyed varying degrees of success. The action was in the wake of a court order in 1995 to shut down around 200 tanneries in the Palar Valley in Tamil Nadu's Vellore district. The court's decision came after complaints that pollution from the tanneries had sullied water resources in the Palar basin affecting irrigation supply for agriculture.

Collective action through the setting up and monitoring of CETPs was the most feasible option in the face of the closure threat. With neither space nor the financial ability to set up individual effluent treatment plants among the smaller tanneries, CETPs were set up. These are now collectively owned and managed by the tanners themselves. Larger units also chose to join the CETP network to minimise individual risks as monitoring effluents is often difficult and expensive. Social ties between tanners have contributed to cooperation and the institutions built around CETPs with locals becoming the main channels of contact for decision makers at the regional level. The state also played a secondary but critical role in extending subsidies and technical support through public research institutions (Kennedy, 1999).

But while CETPs are intended to meet a prescribed norm, it soon emerged that there was a need to deal with the 'free rider' problem due to difficulties in ascertaining the quantity or quality of wastewater each tannery releases into the system. Monitoring committees have been formed to conduct periodic as well as surprise inspections. Violations such as mixing sludge with wastewater or producing in excess of declared capacity are acted upon through forced closures for a limited period (usually one week). Yet, cases have been noted where leniency has been shown toward offenders. Such factors, among many others, such as techniques and technology used, volumes of production and so on, have contributed to the failure of collective action (Tewari and Pillai, 2005).

The setting up of new institutions around the CETPs and the treatment of effluents through collective action may have been considered an overall success in the Palar Valley, but it is still patchy. CETPs have been known to opt for cheaper technologies, for instance using a normal wooden drum that costs around US$10,000 that lasts for 5–7 years instead of an eco-friendly drum that has a lifespan of 50 years but at a cost of $50,000. According to a study conducted by the Central Pollution Control Board in 2005, of the 10 CETPs operating in the Vellore district, very few adhered to the BOD standards, while none met the TDS standards prescribed by the Tamil Nadu Pollution Control Board (CPCB, 2005).

A more successful story with respect to collective action for environmental compliance by the leather industry revolves around the ban imposed by Germany on pentachlorophenol (PCPs) and Azo dyes in the 1990s. During the early stages of adjustment, the ban was implemented through voluntary action on the part of small tanneries, whose compliance was made possible due to the threat of financial losses if they continue to supply non-compliant leather to their clientele. The ban was introduced at a time when the leather industry was India's fourth largest foreign exchange earner. Germany was India's largest leather export market, accounting for 22 per cent of India's total leather exports then. At the behest of both the Ministry of Commerce and the Ministry of Environment and Forests, the state banned not just certain products containing the chemicals, but also the use of the banned chemicals altogether despite strong opposition from multinationals and other powerful vested interests such as the Dye Manufacturers Association of India.

The PCP ban which had called for the eradication of a chemical, for which substitutes were locally available, came five years before the more devastating Azo dye ban, for which substitutes were not readily available and which affected multiple sectors. The government, however, on its part also slashed import duties on safer dyes and alternative chemicals, thus softening the blow. PCPs and Azo dyes are used in the tanning process, which made it difficult, to identify which units were using the banned substances. The problem was compounded by India's lack of an infrastructural set-up or expertise to test samples. Here again, the government stepped in and played an instrumental role in obtaining the transfer of testing technology from Germany.

In addition, both public and private leather research organisations also helped with the introduction of the new standards while exporters, suppliers and their respective associations banded together to help firms meet the stringent standards that were imposed in the wake of the ban. Compared to the early 1990s when more than half the samples failed the tests for PCPs and Azo dyes, the failure rates for tests subsequently fell to less than 7 per cent for PCP and less than 1 per cent for Azo dyes by 1998.

c) *Lead smelters in West Bengal*

Secondary lead smelting units play an important role in the recycling of hazardous wastes generated in the battery industry. However, the resultant emissions of flue gas and dust has placed the industry in the 'red' or 'most hazardous' category. A large proportion of the industry is dominated by small, unorganized sector workers in areas such as Kolkata in West Bengal. The lead content in battery scrap is about 75–80 per cent and smelting involves separating metallic lead from non-metallic materials and other unrelated metals. The process requires the addition of fuel and flux, cooling and casting of molten lead into lead ingots in a furnace with charcoal. There are at least two or three smelting cycles involved before most of the lead is removed, much of it manually.

A study in two municipal wards in Kolkata showed that the West Bengal Pollution Control Board (WBPCB) was instrumental in developing remedial technologies that were relatively cheaper and suitable for the small scale sector. After much community pressure and imposition of stringent regulations which mandated the need for pollution control devices to be installed by the WBPCB, all units were forced to shut down. While 12 units reopened after complying with conditions and reopened, others either opted to shut their operations or relocate to the city fringes and areas that were less accessible to regulatory authorities (Chakrabarti and Mitra, 2005).

Despite the limited data available, the study was able to establish that individual units could achieve positive net returns by operating illegally for a single shift without the pollution control devices; or for two to three shifts with the pollution control device installed. Thus, units that operate on two shifts per day (around 6–7 hours producing 1 metric tonne of lead waste per shift) and on an average a total of 300 days per year was found to generate a substantial amount of additional revenue over the capital outlay for the installation of the pollution control devices. In fact, it emerged that it was far more profitable to run two shifts with the pollution control device, rather than a single illegal shift. Indeed, those who did install the devices were able to expand the scale of their operations, raise their output and edge out the competition from non-adopters who run an illegal shift per day.

In addition, given the occupational hazard associated with the lead smelting industry, it was found that units that had installed the pollution control device saw significant reduction in labour turnover rates. Absenteeism on account of ill-health also fell, enabling labourers to earn more. Other environmental and social benefits have also been attributed to the installation of the pollution control devices. All short-term effects of lead-poisoning, commonly experienced in the pre-installation period for instance, were found to have declined or been eradicated, and positive changes were observed in the natural environment.

Conclusion

The above case studies seem to indicate that when small firms are organised in clusters, there is some hope of a solution towards reducing pollution. But even then, many challenges remain. Other studies, such as Blackman's (2000) analysis of the brick kiln industry in Mexico, showed that several key conditions have to be in place in order for environmental control efforts to achieve some degree of success. These include the presence of an external impetus, collective action stemming from self-interest as well as low compliance costs. In addition, the benefits of staying within the cluster due to increasing returns from economies of scale by pooling may have also contributed to the durability of the arrangements.

In decentralised operations such as recycling and e-waste management, the challenges may be more daunting notwithstanding the efforts of NGOs and other groups. On the other hand, there seems to be some evidence that the existence of a shadow economy tends to result in higher levels of environmental degradation especially in urban slums. Increasing incentives to improve transparency and reduce crime may have an important impact on reducing pollution at least in some sectors, such as recycling, metal working and other operations in urban areas (Kojima and Jain, 2008; Biswas *et al.*, 2012).

In some domains, even with the absence of spatial clustering, small producers may find it in their interest to form guild-like structures in order to consolidate skill sets and help organize marketing efforts. These issues are yet to be explored but some hope can be drawn from the successes of community mapping exercises and other forms of networking using new media. This may offer yet another opportunity for reducing pollution and use of resources through technology transfer.

Acknowledgements

This chapter benefited greatly from the research carried out by Divya Badami Rao.

Endnotes

[1] See MSME (2012).
[2] See Mahalingam (2012).

References

Beck, Thorsten and Asli Demirguc-Kunt. "Small and medium-size enterprises: Access to finance as a growth constraint." *Journal of Banking & Finance* 30, 11 (2006): 2931–2943.

Biswas, Amit K., Mohammad R. Farzanegan and Marcel Thum. "Pollution, Shadow Economy and Corruption: Theory and Evidence." *Ecological Economics* 75 (2012): 114–125.

Blackman, Allen. "Informal Sector Pollution Control: What Policy Options Do We Have?" *World Development* 28, 12 (2000): 2067–2082.

CPCB (Central Pollution Control Board). "Performance Status of Common Effluent Treatment Plants in India." New Delhi, 2005. Available online at http://cpcb.nic.in/upload/Publications/Publication_ 24_PerformanceStatus OfCETPsIinIndia.pdf. Last accessed on 13 August, 2013.

Chakrabarti, Snigdha and Nita Mitra. "Economic and Environmental Impacts of Pollution Control Regulation on Small Industries: A Case Study." *Ecological Economics* 54, 1 (2005): 53–66.

Crow, Michael and Michael B. Batz. "Clean and Competitive? Small-Scale Bleachers and Dyers in Tirupur." In *Small Firms and the Environment in Developing Countries: Collective Impacts, Collective Action*, edited by Allen Blackman, p. 147. Washington, DC: Resources for the Future Press, 2006.

Dasgupta, Susmita, Hemamala Hettige and David Wheeler. "What Improves Environmental Compliance? Evidence from Mexican industry." *Journal of Environmental Economics and Management* 39, 1 (2000): 39–66.

Divan, Shyam and Armin Rosencranz. *Environmental Law and Policy in India: Cases, Materials, and Statutes.* New Delhi; New York, Oxford University Press, 2002.

Erkman, Suren and Ramesh Ramaswamy. "Case Study of the Textile Industry in Tirupur." In *Applied Industrial Ecology — A New Platform for Planning Sustainable Societies (Focus on Developing Countries with Case Studies from India)*, by Suren Erkman and Ramesh Ramaswamy, pp. 44–70. Bangalore: Aicra Publishers, 2003.

Kennedy, Loraine. "Cooperating for Survival: Tannery Pollution and Joint Action in the Palar Valley (India)." *World Development* 27, 9 (1999): 1673–1691.

Kojima, Michikazu and Amit Jain. "Controlling Pollution in Small-Scale Recycling Industries: Experiences in India and Japan." In *Promoting 3Rs in Developing Countries: Lessons from the Japanese Experience*, edited by Michikazu Kojima. Chiba, IDE-JETRO, 2008.

Mahalingam, Kripa. "Hanging by a Thread." *Outlook Business*, India, January 21, 2012. Available online at http://business.outlookindia.com/ article.aspx?279668. Last accessed on 13 August, 2013.

MSME (Ministry of Micro, Small and Medium Enterprises). "Annual Report (2011–12)." Government of India, New Delhi, 2012.

Parker, Craig, Janice Redmond, and Mike Simpson. "Review of Interventions to Encourage SMEs to Make Environmental Improvements." *Environment and Planning C: Government & Policy* 27, 2 (2009): 279–301.

Preetha, M. Soundariya "Fading Fortunes in Tirupur." *The Hindu*, March 11, 2012. Available online at http://www.thehindu.com/business/Industry/ article2985381.ece. Last accessed on 12 August, 2013.

Rangarajan, K. "City-Region of Tirupur, Tamil Nadu." *Paper presented at UNIDO conference on "The System of Governance in Dynamic City Regions."* Bangalore, July 13–15, 2005.

Reddy, Y. Maheshwara "Discharged from Tirupur, Dyeing Units Arrive in Bangalore." *Daily News and Analysis*, May 3, 2012. Available online at http://www.dnaindia.com/bangalore/report_discharged-from-tirupur-dyeing-units-arrive-in-bangalore_1683851.

Swaminathan, Padmini and J. Jeyaranjan. "The Knitwear Cluster in Tiruppur: An Indian Industrial District in the Making?" Working Paper No. 126, Madras Institute of Development Studies, Chennai, 1994.

Tewari, Meenu and Poonam Pillai. "Global Standards and the Dynamics of Environmental Compliance in India's Leather Industry." *Oxford Development Studies* 33, 2 (2005): 245–267.

8. Environmental Management 3.0: Connecting the Dots between Pollution, Sustainability, Transparency and Governance in Indonesia

Shakeb AFSAH and Nabiel MAKARIM

The 1972 Stockholm Environmental Conference marked the first formal commitment by the government of Indonesia to address the environmental issues it had to deal with in the 1970s. Now 40 years on, Indonesia is at the right juncture to reflect on its environmental institutional history, the lessons learned and confront the unfinished and on-going business of environmental management. In moving forward, the country faces many challenges, some of which are even larger than those it had to confront in the past. But first, here is a quick review of how far Indonesia has progressed over the last four decades.

Review of Indonesia's Environmental Policy History[1]

Like most of the OECD countries in the 1970s, Indonesia tried to bolster its national environmental management system through the creation of the Ministry of Environment, whose role was to create the regulatory framework and set up emission standards for monitoring and enforcement purposes. This was a slow process that started with the establishment of the Office of Natural Resources and Environment (ONRE) in 1972. ONRE however had no regulatory authority and was part of the National Development Planning Agency (BAPPENAS), which was in charge of the development framework for the country's natural resource management.

Without broad scale regulation and monitoring, the rapid economic growth of the 1970s took its toll on the environment. ONRE had no authority to undertake policy and regulatory efforts to mitigate the impact of environmental deterioration due to the country's rev-up pace of industrialisation. Increasing environmental concerns did however lead to the creation of the Ministry of Environmental and Development (MEDS) in 1978. This was widely considered to be a major milestone but it too had little impact on pollution control as MEDS did not have the strong regulatory clout needed to carry out its policy goals to the best of its abilities.

It took another four years for MEDS to finally enact its first major law which was the Environmental Management Act (EMA) of 1982 that set the foundation for the issuance of regulatory standards, permits and licenses. To execute the functions defined in EMA 1982, MEDS was restructured in 1983 to create the Ministry for Population and Environment (MoPE) whose role was to formulate policies and coordinate the implementation of regulations. MoPE was however not a line agency and the authority to enforce environmental regulations remained with the respective sectoral ministries. The responsibility for enforcing emissions and effluent standards for industrial pollution, for instance, came under the purview of the Ministry of Industries, this gave rise to a conflict in interests. In reality, MoPE was a rather weak public agency without a mandate for genuine environmental enforcement. As a result, the new environmental legislative efforts barely showed any measurable, let alone credible results on the ground.

Even though its enforcement hands were tied, MoPE, to its credit, did persist with attempts to introduce new regulations. These efforts paid off with the launch of the first environmental impact assessment (EIA) regulations (AMDAL) in 1986, which was followed by the introduction of environmental standards for ambient air and water quality as well as effluent and emissions standards over the next five years. These regulations typically fell in two broad categories: AMDAL, which monitored economic activities at the planning and construction stages, and the setting of regulatory standards that focused on minimising environmental impacts in the subsequent operational phases.

To implement these regulations, the Indonesian government created a new agency in 1990 known as the Environmental Management Impact

Agency (BAPEDAL) which was responsible for implementing the national environmental regulations. The authority ascribed to BAPEDAL looked impressive on paper, but in reality, it was rather difficult to enforce its regulatory standards and compliance on errant polluters without the requisite punitive efficacy under the existing legal system. At this point, it became clear that a well-functioning national legal and good governance framework was needed to parlay environmental regulations into genuine results on the ground.

Further institutional and organisational changes, which included two key reforms, were added in the aftermath of the financial crisis of 1997–1998. The first was the consolidation of BAPEDAL into the Ministry of Environment in 2002. Secondly, the authority to regulate and enforce environmental quality standards was decentralized and extended to units of local governments. Additionally, a new national environmental law was introduced in 2009, which, for the first time, criminalised environmental impairment and empowered the Ministry of Environment to tackle issues relating to climate change via its policies and programmes.

The upshot of these changes meant that there had been no dearth of regulations and environmental quality standards in Indonesia. The key challenge is one of implementation and enforcement — an issue that has ramifications on both the broader institutional and political fronts.

Environmental Regulations and Politics

From 1989 to 1993, four landmark environmental cases were brought before the country's courts by NGOs and local communities against industrial polluters (Nicholson, 2005). In all four instances, the NGOs and the local communities lost their cases and it soon became clear to the regulators that regulations on paper alone were inadequate to rein in pollution to the national environment. Although the rapid economic growth in the industrial sector during the 1990s led to more discernible contamination to the country's main river systems, the authorities were unable to hold any of the polluters legally accountable for their environmental infringements. At the same time, politicians were also unwilling to proactively lend their support to environmental issues lest they be seen as anti-industry in their stance. Their ambivalence is well captured by Frances Cairncross in her book "Costing the Earth: The Challenge for Governments, the Opportunities for Business" (1993). She writes:

> *Environmental issues will not go away. Politicians who hope that they will win green votes, though, may be disappointed. The environment is what public-opinion pollsters call a "consensual" issue: one that a politician can lose votes by being against but not gain votes by supporting. Moreover, those politicians who try hardest to appear "green" will often be the very ones picked out by environmental lobbying groups and upbraided for not being even greener. Environmental issues pose immensely difficult questions for politicians*

Clearly environmental issues are not politically rewarding, and therefore creative strategies are needed to have any real impact.

ECD and Indonesia: A comparative perspective

When the OECD and developing countries like Indonesia made their initial commitments to environmental goals in the 1970s, it was generally thought that the creation of environmental departments, ministries and agencies empowering them with the authority to impose regulations and standards would be sufficient to deal with environmental issues. However, the experiences of Europe, US, Canada and other OECD countries offer quite a contrast to the situation in developing countries.

As shown in Figure 8.1, like the US, Indonesia jumpstarted its environmental efforts in the early 1970s. The difference was that the former — as was in the case of many OECD countries — already had robust and broad based systems of law and governance in place.

In contrast, similar attempts by Indonesia were met with limited success despite what on paper looked like creditable regulations and commendable laws. The lack of success had essentially stemmed largely from inadequacies in the national legal framework to deal effectively with environmental offenders.

Implications for the Future

Despite the systemic flaws, Indonesia has however already shown considerable creativity in its efforts to bolster its environmental policies. Most notable is its environmental disclosure strategy that is designed to circumvent inherent weaknesses in both governance and rule of law. In 1986, the state launched a Clean City Programme (ADIPURA) that

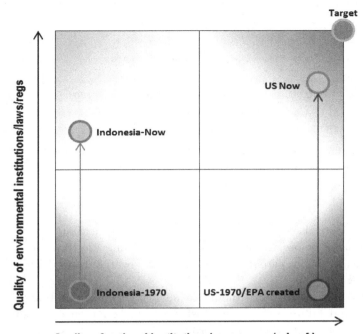

Figure 8.1: Environmental Results Framework.
Source: Compiled by authors.

gave awards to cities based on the quality of their solid waste management practices. The mayors of award winning clean cities were publicly lauded by President Suharto which meant that there was a good likelihood that their appointments would be extended. That was followed in 1995 by the Programme for Pollution Control Evaluation and Rating (PROPER) programme which uses a system of colour codes that were designed to reflect the quality of environmental compliance demonstrated by industry players. The public announcements of these easy-to-understand colour codes immediately brought many companies to the media's attention — which, in turn, also brought to bear implications for their reputation in the eyes of both the public as well as financial markets. The PROPER programme, which remains a flagship initiative taken by the Ministry of Environment, has successfully reduced pollution levels and increased compliance with environmental regulations by up to 80 per cent

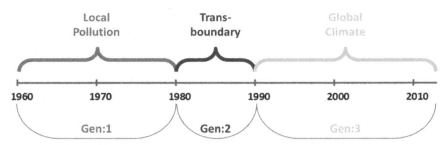

Figure 8.2: The Three Generations of Environmental Challenges.
Source: Compiled by authors.

in some industrial sectors. This success was achieved without a single case being brought before the courts, thereby avoiding any protracted legal tangles under an apparent system of weak governance and ambivalent jurisprudence.

But in moving forward, Indonesia must take a fresh look at both its successes and failures. While it must further strengthen successful programmes such as ADIPURA and PROPER, it must also expand the scope of public disclosure embedded in these initiatives to deal with a broader set of environmental challenges. In its new democratic environment, which has seen considerable authority devolved to local provinces and agencies, there are more opportunities to leverage on information disclosure and transparency efforts to improve governance and further empower local authorities.

As shown in Figure 8.2, the complexities of environmental issues have expanded from local pollution to those with trans-boundary, regional and global impact. Indonesia, like most countries must now retool its environmental management strategies to also address trans-boundary and global climate change challenges even as it continues to tackle on-going local pollution concerns. It needs to take a careful look at its successes and failures and develop a more coherent environmental strategy for the next twenty years. So far, Indonesia's experience has shown that environmental successes require three key ingredients — a trusted environmental agency; timely dissemination of information and a more environmentally aware public. We now show how these insights can be applied to the thinking and execution of a successful environmental management plan for the country.

Environmental Management 3.0

We are now living in the information age where the flows and analyses of data have the ability to better empower communities and stakeholders in ways that can also simultaneously promote good governance, strengthen accountability and minimise the impact of pollution on the environment. To leverage the full capability of our internet-based information system, there are five strategic considerations. These are:

1. Maximise the use of new monitoring technology for data collection, processing and knowledge management;
2. Review institutional rules to enhance the authority to collect data and disseminate information;
3. Adopt strategic communication channels to establish stronger links between politics and environment;
4. Empower communities, public and the media proactively by directly delivering information through the internet, cell phones and other new technologies.
5. Promote good governance and accountability by disclosing information on the performance of key decision-making state agencies who oversee programmes such as PROPER and ADIPURA.

Application to Indonesia

The Environmental Management 3.0 framework, which builds on the successes of PROPER and ADIPURA programmes, also fits well with the trend of national reforms and decentralisation of state controls by the current government. Given the weaknesses of Indonesia's legislative structure, it is also important to frame any environmental strategy with political ramifications in mind.

Ever since the shifts towards decentralisation were introduced after the financial crisis of the late 1990s, many aspects of environmental management were delegated to the heads of regencies (BUPATI) and mayors of cities (WALIKOTA). However, it would appear that these local leaders will act to protect the environment only when four conditions are met. These include (1) strong incentives and both state and public recognition, (2) adequate financial resources, (3) sufficient human resources and proper training and (4) appropriate institutional rules and legal authority.

Accordingly, a two-part strategy will be needed to address these issues in order to achieve better outcomes. First of all, successful existing programmes such as ADIPURA and PROPER must continue to shift their focus to the local level. And secondly, the framework of environmental performance evaluation and disclosure should be broadened to include areas such as deforestation and urban development in which jurisdiction lies with local leaders (BUPATIS and WALIKOTAS).

Enhancement of PROPER and ADIPURA Programmes

To sidestep the predicament of weak legal enforcement, the Ministry of Environment has switched to reliance on public disclosure and reputational incentives to combat environmental degradation. Two of these most prominent programmes are the Clean City Programme (ADIPURA) and the Programme for Pollution Control Evaluation and Rating (PROPER).

ADIPURA: This programme was first introduced in 1986 with the primary goal of improving solid waste management at the city level. Each city was evaluated for its level of effort and quality of physical cleanliness based on detailed field inspections and data collection from government agencies. It was successfully implemented until the onset of the financial crisis is 1997. Between 1998 and 2001, the ADIPURA programme was halted in its tracks as Indonesia became embroiled in issues over post-crisis democratic and economic reforms. It was restarted in 2002 and since then, ADIPURA has seen its coverage expanded to 375 cities as of 2011–2012.

The main objectives of the ADIPURA programme are to improve the general cleanliness and enhance the greenery of cities as well as create incentives for local governments and citizens to maintain high levels of environmental stewardship on a continual basis. ADIPURA places considerable importance on public awareness and participation and encourages a close partnership between the local government and the general public.

Since its re-launch in 2002, ADIPURA has further refined its evaluation process and now uses two sets of performance indicators — (1) the quality of physical infrastructure, which includes residential areas, roads, markets and shopping areas, commercial centres, hospitals, schools, green cover and the transportation sector (including bus terminals, train stations and ports) and (2) institutional, management and public responsiveness of local agencies.

The institutional issues cover sub-topics like organisational structure to support waste management; local regulations, budgeting and human resource matters and infrastructure investments, while management issues include long and short-term planning, follow-up implementation and quality control practices. ADIPURA also puts considerable weight on public responsiveness and it includes specific criteria on how public complaints and community participation are handled. Finally, ADIPURA has also expanded its scope from solid waste management to include the monitoring of air quality and surface pollution.

The evaluation of performance is based on a well-structured scoring system. The range of the score varies from a minimum of 30 points to a maximum of 90 with five discreet performance levels. These are: (1) very poor with a score in the range of 30–45, (2) poor with score from 46–60, (3) average if the score is 61–70, (4) good is in the range of 71–85, and finally (5) very good when the score is in the range of 86–90.

The scoring process is subjective and the evaluation conducted by both inspectors from the Ministry of Environment and provincial officials. Inspectors are known to conduct multiple inspections before the final score is assigned. In addition to the data from field inspections, local governments also fill in questionnaires to submit to the ADIPURA team for evaluation and verification. The data submitted by local authorities are signed off by the mayor or the head of the regency.

The evaluation criteria for clean cities also depend on the size and geographic locations. Cities are organized into four categories based on population size — metropolitan (>1 million), large cities (0.5–1 million), medium-size cities (0.1–0.5 million) and small towns (20,000–100,000). Some evaluation indicators are also different for coastal cities.

The ADIPURA programme has come under intense political attention due to the deliberate timing of the Clean City announcements from the Indonesian president each year in June on Earth Day. The ADIPURA awards often receive widespread media coverage in both national and local dailies. As a result ADIPURA, which uses information disclosure and reputational incentives, has successfully transformed environmental management into a true political asset for mayors and regents at the local level. The political pull of an ADIPURA award is so strong that a mayor was even charged in 2010 for bribing a government official in order to secure the clean city status (Widianarko, 2011).

PROPER: Like ADIPURA, the PROPER programme also leverages on information disclosure and reputational incentives to combat industrial pollution. Under PROPER, companies are rated using a five-colour rating scheme (Gold, Green, Blue, Red and Black).

The PROPER programme was conceived in 1993 and publicly launched in 1995. Its initial scope was limited to the evaluation of water pollution from industrial sources following the boom in the manufacturing sector during the 1980s. Regulatory standards for water quality were already in place but there was little incentive for industries to comply due to a lack of legal enforcement.

There were two main reasons for the weak regulatory enforcement. First, environmental agencies, as we highlighted earlier, did not have adequate authority to bring cases to court. Secondly, the primary focus of the national government was on economic growth. Hence, the political will to take on the private sector was often lacking. Not surprisingly, the unofficial mantra of "grow now, clean up later" took precedent which placed numerous road blocks to any serious efforts at environmental control and enforcement.

Faced with such limited options, the regulators decided to take a different tack by appealing directly to the public through media channels to put pressure on delinquent industrial polluters through a ratings system. Under PROPER, the environmental performance of each participating industrial enterprise is gauged using five color-codes that were easy for the general public to understand. Each colour rating is based on both quantitative and qualitative assessments and the broad definition of each colour-code is shown in Table 8.1.

Table 8.1: PROPER Color Codes and Basic Definition.

Color Rating	Performance Criteria
1. Black	Company makes no effort to control pollution, or causes serious environmental damage.
2. Red	Company makes some effort to control pollution, but not sufficiently to achieve compliance.
3. Blue	Company only applies efforts sufficiently to meet standards.
4. Green	Pollution level is lower than the discharge standards by at least 50%. The company also ensures good housekeeping, proper disposal of sludge, accurate pollution records and a reasonably maintained waste water treatment system.
5. Gold	All requirements of Green, plus similar levels of pollution control for air and hazardous waste. The company meets high international standards by adopting clean technology, recycling and waste pollution prevention measures.

Source: Afsah, *et al.*, 2013.

The first three colours — Black, Red and Blue — are strictly based on environmental regulatory requirements, while Gold and Green ratings are based on voluntary measures taken to enhance efficiency in resource management, recycling, reuse, community development and social responsibility efforts.

The colour approach was carefully selected to ensure that the general public could easily understand and assess for themselves the environmental performances of the companies that came under the purview of the programme. This was important conceptually as environmental issues are often very technical and difficult for the general public and the media to grasp. The mapping of technical environmental data and translation into colour codes however needed a robust and defensible methodology as well as a system of data collection and analysis that was sufficiently transparent and reliable to pass scrutiny.

This is why the PROPER programme employs a blend of quantitative and qualitative criteria to come up with the ratings system with numerical data and cut-off points applied to different colour codes. For Gold and Green ratings, a separate set of non-regulatory indicators and criteria were developed and adopted.

The cut-off points for Blue, Red and Black ratings are based on quantitative data largely monitored on a monthly basis. For example, an enterprise is typically required to monitor its air emissions, water pollution levels and ambient water and air quality at multiple locations at a site. Depending on the scale of the operations and the industrial sector, a company may be required to monitor a few locations to several dozen monitoring points. According to the rating methodology, a company would earn a Blue rating if: (1) its monitoring and reported data for each monitoring point is 100 per cent complete, (2) if data show a compliance rate of 90 per cent or higher for concentration standards, and (3) it complies with the pollution load standard 100 per cent of the time. Additionally, the company must have all the permits current and meet all the requisite requirements with regards to hazardous waste management.

A rigorous and transparent rating methodology is essential for the long-term success of any public disclosure programme like PROPER and ADIPURA. For an environmental disclosure programme to work, the public at large must trust the environmental ratings. And so far, PROPER has done a reasonably good job of maintaining the public's trust. When the PROPER programme was first launched in 1995, there were only 187 companies in the programme. The number has since risen to 1,317 companies in 2012 with the Ministry of Environment planning to increase the number of participating enterprises to 2,000 by 2014.

In terms of results, the PROPER programme has contributed significantly to the doubling of environmental compliance from around 35 per cent in 1995 to nearly 70 per cent in 2012 based on companies with BLUE ratings without any need for legal sanctions or legal enforcement measures, which by all accounts is a commendable if not a remarkable feat in itself. It shows that information disclosure programmes anchored to an environmental regulatory system can play a crucial complementary role as auxiliary but more effective enforcement tool. It evidently shows that public disclosure can serve as a more viable and cost-efficient alternative to legal enforcement which is often costly, combative, politically risky and time consuming for regulators.

Political Lessons from ADIPURA and PROPER

It is well known that politics often trump most regulatory efforts to minimise industrial pollution and other environmental impact. In other words, even with the best of environmental regulations, the political will to undertake rigorous enforcement can be restricted. As a result both inspections to uncover non-compliance and the severity of financial penalties are often so weak that errant polluters have little incentives to undertake the capital and operational expenditure needed to comply with various environmental quality standards. This was clearly the case initially in Indonesia.

As early as 1982 (Environmental Law no. 4), Indonesia had fairly decent environmental laws in place. By the early 1990s, there were sector specific environmental quality standards for water pollution, air emissions and ambient air and water quality (Rock, 2002). These laws have been continually enhanced with revisions of major laws in 1997 and more recently in 2009. The 2009 revision of the Environmental Law No. 32 is particularly noteworthy because it provides clearer authority to public agencies, local governments and the civil society to initiate legal action against polluters. Additionally it penalises public officials who issue environmental permits without following proper procedures.

The ADIPURA programme is now more than 25 years old while the PROPER programme has lasted more than 15 years. Both programmes have not only survived the throes of the Asian financial crisis and democratic reforms in the country but also become flagship programmes of the Ministry of Environmental under multiple administrations and change of ministers. This kind of political durability is uncommon in Indonesia and the fact that they have withstood the test of time goes to prove that both ADIPURA and PROPER are reliable models for environmental governance in the populous Southeast Asian nation.

Both ADIPURA and the PROPER programmes were politically successful because environmental regulators chose to invest in their relationship with their long-term constituencies and stakeholders — namely, the media and the general public.

Using public disclosure as the primary tools to earn the trust of these stakeholders was a smart move by the regulators due to its intrinsic political appeal. The use of disclosure tactics has three attributes that explain the roots of such an appeal. First, information sharing is an important channel for public agencies and politicians to accumulate political capital as such programmes are viewed favourably by the press and the general public. Second, performance measurement and information disclosures signal the willingness of public agencies to be transparent and be held accountable. And finally, the various stakeholders have come to regard the comparative performance analyses under the PROPER rating system as a very useful tool for managerial and political decisions.

This is however not a time to rest on laurels. The media, general public and non-governmental organisations are often tough constituencies which make it imperative to maintain their long-term trust. If the Ministry of Environment falters on the quality of its data gathering and dissemination and hence the efficacy of the ratings systems, the effectiveness of public disclosure will suffer and lead to backsliding to the conditions of rampant pollution during the 1980s and 1990s.

Signs of Cracks in ADIPURA and PROPER

It is common knowledge that PROPER enjoyed positive media coverage until the term of Minister Rachmat Witoelar in 2004–2008. The 2008 announcement of a BLUE rating awarded to PT Lapindo, the company linked to a widely covered mud eruption accident (Davies *et al.*, 2007), turned out to be a lightning rod for public criticism and negative press (Simamora, 2008a; 2008b, The Jakarta Post, 2008). Though the PROPER team clarified that the site of the mud volcano was not in the PROPER programme, this incident shed light on the political vulnerability of its ratings system and its inadequacies.

While it became clear in 2008 that as the rating methodology had expanded its scope after the financial crisis, the specifics of the rating criteria became less transparent, more qualitative and open to judgment and interpretations making the PROPER programme susceptible to public criticism.

This weakness was evident in the media coverage of PROPER ratings in 2009 which saw louder and more wide-ranging criticisms (Simamora, 2009a) after a leading anti-mining NGO was prominently quoted in *The Jakarta Post* (Simamora, 2009b). Headlines for coverage of the PROPER 2009 announcement were overall extremely negative leading to doubts over the credibility of the programme. The 2010 announcement did not receive much media coverage except for one positive report in the *Jakarta Globe* (Satriastanti, 2010) — an indication perhaps of the ambivalent attitude towards the programme among journalists.

The announcement of the PROPER ratings on the 1st of December, 2011 was also limited but rather negative and redolent of the press coverage in 2008 and 2009. Most noticeable is the coverage in the Jakarta Globe with an extremely negative headline "Corporate Green Ratings Slammed as Cover for Polluting Indonesian Companies" (Satriastanti, 2011). And most recently in December 2012, the most prominent national daily *Kompas* ran gave a rather negative review of the programme (Kompas, 2012). Clearly, such headlines cast aspersions on the credibility of the entire PROPER programme — sowing doubts over the effectiveness of the environmental disclosure programmes.

Additionally, we expect NGO-driven political pressure to escalate in the coming years, particularly with regards to PROPER ratings of mining companies. The reason is rather straightforward — the average environmental performance of the mining sector in the PROPER programme continues to be significantly better than the rest of the sectors. The rate of compliance in 2010–2011 for the mining sector is 85 per cent compared to 66 per cent for the rest of the other sectors such as manufacturing, energy production, agriculture, hotels and others (MoE, 2011). Additionally, the share of companies with Green ratings in the mining sector is 20 per cent compared to only 10 per cent in the other sectors. In other words, Indonesian mining companies have typically outperformed other sectors and are more responsive to performance incentives under the PROPER programme.

This is to be expected since mining companies are often the targets of environmental NGOs. As a result, a Red or a Black rating for a mining company carries considerable reputational, regulatory and business risks. Hence, mining sites have strong incentives to perform at Blue or higher levels. In comparison, a medium-sized manufacturing enterprise is unlikely to face NGO pressure despite more Red and Black rated non-mining enterprises due to their lower visibility. The PROPER programme in this respect has become anathema to anti-mining NGOs in Indonesia, who are of the view that the high PROPER ratings only served to douse their activism efforts. It is, therefore, not surprising that anti-mining groups like JATAM are pushing to put to a halt the PROPER programme. We expect this anti-PROPER stance of NGOs to become more strident in their efforts at discrediting the PROPER ratings.

The ADIPURA programme has also gone through a bad patch recently after the Corruption Eradication Commission of Indonesia (KPK) launched an investigation in early 2011 over allegations that the mayor of Bekasi had bribed the officials of the Ministry of Environment to clinch the prestigious Clean City Award.

These recent developments are important reminders of the fragility of the environmental disclosure and ratings programmes in Indonesia. Despite more than 15 years of institutionalisation, environmental governance remains a constant challenge and it will be a mistake for the Ministry of Environment to drop its guard.

Indonesia Needs Environmental Management 3.0

If the credibility of the ADIPURA and the PROPER programmes are compromised, it would be a throwback to the pre-1990s when industrial pollution was widespread. Given the risks, the Ministry of Environment is well aware of the importance of maintaining public credibility of its flagship programmes and is already undertaking efforts to bolster the effectiveness of the ADIPURA and the PROPER programmes. The PROPER team is committed to expanding the participation of enterprises in the rating programme. Additionally, it is strengthening the rating methodology and criteria to better reflect the scope of new environmental regulations as well as emerging regional and global environmental concerns. In this section we discuss some of the specific steps the Ministry of Environment can undertake to maintain the credibility and effectiveness of its environmental disclosure programmes.

Enhancement of ADIPURA and PROPER

In moving forward, both disclosure programmes need to take clear steps to further strengthen the transparency of its backend data collection as well as the evaluation system that ultimately determines the clean city awards in the case of ADIPURA and the colour rating system for the PROPER programme.

In the case of PROPER, the ministry currently only reveals the final ratings to the public. However, each company privately receives a detailed report card that clearly explains the factors being assessed and findings that determine the final rating. Generally the media are very interested in the details behind the final ratings. Such details are readily available in the PROPER report card. These report cards for Blue, Red and Black ratings are typically organised under four sections. The first section presents the status of compliance with the EIA (AMDAL) regulations. Here, the report card shows if a company has an approved AMDAL and whether or not it monitors and reports its data on a regular basis to the Ministry.

The second and third sections cover the issue of water pollution control and air emissions. It includes specific compliance issues like monitoring of all compliance points, technical provisions like installation of monitoring instruments and the level of compliance with concentration, flows and pollution load standards for individual parameters as required by each applicable regulation and permit. The fourth section typically includes compliance with various permits related to hazardous waste management covering items like storage, waste utilisations, transportation, waste balance and accounting.

Due to the increased scrutiny of the media and NGOs, it is critical for the Ministry of Environment to find ways to raise the transparency of its ratings and the underlying data. The PROPER team should take cues from similar programmes in Ghana,[2] where the government releases the final ratings along with the sub-ratings for seven issues including compliance with permits and legal requirements, hazardous and toxic waste management, compliance with water pollution and air emissions standards, self-monitoring and reporting, environmental best practices, public complaints and corporate social responsibility.

The PROPER team can take further steps and create provisions for the media and the general public to view the backend data that companies report and also share the findings of onsite inspections. These steps will improve the transparency of the rating system and shore up its credibility and hence fortify the trust that is essential for the long-term success of the flagship environmental disclosure programmes.

Similarly for the ADIPURA programme, the Ministry of Environment must undertake steps to increase the transparency of the ADIPURA programme's evaluation process by creating provisions to share the primary data collected through its site inspections and questionnaires. This is particularly important because there are multiple media reports that refute the clean city credentials of ADIPURA award winners (Rulistia, 2012). For ADIPURA the challenge is very clear — if a city receives an award, it is very easy for a third party to refute it by simply showing a picture of polluted water, piled-up garbage or other similar contradictory evidence. Therefore, the demand for data quality control, accuracy and due diligence is very necessary for the ADIPURA team.

The Ministry of Environment has already undertaken steps to counter the allegations of corruption in the ADIPURA awards and restore the credibility of the programme (Simamora, 2011a). It created a council consisting of former ministers and other environment experts. But the Ministry of Environment must take the extra efforts to further increase the transparency of its evaluation system (Simamora, 2011b).

The ADIPURA programme has a fairly rigorous system of onsite inspections. As described earlier, multiple site-specific observations are deployed to create a rich database of the quality of cleanliness in a city. For example, the evaluation of roads is structured into two components — main arteries and connectors. Inspectors then identify an area to evaluate the quality of roads and drainage. For the roads, evaluations issues include garbage, green cover, and the quality of sidewalks. Inspectors review if the garbage was piled-up and scattered or if it was properly collected and stored for transportation. Based on such observations, inspectors give a score that is factored into the final evaluation to qualify for the ADIPURA award and recognition.

The ADIPURA's data collection system is quite detailed. Unfortunately, it is not clear whether or not the media and the general public understand the complexities. The ADIPURA team should treat this as an opportunity to further increase the transparency of its evaluation process and create new provisions that will enable journalists and other stakeholders alike to access the raw data. This kind of process will give assurance to the media and the general public about the veracity of the ADIPURA awards.

The more the media feels that it has access to the backend data, the more trust it will garner with the ADIPURA and PROPER programmes. This will lead to more positive media reports, which in turn will strengthen the long-term relationship with its key constituents including the general public. With stronger public trust, the Ministry of Environment will in turn be able to further strengthen its regulations and enforcement efforts in the long run.

Conclusions

Indonesia is internationally recognised for its environmental disclosure and ratings programmes. The relative successful inroads attained by programmes such as ADIPURA and PROPER are ample proof that it is possible to achieve a high level of environmental compliance without taking errant companies through the costly and politically risky legal enforcement process via the court systems.

Indonesia's experience shows that public disclosure and environmental transparency is an effective substitute when legal enforcement is difficult. Legal enforcement is challenging in Indonesia and other developing countries due to a lack of political capital or inadequate institutional capacities. Industry players and associations tend to enjoy better clout compared to environmental agencies. To its credit, Indonesia's Ministry of Environment had recognized such shortcomings by reaching out to the media and the general public to boost its political position.

Through public disclosure programmes like ADIPURA and PROPER, Indonesia has created a new paradigm for environmental governance. It shows that an environmental agency can truly empower itself politically if it decides to use the media and reach out to the general public through information disclosure. However, the long-term success of this strategy requires the Ministry of Environment to adopt greater transparency of the information and analyses it discloses to the public. While some fault lines may have emerged in the recent past with regards to the ADIPURA and PROPER programmes, the Ministry of Environment has already taken concrete steps to tackle these emerging challenges. However, it must further its efforts and work towards strengthening the transparency of these programmes

Endnotes

[1]   This section is adapted from Shakeb Afsah *et al.*, *Environmental Regulation and Public Disclosure: The Case of PROPER in Indonesia* (Routledge: Resources for the Future Press, 2013).
[2]   See EPA Ghana AKOBEN Programme (2010) for further examples.

References

Afsah, Shakeb, Allen Blackman, Jorge H. Garcia and Thomas Sterner. *Environmental Regulations and Public Disclosure: The Case of PROPER in Indonesia*. Routledge/Resources for the Future Press: Oxon, 2013.

Cairncross, Frances. *Costing the Earth: The Challenge for Governments, the Opportunities for Business.* Harvard Business School Press, 1993.

Davies, R. J., Swarbrick, R. E., Evans, R. J. and Huuse, M. "Birth of a mud volcano: East Java, May 29, 2006." GSA Today 17 (2): February 4, 2007.

EPA Ghana AKOBEN Programme. "What is AKOBEN Programme?" 2010. Available online at http://www.epaghanaakoben.org/. Accessed 13 August, 2013.

Kompas. "PROPER: Emasbagi Industri Ekstraktif Menyesakkan." December 4, 2012.

MoE (Ministry of Environment). "PROPER 2010/11 Press Release." Indonesia Ministry of Environment, 2011. Available online at http://proper.menlh.go. id/portal/filebox/130325060205Press_ release_ PROPER_ 2011.pdf

Nicholson, David. "Environmental Dispute Resolution in Indonesia." PhD Thesis, Leiden University, January 13, 2005. Available online at https://openaccess. leidenuniv.nl/bitstream/handle/1887/580/Thesis_Nicholson.PDF;jsessionid= 16CC5C591D2DD324F3CA3FFDF6245697?sequence=12. Accessed on 13 August, 2013.

Rock, Michael T. "Searching for Creative Solutions to Pollution in Indonesia." In *Pollution Control in East Asia: Lessons from the Newly Industrializing Economies* edited by Michael T. Rock. Washington DC: Resources for the Future, 2002.

Rulistia, Novia D. "Sanitary Problems Linger Despite Awards." *The Jakarta Post,* June 21, 2012. Available online at http://www.thejakartapost.com/news/ 2012/06/21/sanitary-problems-linger-despite-awards.html. Last accessed on 12 August, 2013.

Satriastanti, Fidelis E. "Two Firms Get Top Marks for Being Green Friendly." *The Jakarta Globe,* November 26, 2010. Available online at http://www.the jakartaglobe.com/archive/two-firms-get-top-marks-for-being-green-friendly/ 408743/. Last accessed on 12 August, 2013.

──────. "Corporate Green Ratings Slammed as Cover for Polluting Indonesian Companies." *The Jakarta Globe,* December 4, 2011. Available online at http://www.thejakartaglobe.com/archive/corporate-green-ratings-slammed-as-cover-for-polluting-indonesian-companies/. Last accessed on 12 August, 2013.

Simamora, Adianto P. "Lapindo Praised Despite Mudflow." *The Jakarta Post,* August 1, 2008a. Available online at http://www.thejakartapost.com/ news/2008/08/01/lapindo-praised-despite-mudflow.html. Last accessed on 12 August, 2013.

──────. "Activists Criticize Environmental Rating." *The Jakarta Post,* August 6, 2008b. Available online at http://www2.thejakartapost.com/node/176865. Last accessed on 12 August, 2013.

──────. "Activists Push Govt to Punish Polluting Firms." *The Jakarta Post,* March 29, 2009a. Available online at http://www2.thejakartapost.com/

news/2009/10/17/activists-push-govt-punish-polluting-firms.html. Last accessed on 12 August, 2013.

———. "Govt Doubtful to Punish 'Dirty' Firms." *The Jakarta Post*, October 16, 2009b. Available online at http://www2.thejakartapost.com/news/2009/10/16/govt-doubtful-punish-dirty039-firms.html. Last accessed on 12 August, 2013.

———. "KPK Searches Ministry for Adipura Scandal." *The Jakarta Post*, January 14, 2011a. Available online at http://www2.thejakartapost.com/news/2011/01/14/kpk-searches-ministry-adipura-scandal.html. Last accessed on 12 August, 2013.

———. "New Council to Restore Award's Tarnished Image." *The Jakarta Post*, March 29, 2011b. Available online at http://www2.thejakartapost.com/news/2011/03/29/new-council-restore-award%E2%80%99s-tarnished-image.html. Last accessed on 12 August, 2013.

The Jakarta Post. "Editorial: A Disastrous Award?" August 6, 2008. Available online at http://www2.thejakartapost.com/news/2008/08/06/editorial-a-disastrous-award.html. Last accessed on 12 August, 2013.

Widianarko, Budi. "Adipura Scandal a Slap in the Face for Indonesia." *The Jakarta Post*, February 6, 2011. Available online at http://www2.thejakartapost.com/news/2011/02/06/adipura-scandal-a-slap-face-indonesia.html. Last accessed on 12 August, 2013.

9. Environmental Law, Policy, Governance and Management for Cities: Getting it Right for a Sustainable Future — The Singapore Experience

LYE Lin-Heng

Sustainable Cities

The issue of the sustainability of cities is complex, as few can agree on what 'sustainability' means and how it is measured in the context of a city (Satterthwaite, 1999; Hall, 1996; Hardoy *et al.*, 1992; Dubois-Taine and Henriot, 2002; UN HABITAT, n.d). Although there is no consensus on the definition of the terms 'sustainable cities' or 'sustainable human settlements,' it is clear that a city encompasses many dimensions, including environmental, economic, social, political, legal, demographic, institutional and cultural.

Fundamentally, cities that strive to be 'sustainable' face the tensions between economic development and environmental stewardship. The Brundtland Commission's definition of 'sustainable development' is familiar to most — "development that meets the needs of the present without compromising the ability of future generations to meet their own needs" (UN, 1987).[1] The juxtaposition of the word 'development' with 'sustainable' highlights the dilemmas that confront all urban environments. As cities are almost invariably the engines of growth that fuel the economy of a nation, they are constantly at the forefront of new and myriad challenges that arise from the need to find food, shelter, employment, transport, energy sources, healthcare and other essential services for an ever-growing population. Indeed, it has been said that "the battle for sustainability will be won or lost in cities" (Djoghlef, 2009). How then, can a city ensure that its manifold activities are sustainable?

171

It should also be noted that the concentration of people, enterprises and motor vehicles in a city, while often viewed as a problem, can also bring certain advantages, such as lower costs per household and per enterprise for the provision of the environmental infrastructure and services — such as public transportation systems, sewage treatment plants and systems for the removal of domestic and industrial wastes (Satterthwaite, 1999). Cities with well-managed public transportation systems reduce stress on the natural environment, as a good public transport system will minimise the need for more private motor vehicles. Likewise, the concentrations of industries in particular industrial zones will facilitate the enforcement of environmental laws by reducing the length of journeys required for inspections by authorities. Indeed, with intelligent planning, the closer people live to their workplace, the greater the potential for resource efficiencies, and an enhanced quality of life.[2]

How then, do we measure the environmental performance of a city? Are the considerations similar between cities in developed and developing economies? Is it a matter of governance? If so, what are the ingredients required for sound environmental governance?

This chapter focuses on the tiny city-state of Singapore, and its transformation from a squalid Crown colony to a "Garden City",[3] its evolution to a "City in a Garden",[4] and now its blossoming into a "City of Gardens and Water" (Lee, 2006).[5] It first examines how Singapore managed to develop economically while cleaning up its environment.[6] It then focuses on the government's blueprint for the next 20 years entitled, *A Lively and Liveable Singapore: Strategies for Sustainable Growth* (hereinafter referred to as "the Blueprint"[7]), jointly published by the Ministry of Environment and Water Resources and the Ministry of National Development in 2009 (MEWRND, 2009).[8] It notes that Singapore has done remarkably well in cleaning up its environment in the course of its development and rightly deserves its place as an exemplar for developing cities. Credit must be given to a very far-sighted team of government leaders and civil servants who have conceived the right policies and implemented them efficiently and effectively. However, it also emphasises that there are still considerable inadequacies such as the lack of laws mandating environmental impact assessments as well as the lack of laws mandating recycling. The chapter concludes with an examination into these shortcomings and how they can be addressed.

Environmental Management Systems (EMS) for Cities: The Singapore Experience

"We have built. We have progressed. But there is no hallmark of our success more distinctive and more meaningful than achieving our position as the cleanest and greenest city in Southeast Asia."

— Mr. Lee Kuan Yew, Prime Minister of Singapore,
at launching ceremony of the "Keep Singapore Clean" Campaign,
1 October 1968

The basic requirements for an EMS

A sound Environmental Management System (EMS) for a city starts with sound environmental management policies. These must then be implemented via effective institutional, administrative, legal and physical infrastructure. A sound EMS for a city should comprise the following:

1. Sound environmental policies implemented through effective institutional and administrative structures
2. Comprehensive land use planning
3. Effective environmental laws and enforcement
4. Physical infrastructure for the provision of essential services such as clean water, electricity, transport and communications
5. Physical infrastructure for pollution control including facilities for the collection and treatment of garbage, sewage and trade effluents, the management of hazardous substances, and control of air emissions.

It should be emphasised that there must be coherence in the various policies and in their implementation among the various institutions, and this must be integrated into national and local policy and legal frameworks. There must also be respect for the rule of law. These will now be examined in the context of Singapore.

An Overview: Singapore

The tiny city state of Singapore, referred to by a former Indonesian president as "the little red dot" (Chang Li Lin *et al.*, 2005) is one of the smallest and most densely populated countries in the world with a land area of only

715 square kilometres (Singapore, 2012)[9] housing a population of 5,312,000 as of 2012 (a density of some 7,430 persons per square kilometre). Strategically sited at the tip of the Malay Peninsula, it is at the crossroads of Southeast Asia. Founded by Stamford Raffles, an employee of the East India Company[10] in 1819 to serve as a trading outpost, it grew quickly into an important Crown Colony. It was occupied by the Japanese during the Second World War, returned to the British in 1945. It achieved self-governance in 1959 and joined Malaysia in 1963 and left on 9th August 1965 to become a sovereign state. It has been governed by the same political party that won the first elections in 1959, the People's Action Party (PAP), led by Prime Minister, Mr Lee Kuan Yew. English is the language of communication and of government, although the national language, as stated in its Constitution, is Malay.

Lacking in natural resources, Singapore has built on its strategic location, natural deep harbour and its people, to develop a robust open economy based on trade and services. Today, it has excellent transportation networks and telecommunication facilities. Its port[11] and airport[12] are among the world's busiest. In 2010 and 2011, it was ranked the world's easiest place to do business by the World Bank out of a list of 183 countries (World Bank-IFC, 2012a). Indeed, it has the remarkable distinction of moving "From Third World to First" in the space of some four decades, as states the title of the autobiography of Lee Kuan Yew, its first Prime Minister (Lee, 2000). Much of this success must be attributed to Lee, who was largely the chief architect of Singapore's success and continues to play a significant role as Minister Mentor.

In its early years, Singapore faced the same problems that beset developing countries today. These include the lack of proper sewage disposal facilities, highly polluted rivers and river basins, indiscriminate waste disposal leading to both land and water pollution, poor health management systems that led to periodic outbreaks of typhoid and cholera, polluted air from aging, inefficient gas works, and frequent flooding due to poor drainage.[13]

Today, Singapore's air and water quality are well within World Health Organisation (WHO) benchmarks.[14] All inland waters are able to support aquatic life, with coastal waters generally meeting recreational water standards. All homes receive piped, potable water; garbage is collected daily by licensed contractors, incinerated and the ash sent to an offshore landfill. The average life expectancy is 82 years while infant mortality is low at 2 per cent for every 1,000 live births (Singapore, 2011). Some 3.9 per cent of its GDP is spent on national healthcare.[15]

Notwithstanding that it is not a producer of oil, Singapore is the world's top bunkering port and the third largest oil refining centre in the world with more than four major oil companies (Shell, Caltex, BP and Exxon-Mobil) operating within its borders with a combined refining capacity of 1.395 million barrels a day.[16] Singapore has become a strong industrial base for electronics and precision engineering, chemical and petrochemicals, pharmaceuticals and biosciences. In recent years, Singapore has emphasised research and development in biomedical sciences, water and environmental technology, healthcare services, educational services, info-communications, logistics and transport as well as precision engineering.[17]

Singapore also has one of the best public housing schemes in the world. 82 per cent of the population live in government-subsidised public housing in more than two dozen new towns built by the Housing and Development Board (HDB).[18] Nearly nine out of ten Singaporeans have own their own homes on 99-year leases — thanks to mandatory employer and employee financial contributions to the Central Provident Fund (CPF), a social security savings programme that can be used for home purchases, healthcare and family protection, retirement and asset enhancement.[19] This policy of home ownership accounts for a large measure of the success of its public housing system. In contrast, most public housing schemes in developing as well as developed countries are leased to the public on short leases.[20]

The city state's transport policies have resulted in a highly efficient public transport road and rail system. The use of private motor vehicles is discouraged by raising the costs of motoring through innovative taxes and electronic road pricing systems.[21] Indeed, Singapore is one of the pioneers of congestion pricing.

Singapore is also well known for its draconian laws. It has made full use of the law to discourage unsociable and irresponsible behaviour. These include fines for littering, as well as for failing to flush public toilets after use. Blatant acts of vandalism are punished by caning as well as fines and imprisonment. Innovative penalties have been introduced, such as the Corrective Work Order (CWO) which requires those found guilty of littering to clean up public places. Vehicles used in illegal dumping may be forfeited. Buses are required to provide litter bins. Offences such as discharging a toxic substance into inland waters carry mandatory jail terms with fines of $100,000 or more[22] for second or subsequent transgressions.

Singapore's strict laws and their enforcement have ensured a low crime rate and provided a safe environment for its residents. Sound financial policies have resulted in the rapid growth of industries and service sectors that have made major contributions to the economy. A 'clean' government has ensured that funds are available for the building of an excellent environmental infrastructure while sound land use planning policies have ensured the preservation of green areas for nature conservation and recreational use. Thus, a 'clean and green' physical environment has been secured. Indeed, in 2009, Singapore was commended for being "one of the cleanest and most welcoming cities in the world" by the World Bank in its World Development Report 2009.[23]

Singapore's environmental management system (EMS)

So how did Singapore pursue a policy of rapid industrialisation while ensuring the cleaning up of its environment? The fact is that a clean and green environment was part of the government's strategy in wooing investors in the early years following independence.[24] It may thus be said that the city-state of Singapore has an effective Environmental Management System (EMS) in place, starting with the identification of the types of industries that are allowed into the city-state and sound land use policies that determine where they are to be sited.

1. Sound Environmental Policies Implemented through Effective Institutional and Administrative Structures

The government leads environmental policy in Singapore. In the early years especially, it was very much a 'top-down' approach. Environmental matters were the province of the Ministry of Health[25] until 1972 when the Ministry of Environment (ENV) was formed.[26] It is significant that the Anti-Pollution Unit (APU) was established two years earlier in 1970 and brought under the purview of the Prime Minister's office. It was not until 1986 that the APU was merged with ENV. This is a clear indication of the importance that PM Lee placed on pollution control. On 1 July, 2002, the ENV was renamed the Ministry of Environment and Water Resources (MEWR), with two statutory boards under its purview — the National Environment Agency (NEA) and the Public Utilities Board (PUB).[27] The two statutory boards have a joint mission: "To deliver and sustain a clean and healthy environment and water resources for all in Singapore." MEWR now seeks "to manage Singapore's limited resources and address Singapore's environmental sustainability challenges through innovation, vibrant partnerships and co-operation across the 3P sectors — private, public and people."[28]

In the early years, the ENV was responsible for providing the infrastructure for environmental management, implementation and enforcement of the laws related to pollution control. ENV's Pollution Control Department managed environmental planning, working closely with other institutions to ensure that there was coordination in (i) the type of industries that were allowed to be established, (ii) where they can be sited and (iii) the control of emissions and effluents. Thus, the ENV worked closely with the Economic Development Board (EDB),[29] the Urban Redevelopment Authority (URA)[30] and the Jurong Town Corporation (JTC)[31] as well as other ministries and state agencies such as the Trade Development Board (now International Enterprise Singapore or IESingapore), the Ministry of Health (MOH), the Ministry of Manpower (MOM), the Maritime and Port Authority (MPA) as well as the Land Transport Authority (LTA). The 'command and control' approach was adopted and continues to be applied.

2. Land-use Planning

It must be emphasised that sound land-use planning plays an important role in effective environmental management. The conflict between development and conservation is particularly acute in an urban environment. Environmental considerations should therefore be incorporated in the early phases of development planning so that appropriate measures can be undertaken to address these challenges. Environmentally sensitive land-use planning provides the opportunity to institute proper measures and controls at an early stage in the development process. Chapter 10 of Agenda 21 (often referred to as 'Earth's Action Plan'), endorsed at the United Nations Conference on Environment and Development at Rio de Janiero in 1992, emphasises the importance of an integrated approach towards the planning and management of natural resources. Singapore's Master Plan, Concept Plan and Development Guide Plans ensure a comprehensive overview of land use for the entire island (Lye, 2007). These land use plans also anticipate and make provision for the city's future needs.[32]

In Singapore, pollution is controlled at the initial stages for all industries — starting first with sound land-use planning; the siting of industries in appropriate areas (highly polluting industries are located away from residential and commercial areas);[33] the mandating of pollution control studies to assess all sources of pollution; and the requirement of mitigating measures to be incorporated into the design and operation of the project.[34] Industries may also be required to self-monitor while the NEA is tasked with carrying out regular checks on source emissions and fuel analyses. Industrial premises that are located close to residential areas and within the water catchment areas may only be occupied by clean or light industries.[35]

3. Laws, Implementation and Enforcement

Singapore has adopted the 'command and control' approach to environmental management. Thus, before a proposed development can be built, the developer must submit its building plans to the Building and Construction Authority (BCA) for approval.[36] These plans must also be submitted to and approved by various other authorities including the Fire Safety Bureau, the National Parks Board (NParks), and NEA's Central Building Plan Unit (CBPU). The CBPU scrutinises all building plans to ensure they comply with sewerage, drainage, environmental health and pollution control requirements. In particular, the CBPU will screen prospective industries to ensure that they:

- Are sited in designated industrial estates and are compatible with the surrounding land use;
- Adopt clean technology to minimise the use of hazardous chemicals and the generation of harmful wastes;
- Adopt processes to facilitate the recycling, reuse and recovery of wastes;
- Do not pose unmanageable health and safety hazards and pollution problems; and
- Install pollution control equipment that meet, discharge and emission standards.

When the factory building is completed, the CBPU will inspect the premises to check if the structure has been built in compliance with the requirements of the Sewerage, Drainage, Environmental Health, and Pollution Control Departments. The factory will only be given a Temporary Occupation Permit or a Certificate of Statutory Completion when all these conditions are met.

Next, the factory's operations must comply with the laws that govern their discharge of air emissions, trade effluent and wastes. These include the Environmental Protection and Management Act (EPMA), Environmental Public Health Act (EPHA), Sewerage and Drainage Act (SDA), Workplace Safety and Health Act (WSHA) and their subsidiary laws.[37] It should be noted that some laws reverse the onus of proof[38] and also allow a lifting of the corporate veil to enable officers and employees of a corporation to be charged for offences committed by the corporation.[39]

4. Building the Environmental Infrastructure

It must be emphasised that the best laws will not work without the provision of the environmental infrastructure — these include sewage treatment plants, scrubbers for air emissions from incinerators, air monitoring stations, effluent treatment plants, sanitary landfills and incinerators for hazardous and bio-hazardous wastes. As these require considerable capital expenditure, the provision of the physical environmental infrastructure is a constant challenge to many cities. While Singapore's economic policies have generated considerable wealth for the city-state, the judicious management of its finances by its "clean" government[40] has ensured that funds are available for the building of a first-rate environmental infrastructure. This, in itself, is an important component of sound environmental management.

Singapore has also resolved its lack of natural water resources by investing heavily in research and technology and the building of sound infrastructure for its water resources and supplies. Today, the country's water supply is derived from four different sources (the "Four National Taps") comprising water from local catchment areas, imported water (from the state of Johore in Malaysia), recycled water (called NEWater) and desalinated water.[41] Singapore also has five incinerators[42] and an offshore landfill site (NEA, 2002c), all of which were built at considerable costs. It has an efficient public transport system,[43] excellent transportation networks and telecommunication facilities.[44]

The healthier air and clean and green environment have made Singapore an increasingly popular base for foreign corporations. In contrast, despite its many advantages, increasing pollution in Hong Kong has driven investors to Singapore (Financial Times, 2006; The Stalwart, 2006). Indeed, studies have shown that good environmental governance is critical and it is "one reason why highly regulated Singapore has proven far better at combating pollution than laissez-faire Hong Kong."[45]

A healthy and pleasant living environment continues to play an important role in ensuring that Singapore remains an attractive place for investors, talented migrants and its own citizens.

Future Challenges

Singapore's environmental governance has focused on the control and management of pollution, the ensuring of a safe and reliable supply of water and the protection of its natural resources.[46] It has developed its industrial base and achieved high economic growth within a short span of four decades.

Environmental management policies were, at the outset, integrated with the economic policies of the country. Programmes were implemented to protect and clean up the environment at the early stages. Cleaning up, greening and protecting the environment were indeed a major part of Singapore's strategies for success. As stated by its first Prime Minister Lee, "In wooing investors, even trees matter."[47]

Today, the challenge of climate change looms large. There is a need to manage the rise of sea levels as well as implement strong policies on resource conservation and waste management.

This chapter now examines the government's priorities and strategies for the next 20 years under the government's Blueprint for Sustainable Development, entitled "A Lively and Liveable Singapore: Strategies for Sustainable Growth".[48] It will examine the strategies articulated, highlight the inadequacies and offer some suggestions for improvements.

The Singapore Blueprint for Environmental Sustainability

It should first be noted that the Blueprint defines "sustainable development" to mean "achieving the twin goals of growing the economy while protecting the environment in a balanced way."[49] To this, one should ask — who defines this 'balance'? Is there a role for the public here in determining what should be priorities in this context? To what extent is there public participation in environmental matters in Singapore? What laws are necessary to help achieve these objectives?

The Blueprint rightly emphasises that Singapore's resources are limited: land supply is scarce; energy, food and water have to be imported. It states that "with a small domestic market, we have to find creative ways to keep our economy growing and thriving while acting as stewards for the environment for present and future generations. Thus, a pragmatic approach has to be taken. While clear goals will be set and progress tracked, plans will have to be implemented in ways that will not sharply increase the costs for businesses, households and commuter." The government will invest SGD$1 billion over five years to support the implementation of plans in its Blueprint[50] which has identified a number of key strategies aimed at:

1. Boosting resource efficiency
2. Enhancing the living environment
3. Controlling pollution and waste management

4. Promoting clean technology and investing in research and development
5. Building capacity and encouraging public participation

These will now be briefly examined.

1. Promoting Energy Efficiency

This is targeted at different areas: industry, water, buildings, public housing and transportation.

Energy efficient industries: As the industrial sector accounts for more than 50 per cent of total national energy consumption, businesses must be encouraged to invest greater attention and resources in energy efficiency. This requires the raising of awareness on best practices, building capacity in energy management, the adoption of energy efficient designs in industrial facilities as well as energy-related benchmarking for key industrial sectors and the promotion of energy management systems within companies. A number of schemes have been devised by the NEA to assist companies[51] including helping investors with funding for new and more energy efficient facilities; co-funding energy audits and offsetting costs in the deployment of energy efficient measures as well as promoting co-generation and tri-generation technology.[52]

Enhancing Water Security and Efficiency: It is anticipated that water needs will increase as water-intensive industries such as petrochemical and wafer fabrication continue to grow. Thus, Singapore has to continuously develop alternative sources of water supply and promote water efficiency. The Blueprint has identified various additional efforts including expanding NEWater capacity to form an island-wide network of pipes while developing localised water supplies through recycling, desalination and promoting industry-led initiatives to identify areas for improvement in water conservation, starting with hotels, schools and commercial buildings. Again, some financial incentives have been provided by the State to drive these initiatives.[53]

Resource-Efficient Buildings: The Green Mark Scheme is a rating system that evaluates the environmental impact and performance of buildings via the Building Control (Environmental Sustainability) Regulations (2008). Buildings are awarded the following ratings if there is energy efficiency improvement:

- Certified Green Mark: 10 to 15 per cent improvement
- Gold Mark: 15 to 25 per cent improvement

- Gold Plus: 25 to 30 per cent improvement
- Platinum: more than 30 per cent improvement

These ratings will be implemented in various ways with incentives to cover new buildings, public sector buildings as well as existing buildings. The government will require all new buildings in key development areas[54] to achieve high Green Mark ratings (Platinum and Gold-Plus) as part of its land sales requirements.[55] These ratings will be tightened further in the longer term. Public sector buildings with more than 5,000 sqm air-conditioned floor area are required to achieve the Green Mark Platinum rating. For existing buildings, the government aims through various incentives to encourage 80 per cent to achieve the minimum Green Mark rating as this will improve energy efficiency by 5–10 per cent.

Resource-Efficient Public Housing:

The Blueprint seeks to make public housing more resource-efficient in three ways:

(a) The Housing and Development Board (HDB) will build a new generation of eco-friendly public housing, incorporating environmentally friendly features and green technology
(b) The HDB will also test-bed solar technology within 30 public housing precincts nation-wide at a cost of $31 million so as to see how it can incorporate solar technology into the design of new apartments.
(c) The HDB has embarked on projects to reduce energy consumption in existing estates by 20 to 30 per cent which include the replacement of outdoor and corridor high-energy lamps and common areas with more energy efficient lighting and lift systems.

Greener, Cleaner and More Efficient Transportation:

Singapore's roads take up 12 per cent of the total land area. The transport sector accounts for 13 per cent of the country's overall energy consumption and 50 per cent of the fine particulates (PM2.5) in the air. The Blueprint calls for a 'cleaner, greener and more efficient transport system' in four ways — by enhancing public transport, improving resource efficiency, tightening emissions regulations[56] and encouraging cycling and walking.

2. Enhancing the Quality of Life — A City of Gardens and Water

The Blueprint states that "we want to see our city nestled in greenery, our waterways come alive and our residents enjoy better access to nature and our rich biodiversity."[57] The key recommendations are:

Parks: More parks and nature-based leisure options will be created and their connectivity enhanced; sky rise greenery will be promoted including green roofs atop multi-storey car parks in public housing estates. More greenery must be provided in new developments and the URA will adopt a landscape replacement policy. All new developments in the downtown core area will have to provide landscape areas equal to the overall development site area in the form of sky-rise greenery and ground level communal landscape area.

Water bodies: The dense network of canals and waterways that have been developed to manage storm water and to meet the city state's water needs will be transformed to support recreational activities. By 2030, more than 130 projects will open up 900 ha of reservoirs and 100km of waterways for recreational uses.

Biodiversity protection and enhancement: Singapore's four legally protected nature reserves[58] and two protected national parks[59] cover more than 4.5 per cent of its land area. Due to the shortage of land, there is a constant tussle between development and conservation. The Blueprint endeavours to "keep the nature areas for as long as possible. The URA will also seek to focus on development in urbanised areas before undeveloped areas are opened up."[60] Where development must take place, measures will be undertaken to reduce the impact on biodiversity by linking parks and nature reserves with park connectors and the planting of suitable trees and shrubs to induce birds and butterflies to fly from park to park. Singapore's NParks has initiated a City Biodiversity Index, which was endorsed at the Nagoya meeting of the parties to the Convention on Biological Diversity in 2010.[61] In its application to Singapore, NParks will utilise parks for ex-situ conservation and to house or re-create ecosystems that have been lost. NParks is also studying the development of eco-links between nature reserves. The Blueprint states that "the government will take into account biodiversity issues when making decisions and adopt holistic approaches towards the conservation of our natural environment."

3. Enhancing Pollution Control and Waste Management

Air emissions will be tightened with PM2.5 (fine particles in ambient air of 2.5 micrometres or less in size) reduced from 16ug/m3 (microgram per cubic metre) in 2008 to 12ug/m3 by 2020 with the level expected to be maintained till 2030 through the introduction of vehicles using cleaner diesel fuels. The NEA also seeks to cap ambient sulphur dioxide (SO2) levels at an annual mean of 15ug/m3 in 2020 to be maintained at this level till 2030. It was recently announced that the NEA aims to raise the emission standard of petrol vehicles to Euro IV by January 2014, up from the current Euro II standard which has been in place since 2001 (Tan, 2012). The agency will work with major emitters such as oil refineries, petrochemical plants and power generation companies to use cleaner fuels and put into place more pollution control measures. Waste management and recycling are emphasised through the promotion of less packaging, the provision of financial support for recycling and the promotion of recycled products.

4. Promoting Clean Technology and Investing in R&D and Manpower

The government will invest more in developing clean technology and sustainable urban solutions as new growth areas expected to contribute to the economy. It will position Singapore as a Sustainable Development Hub, which will serve as a base for research and export of new technologies as well as an innovative thought centre on high-density living and sustainable development. The Economic Development Board (EDB) will seek to create a vibrant research environment in clean technology with considerable funds set aside for clean energy and water technology sectors, innovative design and integration of solar panels into buildings (Solar Capability Scheme) and research devoted to refinement of land use planning and high-density living.

5. Public Participation and the formation of local environmental non-governmental organisations (NGOs) will be encouraged, as well as partnerships with corporations and schools.

Evaluation and Critique

While the initiatives and strategies mentioned are highly laudable, there are two major inadequacies that need to be addressed:

1. Lack of laws mandating environmental impact studies/assessments; and
2. Lack of laws mandating recycling

1. Environmental Impact Assessments (EIA) and Public Participation

The essence of the EIA's assessment is to "Look before you Leap" which is a very important tool in planning for development projects. Environmental assessment is a process that ensures that the environmental implications are taken into account before decisions are made. It involves a series of steps to carefully analyse the potential impacts of a project on the environment. These steps include: screening, scoping, baseline studies and evaluation, impact prediction, community consultation and stakeholder engagement, mitigation, development of an environmental management plan, post-project audit and evaluation. A report must be prepared and disclosed to the public, who would be invited to give their comments in a public consultation exercise. The decision whether to proceed still lies with the government. However, this public examination and consultation will ensure that the decision is made with the fullest possible information, such that if the project is to proceed, effective mitigation measures can be implemented.[62] Many multilateral environmental instruments have called for states to implement EIAs. Principle 17 of the Rio Declaration on Environment and Development (1992) states that "environmental impact assessment as a national instrument shall be undertaken for proposed activities that are likely to have a significant adverse impact on the environment and are subject to a decision of a competent national authority." The ASEAN Agreement on Nature and Natural Resources (1985), the Convention on Biological Diversity (1992) and Agenda 21 (1992) which Singapore signed, ratified and endorsed respectively all emphasise the importance of EIAs and public participation.[63] The United Nations Environment Program (UNEP) which promotes the application of the EIA process in major projects has recommended that it should be used during the entire project cycle from planning through operation, to eventual closure.[64]

The nearest approximations of the EIA in Singapore are contained in sections 26 and 36 of the Environmental Protection and Management Act (EPMA). Section 26 relates to impact analysis studies of hazardous installations.[65] It empowers the Director of Pollution Control to require the owner or occupier of a hazardous installation to carry out impact analysis studies and identify all possible hazards; estimate their frequency or probability; quantify the consequences and risk levels; evaluate the effects of fires or other disasters and identify all necessary preventive measures. The Director may also require that measures be undertaken to prevent, reduce or control potential hazards. Section 36 empowers the Director to require any person intending to carry out any activity that is "likely to cause substantial pollution" to first conduct a study on environmental pollution control and to submit a proposal for the reduction or control of pollution.

Both provisions fall short of an EIA as they focus only on industries or projects with high polluting capacity whereas EIAs require a comprehensive, integrated and detailed study of all potential impacts on the environment including ecological and sociological impacts. It is also a hallmark of EIA laws that they allow some measure of public participation, whereas sections 26 and 36 do not involve any third parties.

Environmental lawyers and planners have lamented the lack of EIA laws in Singapore.[66] Some of the controversies which raised the issue of the EIA include the following:

(1) *The 1992 proposal to convert part of the Lower Peirce Reservoir (gazetted as a nature reserve) into a golf course.* In response to calls for environmental impact studies to be undertaken, the authorities agreed to commission an EIA but declared the results to be confidential. This prompted the Nature Society to undertake and publish its own EIA Report which revealed that considerable damage to the eco-system and loss of biological diversity would ensue and would be irreparable.[67] While the project has been shelved for the time being, it is clear that such issues may well rise again in the future, and indeed it has.

(2) *Chek Jawa:* The EIA issue emerged again in 2001 with the government's proposal to reclaim a stretch of beach at Tanjong Chek Jawa on the offshore island of Pulau Ubin.[68] The proposed reclamation of Chek Jawa generated much interest and controversy. Concerned citizens, educators and non-government organisations tried hard to persuade the authorities to reverse its decision.[69] However, the Urban Redevelopment Authority maintained that reclamation would proceed. Fortunately, at the very last minute, the authorities relented and announced that Chek Jawa would not be reclaimed, at least for the next ten years. While the respite is clearly welcome, albeit for an uncertain duration, the fact remains that unlike the Lower Peirce Reservoir site, Chek Jawa was not legally protected, and the lack of any procedures for a proper EIA to be undertaken resulted in considerable damage to the eco-system, as specimens of flora and fauna were removed from the beach by members of the public with impunity. Chek Jawa is still

not legally protected. With the decision not to proceed with the recla-mation, NParks was placed in charge of Chek Jawa. A walkway for public viewing of the beach has since been built at a considerable expense to encourage public appreciation for this nature site and at the same time, reduce further damage to the eco-system.[70]

(3) *Bukit Brown Cemetery:* This is the latest controversy which erupted in 2012 stemming from the government's announcement that the site, which contains over 100,000 graves and is the largest Chinese ceme-tery outside China, was zoned for housing needs in the future. In the meantime, some 5,000 graves will be exhumed to make way for road expansion works. The Nature Society and the Singapore Heritage Soci-ety objected, maintaining that the site should be preserved as both a heritage and nature site. There was no public consultation prior to the announcement. Again, the EIA process would have required that the views of the public be sought and various alternatives to the road expansion carefully considered, such as the building of an underground tunnel or a viaduct.[71]

Today, EIAs continue to be done on an *ad hoc* basis although access has been given increasingly to non-government organisations such as the Nature Society. Announcements have been made on the Government Gazette informing readers where the EIA report can be viewed.[72] However, as there is no legislation mandating environmental impact studies, there is no sys-tem in place for the proper facilitation of such studies. There is no spelling out of the roles of the different parties, the right of the public to be informed and to be allowed to participate in the process of deliberation. This is a major inadequacy in our laws.

The challenges of further urbanisation and depletion of the natural environment have led to calls for more rigorous environmental planning procedures.[73] These include:

- Establishing a coordinating body which deals comprehensively and authoritatively with environmental planning matters;
- Establishing a definitive set of procedures that require developers and public agencies to adhere to and ensure a high degree of environmental sensitivity when undertaking major infrastructure construction;
- Ensuring the systematic collection and sharing of environmental data among the various agencies; and
- Introducing environmental impact studies as an integral part of the planning process.

There are also calls for ethical public land stewardship in Singapore, using the concept of the public trust whereby the state is viewed as a trustee of all publicly-owned lands for present and future generations of citizens, and is under an obligation to give due consideration to ecological concerns as well as facilitate public consultations in its deliberations on land use (Chun, 2005; Lye, 2010).[74] Indeed, the EIA and public participation in its deliberations should be viewed positively as a means for the authorities to obtain all relevant information so as to assist in their making of sound and reasoned decisions after considering all possible alternatives and mitigating factors. Thus, there are cogent and pressing reasons for the argument that EIAs should be legally mandated. The usual concerns that the consultative process may prolong the development and obstruct decision making can easily be resolved by clear laws and procedures with strict timelines for public consultation and feedback.

2. Lack of Laws for Recycling

There are no laws mandating recycling in Singapore which is a stark contrast to other Asian countries such as Taiwan, South Korea and Japan. The Environmental Public Health Act and its regulations govern the management of solid wastes in Singapore.[75] Refuse and garbage is collected daily by licensed general waste contractors.[76] The island is divided into nine geographical sectors and pre-qualified waste collection companies compete to provide refuse collection services for the designated domestic and trade premises. Successful bidders are awarded tenders to serve the respective sectors for a period of five to seven years. They are also required to provide door-to-door collection services for recyclable materials from households in their sectors under the National Recycling Programme.

In the case of condominiums and private apartments, the Building Maintenance and Strata Management Act[77] stipulate the need for management corporations to separate and prepare wastes for recycling. In the case of HDB apartments, a recycling bin is provided for every five blocks and these are collected every fortnight. This is clearly inadequate!

Apart from the above, there are no laws for the mandatory separation of wastes and recycling which is still voluntary. Incineration produced some 963 million kWh of electricity accounting for 2 per cent to 3 per cent of the total electricity generated in Singapore. However, more energy can be produced from incineration if wet wastes such as food and other organic wastes are first sorted out and separately treated. Legislation mandating such practices would greatly ease the efforts of the private sector to collect and appropriately treat such wastes. There was only one plant that treated food wastes by converting them to compost through a process of bio-methanisation. It generated energy that was sold to the power grid. Regrettably, it was compelled to close down as it could not obtain sufficient food wastes.[78] This was clearly due to the lack of laws mandating the separation of wastes.

As wastes in Singapore are incinerated, thereby reducing their bulk very substantially, this may be a factor accounting for the reluctance to pass recycling laws. However it must be emphasised that the shortage of land requires that its sole offshore landfill site should be filled up as slowly as possible. Another factor is that a substantial number of apartments in Singapore are built with a private garbage chute in the kitchen area. This is a major impediment to recycling, as residents dispose of wastes in the privacy of their own homes. It would make the enforcement of recycling laws extremely difficult. In recent years, some attempts have been made to locate garbage disposal chutes in the common areas of apartments and to have separate chutes for garbage and for recyclable wastes. This is a welcome move but much more is needed. It must be emphasised that laws can still be passed for industrial and commercial buildings, restaurants and food courts. It is notable that the Blueprint does not mention that new buildings should not be built with private garbage chutes. It does not appear that there are any planning controls on this. Indeed, a new HDB estate, Casa Clementi, was built with just one garbage chute, located outside the apartments.

Conclusion

The issue of the sustainability of cities is highly complex and dependent on many factors. This chapter has examined the Environmental Management System (EMS) implemented in the city state of Singapore. Whether an EMS can be effectively implemented depends on many factors, particularly the political, social and economic contexts of that city. An effective EMS is a major step towards sustainability. It is part of good governance. Good governance also requires an honest and capable government with political will. It is submitted that while Singapore has done very well for the most part in protecting its environment and should be lauded for its honest and efficient government and administrative agencies, the lack of environmental impact assessment (EIA) laws and absence of recycling laws are major inadequacies that should be remedied.

The authorities should view the EIA as a positive step in helping them in decision making, as the consultative process furnishes them with all relevant information. The wisdom of the EIA allows sound mitigating measures to be undertaken if the project has to proceed. It is also consistent with the wishes of a new citizenry which is better educated and takes a keener interest in the country's development and environment. This paves the way for more meaningful public participation and engagement, and is aligned with the view that the environment belongs to the citizens, with the government playing the role of a trustee for present and future generations of Singaporeans. It follows that, as beneficiaries, they ought to be consulted.

Laws should also be passed for the recycling of wastes. Only then can Singapore fully claim that it is a 'sustainable city' and that its green plans are in accord with the spirit and intent of Agenda 21, which Singapore endorsed at the United Nations Conference on Environment and Development (Earth Summit) held in Rio de Janeiro in 1992.

Endnotes

[1] That same year, the term 'eco-city' was coined with the book *Ecocity Berkeley: building cities for a healthy future*, by Richard Register. This chapter does not attempt to discuss eco-cities, as the few examples today are still in an embryonic stage. See "Sustainable Cities: Oxymoron or the Shape of the Future?", See Annissa *et al.* (2011). See also NUS (2009); Singapore (2009). Singapore and China are in collaboration to build two eco-cities in Tianjin (Sino-Singapore Tianjin Eco-City) and Nanjing (Eco-Hightech Island). See Singapore (2012); Huang (2010).

[2] According to Columbia University's Earth Institute, New York City is one of the most energy-efficient places in the United States, consuming a quarter of the national average in energy consumption and emitting a quarter of the national average of carbon dioxide. See CU (2011) and Naparstek (2009).

[3] "Lee Kuan Yew wanted Singapore to become a garden city, to soften the harshness of life in one of the world's most densely populated countries", Han *et al.* (1998: 1).

[4] See MND (n.d).

[5] "Efforts will include linking up Singapore's waterways, turning them into recreational spots and blending them in with parks and green spaces" (Lee, 2006).

[6] See Lye (2002, 2008a and 2013); Tookey (1998); and Foo *et al.* (1995).

7 The paper states "This is our blueprint to realise this vision. It contains the strategies and initiatives we believe are needed for Singapore to achieve both economic growth and a good living environment over the next two decades." (p. 11)

8 This blueprint was co-chaired by the two Ministers, with a three-member committee comprising the Minister for Transport, the Minister for Finance, as well as the Senior Minister for Trade and Industry. There were consultations with business and community leaders and members of the public.

9 Singapore has added to its land area from time to time, by reclamation of land from the sea. In the 1960s, its land area was 581.5 square kilometres (224.5 sq mi).

10 Stamford Raffles was Lieutenant-Governor of Java from 1813 to 1816 and was knighted in 1816 by the Prince Regent on his return to England. See NNDB (2012) and ERB (2012).

11 See MPA (2009) Singapore was the world's busiest port since 1986, but it is now ranked third busiest after Shanghai and Ningbo-Zhoushan. See http://www.marineinsight.com/marine/top-10-biggest-ports-in-the-world-in-2011/.

12 See Changi (2012).

13 See (MOE, 1997).

14 See (NEA, 2008/09).

15 See MOH (2012).

16 According to the 2012 BP Statistical Energy Survey, Singapore had a 2011 refinery capacity of 1,395,000 barrels per day, 1.5 per cent of the world total. See BP (2012) The major oil refineries in Singapore have the following capacities: ExxonMobil Jurong Island Refinery (605,000 bbl/d), Shell Pulau Bukom Refinery (500,000 bbl/d) and Singapore Refining Corporation (SRC) Jurong Island Refinery (290,000 bbl/d) (Reuters, 2011).

17 See EDB (2012).

18 See HDB (2012). Only Singapore citizens and permanent residents are allowed to purchase HDB apartments.

19 See CPFB (2012).

20 See AHI (2012).

21 See Lye (2001; 2009).

22 See Lye (2008).

23 See World Bank (2009).

24 See Lee Kuan Yew (2000).

25 For an early history of Singapore's environmental organisation, see Chapter 2, "How it Began" in *Singapore — My Clean and Green Home,* Ministry of the Environment, 1997, published to commemorate the 25th Anniversary of the Ministry.

26 This was the year of the United Nations Conference on the Human Environment at Stockholm meeting, attended by many heads of state, that resulted in

the Stockholm Declaration on the Human Environment and the formation of the UN Environment Programme (UNEP: 1972). Thereafter, many countries, including Singapore, set up a separate institution/ministry focusing on the environment.

[27] MEWR (2012).

[28] *Ibid.*

[29] The EDB was established in 1961 to promote industrial development by encouraging and facilitating foreign investors to locate their manufacturing in Singapore. See EDB (2012b).

[30] The URA is Singapore's national land use planning and conservation authority. It adopts a long term and comprehensive planning approach in formulating strategic plans such as the Concept Plan and the Master Plan, to guide the physical development of Singapore in a sustainable manner. See URA (2010).

[31] Singapore's first industrial estate was sited in Jurong. The JTC was established in 1968 and pioneered the building of the industrial infrastructure, producing low cost factories and housing for workers in the early years. JTC continues to play a vital role today. See JTC (2012).

[32] See URA (2012).

[33] Highly pollutive industries must be sited in specially designated areas such as Jurong Island with measures to control, manage and minimise pollution as well as to maximise industrial and technological synergies. In particular, the PCD will examine measures to control air, water and noise pollution, the management of hazardous substances, and the treatment and disposal of toxic wastes.

[34] See NEA (2002a), and Lye (2008).

[35] See NEA's Code of Practice http://app2.nea.gov.sg/codeofpractice.aspx.

[36] See *Building Control Act* (Cap. 29, 1999 Rev. Ed. Sing.).

[37] Singapore's laws, including subsidiary legislation can be found at AGC (n.d.).

[38] See s. 17 EPMA — if a toxic substance is found in the drains of a factory, the factory owner is presumed to have caused it.

[39] See s. 71, EPMA.

[40] Singapore has frequently been voted 'the least corrupt in Asia'; see *ibid.*; see Asia One (2011).

[41] See PUB (2012).

[42] See Let's Recycle (2010).

[43] See LTA (2012).

[44] See Point Topic (2011); see also IDA (2012).

[45] See TIME (2006).

[46] See also Lye (2002; 2003).

[47] Senior Minister Lee Kuan Yew on the 35th Anniversary of the Economic Development Board (August 1, 1996). See Koh Kheng Lian (n.d.).

[48] See *Sustainable Singapore* (n.d.).

49 *Ibid.*, p. 6.
50 *Ibid.*, p. 116.
51 See Energy Efficient Singapore (n.d) and their publication *E2 Singapore* at Energy Efficient Singapore (n.d).
52 See the Design for Efficiency Scheme (DfE), Energy Efficiency Improvement Assistance Scheme (EASe) and the Investment Allowance Scheme.
53 The Water Efficiency Fund helps industries defray part of the capital costs of water recycling programmes; the Water Efficient Buildings programme encourages the use of water-efficient fittings and assists building owners in monitoring their water consumption.
54 These include Marina Bay and the Central Business District, Jurong Gateway, Kallang Riverside and Paya Lebar Central (Blueprint, p. 47).
55 It is unclear what will happen if these new buildings fail to achieve these ratings.
56 Singapore will be adopting the World Health Organisation (WHO) Air Quality Guidelines (AQG) for particulate matter 10 (PM10), Nitrogen Dioxide, Carbon Monoxide and Ozone, and the WHO AQG's Interim Targets for PM2.5 and Sulphur Dioxide, as Singapore's air quality targets for 2020. See NEA (2002b).
57 See 'Sustainable Singapore', p. 66.
58 These are the Bukit Timah Nature Reserves, Central Catchment Nature Reserve, Sungei Buloh Wetland Reserves, and Labrador Nature Reserves. See Lye (2008b).
59 These are the Botanic Gardens and Fort Canning Park.
60 See 'Sustainable Singapore', p. 73.
61 See CBD (n.d).
62 See guidelines from the European Union; available online at http://ec.europa.eu/environment/eia/.
63 See Article 14 of the ASEAN Agreement; Article 14 of the *CBD*; and Section III of the Agenda 21.
64 See http://www.unep.fr/pc/pc/tools/eia.htm.
65 The *Code of Practice on Pollution Control*, *supra* note 88 at 11, refers to Quantitative Risk Assessments ("QRA Study") without making reference to section 26 of the *EPMA*.
66 See Foo *et al.* (1995) see Malone-Lee (2002) Lye (2010).
67 See *Proposed Golf Course at Lower Peirce Reservoir — An Environmental Impact Assessment* (Singapore: Nature Society, 1992).
68 "Discovered only last December, the unique mud and sand flat at Chek Jawa may be the last of its kind here. Too bad its destined for the bulldozer." See Wee (2001); see also Chun (2006), and Lye (2010).
69 See *The Straits Times* (2001).
70 Websites have been set up for Chek Jawa; see Chek Jawa (n.d. 2; 3).

[71] See NSS (n.d) See "Call for Moratorium over Plans for Bukit Brown" April 24, 2012; available online at http://sosbukitbrown.wordpress.com/author/bukit brown/page/2/.

[72] See the EIA commissioned by Jurong Town Corporation, relating to the reclamation of Pulau Ular. This appeared in the Government *Gazette* on 13 July 2006, informing the public that the EIA can be viewed at their office. See *Government Gazette* (2006). See also *Habitat News* (2006). Available online at http://habitatnews.nus.edu.sg/news/pulauhantu/2006/01/call-to-view-marine-eia-for-proposed.html.

[73] See Malone-Lee (2002), see also Chun (2005), and Lye (2010).

[74] See also Lye (2010).

[75] These include the *Environmental Public Health (Public Cleansing) Regulations* (2000 Rev. Ed. Sing.); and the *Environmental Public Health (General Waste Collection) Regulations* (2000 Rev. Ed. Sing.).

[76] See NEA (n.d1)

[77] See NEA (n.d2)

[78] "Recycling firm IUT Global being wound up", 22 March 2011, *The Business Times* — IUT's owner said the only way for recycling companies to make money in Singapore is to have laws. 'We get most of our food waste from the industrial and commercial areas, but there is about 30–40 per cent impurities, such as glass and plastics, in it. Sorting out that waste only added to our labour costs, and increased our operating costs.' He earlier explained that the lack of recycling laws here also meant that IUT cannot collect from the many places that generate food waste, such as hawker centres. See http://www.timesdirectories.com/environmental/news/xxx/711763.

References

AHI (Affordable Housing Institute). "Home." 2012. Available online at http://affordablehousinginstitute.org/. Last accessed on 6 November, 2012.

Alusi, Annissa and others. *Sustainable Cities: Oxymoron or the Shape of the Future?* Boston, MA: Harvard Business School Press, 2011. Available online at http://www.hbs.edu/research/pdf/11-062.pdf. Last accessed on 6 November, 2012.

Asia One. "Singapore No Longer Top of Least-Corrupt Countries." December 2, 2011. Available online at http://news.asiaone.com/News/AsiaOne%2B News/Singapore/Story/A1Story20111202-314074.html. Last accessed on 30 October, 2012.

BP (British Petroleum). "Statistical Review of World Energy." 2012. Available online at http://www.bp.com/liveassets/bp_internet/globalbp/globalbp_uk_english/reports_and_publications/statistical_energy_review_2011/STAGING/

local_assets/pdf/statistical_review_of_world_energy_full_report_2012.pdf. Last accessed on 30 October, 2012.

CBD (Convention on Biodiversity). "City Biodiversity Index (or Singapore Index)." n.d. Available online at http://www.cbd.int/authorities/getting involved/cbi.shtml. Last accessed on 6 November, 2012.

Chang, Li Lin and Tommy Koh, eds. *The Little Red Dot- Reflections by Singapore's Diplomats*. Singapore: Institute of Policy Studies and World Scientific Publishing Co. Ltd, 2005.

Changi. "About Changi Airport: Awards." 2012. Available online at http://www.changiairport.com/our-business/about-changi-airport/awards. Last accessed on 29 October, 2012.

Chek Jawa. "Chek Jawa Homepage." Available online at http://chekjawa.nus.edu.sg/. Last accessed on 26 August, 2013.

_____. "Remember Chek Jawa" Available online at http://rememberchekjawa.wordpress.com/%3E. Last accessed on 26 August, 2013.

_____. "Wild Singapore." Available online at http://www.wildsingapore.com/places/cj.htm. Last accessed on 26 August, 2013.

Chun, Joseph. "Reclaiming the Public Trust in Singapore." *Singapore Academy of Law Journal* 17 (2005): 717–737.

_____. "Beyond Real Estate: Sowing the Legal Seeds for an Ethical Public Land Stewardship in Singapore." *Macquarie Journal of International and Comparative Environmental Law* 3, No. 1 (2006): 1–34.

CPFB (Central Provident Fund Board). "Overview." 2012. Available online at http://mycpf.cpf.gov.sg/CPF/About-Us/Intro/Intro.htm. Last accessed on 29 October, 2012.

CU (Columbia University). "Events: New York a Sustainable City." 2011. Available online at http://www.columbia.edu/event/new-york-city-sustainable-city-48283.html. Last accessed on 22 October, 2012.

Djoghlef, Ahmed. "Statement Made by Executive Secretary at the Convention on Biological Diversity." 2009. Available online at http://www.cbd.int/doc/speech/2009/sp-2009-02-10-cbi-en.pdf. Last accessed on 6 November, 2012.

DSS (Department of Statistics Singapore). "Statistics." 2012. Available online at http://www.singstat.gov.sg/stats/keyind.html. Last accessed on 29 October, 2012.

Dubois-Taine, Genevieve. "Introduction." In *Cities of the Pacific Rim — Diversity and Sustainability*, edited by Genevieve Dubois-Taine and Christian Henriot. Paris: Institut Des Sciences De L'homme, 2002.

EC (European Commission). "Environmental Assessment." 2012. Available online at http://ec.europa.eu/environment/eia/. Last accessed on 6 November, 2012.

EDB (Economic Development Board). "Why Singapore." 2012a. Available online at http://www.edb.gov.sg/content/edb/en/why-singapore.html. Last accessed on 6 November, 2012.

————. "About." 2012b. Available online at http://www.edb.gov.sg/content/edb/en/about-edb.html. Last accessed on 29 October, 2012.

Energy Efficient Singapore. "Home." Available online at http://app.e2singapore.gov.sg/. Last accessed on 19 August, 2013.

————. "E2 Singapore." Available online at http://app.e2singapore.gov.sg/DATA/0/docs/Booklet/E2S%20Publication.pdf. Last accessed on 19 August, 2013.

ENV (Ministry of the Environment), Government of Singapore. "Singapore — My Clean & Green Home." 1997.

ERB (Encyclopedia Britannica Online). "Sir Stamford Raffles." 2012. Available online at http://www.britannica.com/EBchecked/topic/489451/Sir-Stamford-Raffles. Last accessed on 23 October, 2012.

Financial Times. "Hedge Funds Flee Hong Kong Pollution for Singapore." *Financial Times*, 2006.

Foo Kim Boon, Lye Lin Heng and Koh Keng Lian. "Environmental Protection — the Legal Framework." In *Environment and the City — Sharing Singapore's Experiences and Future Challenges*, edited by Ooi Giok Ling. Singapore: Institute of Policy Studies, Times Academic Press, 1995.

Government Gazette. July 13, 2006. Available online at http://www.egazette.com.sg/Document/gg/2006/065016.pdf.

Habitat News. "Call to view the marine EIA for proposed reclamation works at Pulau Ular." January 13, 2006. Available online at http://habitatnews.nus.edu.sg/news/pulauhantu/2006/01/call-to-view-marine-eia-for-proposed.html. Last accessed on 26 August, 2013.

Hall, Peter. *Cities of Tomorrow.* Oxford: Blackwell, 1996.

Han Fook Kwang, Warren Fernandez and Sumiko Tan. *Lee Kuan Yew: The Man and His Ideas.* Singapore: Singapore Press Holdings, 1998.

Hardoy, Jorge E., Diana Mitlin and David Satterthwaite. "Sustainable Development and Cities." In *Environmental Problems in Third World Countries.* London: Earthscan Publications, 1992.

HDB (Housing and Development Board). "HDB History." 2012. Available online at http://www.hdb.gov.sg/fi10/fi10320p.nsf/w/AboutUsHDBHistory?OpenDocument. Last accessed on 29 October, 2012.

Huang, Jo-ann. "Singapore-Nanjing Eco High-Tech Island to Attract More Foreign Investment." *channelnewsasia.com*, 2010. Available online at http://www.channelnewsasia.com/stories/singaporebusinessnews/view/1075103/1/.html. Last accessed on 22 October, 2012.

IDA (Infocomm Development Authority of Singapore). "About Us." 2012. Available online at http://www.ida.gov.sg/About-Us.aspx. Last accessed on 6 November, 2012.

IFC-World Bank. "Economy Rankings Benchmarked to June 2011." 2012a. Available online at http://www.doingbusiness.org/rankings. Last accessed on 30 October, 2012.

IFC-World Bank. "Doing Business 2010: Reforming through Difficult Times." 2012b. Available online at http://www.doingbusiness.org/rankings. Last accessed on 6 November, 2012.

JTC (Jurong Town Corporation). "About JTC: Our History." 2012. Available online at http://www.jtc.gov. sg/About-JTC/Pages/Our-History.aspx. Last accessed on 30 October, 2012.

Koh, Kheng Lian. "Garden City to Model Green City." ESCAP Virtual Conference. Available online at http://www.unescap.org/drpad/vc/conference/bg_sg_14_gcm.html. Last accessed on 1 September, 2012.

Lee, Kuan Yew. *From Third World to First — The Singapore Story: 1965–2000 — Singapore and the Asian Economic Boom*. New York: Harper Collins Publishers, 2000.

———. "Greening Singapore." Chap. 13 In *From Third World to First: The Singapore Story: 1965–2000*. New York: Harper Collins Publishers, 2000.

Lee, Lynn. "PM's Call: Make Singapore a City of Gardens and Water." *The Straits Times*, 2006.

Let's Recycle. "Singapore's Tuas Incinerator officially opened." August 4, 2010. Available online at http://www.letsrecycle.com/news/special-reports/singapores-tuas-incinerator-officially-opened. Last accessed on 19 August, 2013.

LTA (Land Transport Authority). "Home." 2012. Available online at http://www.lta.gov.sg/content/ltaweb/en.html. Last accessed on 30 October, 2012.

Lye, Lin-Heng. "Transport-Based Air Pollution Management — The Singapore Experience." *Asia Pacific Journal of Environmental Law* 6, No. 3 (2001): 333–348.

———. "Singapore." In *Environmental Law and Enforcement in the Asia-Pacific Rim*, edited by Terri Mottershead. 395–434. Hong Kong: Sweet & Maxwell, 2002.

———. "Environmental Pollution Laws in Singapore." *American Bar Association Newsletter*, Section on Environment, Energy & Resources, Special Issue on Environmental Protection in the Asia-Pacific Region, February 2003.

———. "Land Use Planning, Environmental Management and the Garden City as an Urban Development Approach in Singapore." Chap. 21 In *Land Use for Sustainable Development Series*, edited by Patricia Kameri-Mbote, Nathalie J. Chalifour, Lin Heng Lye and John R. Nolon. 374–396. New York: Cambridge University Press, 2007.

———. "A Fine City in a Garden-Environmental Law and Governance in Singapore." *Singapore Journal of Legal Studies* (2008a): 68–117.

———. "Nature Conservation Laws — the Legal Protection of Flora and Fauna in Singapore." In *Singapore Red Data Book*. 2008b.

———. "Environmental Law, Singapore." In *Kluwer International Encyclopedia of Laws* (2008c) edited by Roger Blanpain, pp. 1–128. New York: Watter Kluwer, 2013.

————. "Environmental Taxation in the Management of Traffic in Singapore." In *Critical Issues in Environmental Taxation: International and Comparative Perspectives*, edited by Janet E. Milne, Lin-Heng Lye, Hope Ashiabor, Kurt Deketelaere and Larry Kreiser. Oxford: Oxford University Press, 2009.

————. "Land Law and the Environment: Re-Examining the Concept of Owner-ship and Forging New Rights and Obligations in a Changed World." *Singapore Academy of Law Journal* (2010): 189–228.

Malone-Lee, Lai Choo. "Environmental Planning." In *Capacity Building for Environmental Law in the Asian and Pacific Region — Approaches and Resources*, edited by Nicholas A. Robinson, Koh Kheng-Lian and Donna G. Craig, pp. 606–615. Manila: Asian Development Bank, 2002.

MEWR (Ministry of Water and Environment), Government of Singapore. "About Us." 2012. Available online at http://app.mewr.gov.sg/web/Contents/Contents.aspx?Id= 189. Last accessed on 6 November, 2012.

MEWRND (Ministry of the Environment and Water Resources and Ministry of National Development), Government of Singapore. "A Lively and Livable Singapore: Strategies for Sustainable Growth." 2009. Available online at http://app.mewr.gov.sg/data/ ImgCont /1292/sustainbleblueprint_forweb.pdf. Last accessed on 23 October, 2012.

MND (Ministry of National Development), Government of Singapore. "From Garden City to City in a Garden." Available online at http://www.mnd.gov.sg/MNDAPPImages/About%20Us/From%20Garden%20City%20to%20City%20in%20a%20Garden.pd. Last accessed on 23 October, 2012.

MOH (Ministry of Health), Government of Singapore. "Our Healthcare System." 2012. Available online at http://www.moh.gov.sg/content/moh_web/home/our_healthcare_system.html. Last accessed on 6 November, 2012.

————. "Population and Vital Statistics." 2013. Available online at http://www.moh.gov.sg/content/moh_web/home/statistics/Health_Facts_Singapore/Population_And_Vital_Statistics.html. Last accessed on 24 August, 2013.

MPA (Maritime and Port Authority). "Premier Hub Port." 2009. Available on-line at http://www.mpa.gov.sg/sites/maritime_singapore/what_is_maritime_singapore/premier_hub_port.page. Last accessed on 20 October, 2012.

Naparstek, Aaron. "New York City Wins the 2009 Sustainable Transport Award." *Streetsblog.org*, January 13, 2009. Available online at http://www.streetsblog.org/2009/01/13/new-york-city-wins-the-sustainable-transport-award/. Last accessed on 22 October, 2012.

NEA (National Environment Agency). "Code of Practice on Pollution Control." 2002a. Available online at http://app2.nea.gov.sg/data/cmsresource/20090312534898283541.pdf. Last accessed on 6 November, 2012.

————. "Singapore to Adopt Higher Air Quality Targets." 2002b. Available online at http://app2.nea.gov.sg/news_detail_2012.aspx?news_sid=20120823135426553232. Accessed on 6 November, 2012.

————. "Semakau Landfill." 2002c. Available online at http://app2.nea.gov.sg/semakaulandfill.aspx. Accessed on 6 November, 2012.

————. "Annual Report." 2008/2009. Available online at http://web1.env.gov.sg/cms/ar2009/content/nea-annual_report.pdf. Last accessed on 29 October, 2012.

————. "Code of Practice for Licensed General Waste Collectors." Available online at http://www.nea.gov.sg/cms/esd/cop_general_waste_collector.pdf. Last accessed on 6 November, 2012.

————. "Guidebook on Setting up Structured Waste Recycling Programme in Condominiums and Private Apartments."

NNDB. "Sir Stamford Raffles." 2012. Available online at http://www.nndb.com/people/709/000104397/. Last accessed on 23 October, 2012.

NSS (Nature Society Singapore). "Nature Society (Singapore)'s Position on Bukit Brown." n.d. Available online at http://www.nss.org.sg/documents/Nature%20Society's%20Position%20on%20Bukit%20Brown.pdf. Last accessed on 6 November, 2012.

————. *Proposed Golf Course at Lower Peirce Reservoir — an Environmental Impact Assessment.* Singapore: The Nature Society, 1992.

NUS (National University of Singapore). "Centre for Sustainable Asian Cities." Singapore: School of Design and Environment, 2009. Available online at http://www.sde.nus.edu.sg/csac/index.htm. Last accessed on 22 October, 2012.

Point Topic. "Broadband Operators and Tariffs." October 4, 2011. Available online at http://point-topic.com/content/operatorSource/profiles2/singapore-broadband-overview.htm. Last accessed on 19 August, 2013.

PUB (Public Utilities Board). "Overview." 2012. Available online at http://www.pub.gov.sg/water/Pages/default.aspx. Last accessed on 30 October, 2012.

Register, Richard. *Ecocity Berkeley: Building Cities for a Healthy Future.* Berkeley, CA: North Atlantic Books, 1987.

Reuters. "Factbox: Major Oil Refiners in Southeast Asia." May 13, 2011. Available online at http://www.reuters.com/article/2011/05/13/us-refiners-seasia-factbox-idUSTRE74C0PV20110513. Last accessed on 29 October, 2012.

Satterthwaite, David. "Cities as Solutions in an Urbanizing World, UN Centre for Human Settlements." In *The Earthscan Reader in Sustainable Cities*, edited by David Satterthwaite. Oxford: Blackwell, 1999.

————. "Sustainable Cities or Cities That Contribute to Sustainable Development?" In *The Earthscan Reader in Sustainable Cities*, edited by David Satterthwaite. Oxford: Blackwell, 1999b.

SHS (Singapore Heritage Society). "SHS Response to Announced Road Alignment at Bukit Brown." 2012. Available online at http://www.singaporeheritage.org/?p=2346. Last accessed on 6 November, 2012.

Singapore. "Centre for Livable Cities." 2009. Available online at http://www.clc. gov.sg/AboutUs/Aboutclc.htm. Accessed on 22 October, 2012.

———. "Statistics." 2011. Available online at http://www.singstat.gov.sg/ stats/keyind.html#popnarea. Accessed on 6 November, 2012.

———. "Tianjin Eco-City." 2012. Available online at http://www.tianjinecocity. gov.sg/. Last accessed on 22 October, 2012.

Straits Times. "Chek Jawa's Natural Beach Should Be Preserved." July 16, 2001. Available online at http://www.ecologyasia.com/news-archives/2001/jul-01/ straitstimes.asia1.com.sg_forum_story_0,1870,57586,00.html. Last accessed on 6 November, 2012.

Sustainable Singapore. "What is Sustainable Development?" Available online at http://app.mewr.gov.sg/web/Contents/ContentsSSS.aspx?ContId=1034. Last accessed on 19 August, 2013.

Tan, Christopher. "Singapore to Raise Vehicle Emission Standard." *The Jakarta Post*, August 9, 2012. Available online at http://www.thejakartapost.com/ news/2012/08/09/singapore-raise-vehicle-emission-standard.html. Last accessed on 6 November, 2012.

The Stalwart. "Hong Kong Pollution Sends Expats to Singapore." May 23, 2006. Available online at http://www.thestalwart.com/the_stalwart/2006/ 05/hong_kong_pollu.htm. Last accessed on 30 October, 2012.

TIME. "Asia's Environment — Visions of Green." October 2, 2006.

Tookey, Douglas. "Singapore's Environmental Management System: Strengths and Weaknesses and Recommendations for the Years Ahead." *William & Mary Environmental Law and Policy Review* 23, No. 1 (1998): 169–270.

UN (United Nations). "Report of the World Commission on Environment and Development — Our Common Future." 1987.

UNEP (United Nations Environment Programme). "The 10yfp Adopted at Rio+20." n.d. Available online at http://www.unep.fr/scp/. Last accessed on 6 November, 2012.

———. "Declaration of the United Nations Conference on the Human Environment." 1972. Available online at http://www.unep.org/Documents.Multi lingual/Default.asp?documentid=97&articleid=1503. Last accessed on 29 October, 2012.

UN-Habitat. "Habitat Debate." Available online at http://www.unhabitat.org/ categories.asp?catid=9. See also http://www.unhabitat.org/pmss/search Results.aspx?sort=relevance&page=search&searchField=title&searchstr ing=habitat+debate&x=26&y=9. Last accessed on 23 August, 2013.

URA (Urban Redevelopment Authority). "About Us: Introduction." 2010. Available online at http://www.ura.gov.sg/about/ura-intro.htm. Last accessed on 30 October, 2012.

———. "Publications: Overview." 2012. Available online at http://www.ura.gov. sg/publications/. Last accessed on 30 October, 2012.

Wee, Lea. "Chek out this Hidden Eden." *The Straits Times.* July 8, 2001. Available online at http://chekjawa.nus.edu.sg/articles/AG/AGart-ref.htm#3. Last accessed on 18 August, 2013.

World Bank. "World Development Report." 2009. Available online at http://siteresources.worldbank.org/INTWDR2009/Resources/4231006-1225840759068/WDR09_01_Overviewweb.pdf. Last accessed on 6 November, 2012.

10. Trade-Offs and Synergies for Sustainable Development and Climate Stabilisation in Asian Regions

Keigo AKIMOTO, Fuminori SANO, Ayami HAYASHI,
Takashi HOMMA, Junichiro ODA, Kenichi WADA,
Miyuki NAGASHIMA, Kohko TOKUSHIGE
and Toshimasa TOMODA

Advances in economic growth have helped to mitigate many of the historical risks that humanity once faced. Human lifespans drastically increased over the past century, thanks to improvements in various technologies. However, there are some countries and regions which are still facing numerous critical risks and issues that can interfere with sustainable development. The increasing pace and levels of consumption that have brought about remarkable global economic growth in recent decades have also caused a fair amount of degradation to the environment thereby raising threats to human society itself. In particular, massive fossil fuel consumption, widespread destruction of forests and other similar phenomena have led to elevated concentrations of atmospheric greenhouse gas (GHG) and palpable climate change. These will have a serious, veritable impact on natural resources and human societies if left unchecked, especially in Asian regions where the fevered pace of economic growth and greenhouse gas (GHG) emissions are expected with worldwide implications.

There are manifold links among multiple objectives in our society. Most of the links involve either trade-offs or synergetic relationships. In addition, conditions can be divergent throughout the world and hence these linkages often vary in different countries and regions. Hence, it is vital to balance such multiple objectives in our quantitative assessments of the complex interrelationships relating to sustainable economic development. This chapter assessed various scenarios using highly consistent integrated assessment models focusing on Asian regions. The assessments of specific

sectors or indicators as well as regional distributions in order to seek specific measures for achieving higher levels of sustainable development with
an emphasis on Asian countries.

Integrated Assessment Model

Overview of the model

In order to assess the different scenarios, several models are used, tracking
indicators such as energy consumption, climate change impact, land and
water use and biodiversity or ocean acidification (Figure 10.1). The models
are essentially soft-linked rather than being fully integrated. Regional divi-
sions vary among the models. For example, the DNE21+ model covers 54
regions (Akimoto et al., 2010; 2008) while the DNE21 model is restricted
to analyses of 10 regions (Akimoto et al., 2004; Fujii and Yamaji, 1998).
The DNE21+ model looks into consumption patterns and use of CO_2 emission technology not only in energy supply but also the demand side of the
equation for its detailed assessments. The DNE21 model covers a long-term
period up to 2150, looking not only at energy sectors but also the larger

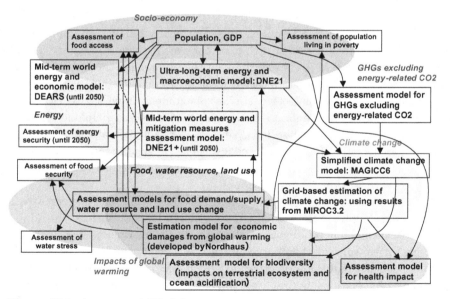

Figure 10.1: Assessment Models.

Source: Compiled by the Authors.

macro-economy while the DNE21+ model covers a medium-term period up to 2050 with a focus on only energy-related technology and sectors.

The land-use and water-use model is an integrated food supply and demand module which covers 32 regions (Hayashi *et al.*, 2013). Crop productivity, including effects of climate change are assessed using a module based on the Global Agro-Ecological Zones (GAEZ) framework (Fischer *et al.*, 2002). The water assessment module estimates annual withdrawals-to-availability ratios using the definition of river basin provided by Oki (2001).

For climate estimations such as atmospheric CO_2 and GHG concentration, radiative forcing and global mean temperature change, a simple climate change model, MAGICC6 (Meinshausen *et al.*, 2011), was used. The grid-based projections for monthly temperature, precipitation and the like are provided by MIROC3.2-Medres (K-1 model developers, 2004) and adopted to approximate weather patterns related to climate change in the region (Hayashi *et al.*, 2010).

Sustainable development indicators

The Millennium Development Goals (MDGs) cover indicators relating to sustainable development. In this study, the indicators listed in Table 10.1 were selected to provide and assess alternative scenarios for sustainable development and their effects on climate change. Many of the indicators are not independent, but involve inter-related as shown in Figure 1 entailing both trade-offs and synergies.

Assumed Alternative Scenarios for Assessments

In order to assess alternative scenarios from several perspectives relating to sustainable development and climate change, the following scenarios were assumed.

Climate stabilisation scenarios

Five levels of GHG emission reduction are assumed for the assessments (Table 10.2) based on recommendations by the United Nations' Intergovernmental Panel on Climate Change (IPCC) and a set of scenarios suggested by the scientific community in 2007.[1] Four scenarios with different emission levels known as Representative Concentration Pathways (RCPs)

Table 10.1: Sustainable Development Assessment Indicators.

Category	Indicator Used
Economics and poverty	Income (GDP per capita)
	People living in poverty (taking into account the impact of climate change and mitigation measures)
	Food access (food consumption per GDP taking into account impact of climate change and mitigation measures)
	Energy access (access to grid electricity; use of biomass for cooking)
Agriculture, land-use, and biodiversity	Agriculture land area (taking into account the impact of climate change)
	Food security (food import per GDP taking into account the impact of climate change and mitigation measures)
Water	People living under water stress
Energy	Sustainable energy use (cumulative fossil fuel consumption)
	Energy use efficiency (primary energy consumption per capita and per GDP)
	Energy security (share of total primary energy consumption from oil and gas imports with country risks factored)
Climate change	Economic impact of mitigation measures (marginal abatement cost or carbon price and GDP loss)
	Global mean temperature change
	Aggregated economic impact of climate change
	Ocean acidification (pH and impact on CaCO3 or aragonite)

Source: Compiled by the Authors.

were chosen: RCP8.5, RCP6.0, RCP4.5 and RCP3PD 2.6 (van Vuuren *et al.*, 2011). The RCP6.0, RCP4.5 and RCP3PD2.6 correspond closely to CP6.0, CP4.5 and CP3.0 scenarios used in this study.

Scenarios for sensitivity analysis

Climate change will be one of the most serious issues that will impact sustainable development negatively if left unchecked. Some of these have been factored into the various scenarios for sensitivity analysis below in Table 10.3.

Historical evidence has shown that a pattern of elevated economic growth tends to lead to slower population growth. In the base scenario (Scenario A), a moderate improvement in technology usage and hence total

Table 10.2: Atmospheric CO_2 Concentration and Global Mean Temperature Change.

	CO_2 Concentration (ppm-CO_2)	GHG Concentration (ppm-CO_2 equivalent)	Radiative Forcing (W/m^2)	Global Mean Temperature Change Relative to Pre-industrial Level (°C)	
	2100	2100	2100	2050	2100
Baseline	820	1010	7.0	2.4	4.1
CP6.0	680	760	5.5 (6.0 in 2150)	2.3	3.3
CP4.5	550	630	4.5	2.1	2.8
CP3.7	480	550	3.7	2.0	2.3
CP3.0	420 (overshoot; 380 in 2150)	480 (overshoot; 450 in 2150)	3.0	1.8	1.9

Note: Equilibrium climate sensitivity is assumed to be 3.0°C for estimates of global mean temperature change. According to IPCC (2007), the range of climate sensitivity is likely to be 2.0−4.5°C, and the most likely value is 3.0°C.
Source: Compiled by the Authors.

Table 10.3: Assumed Socio-Economic Scenarios Relating to Technology Improvement and Energy Security.

Scenarios for Sensitivity Analysis	Description
A: Base scenario	Moderate per-capita GDP growth and moderate population growth
B: High economic growth scenario	High per-capita GDP and low population growth
C: Energy security prioritised scenario	High priority on energy security

Source: Compiled by the Authors.

factor productivity is assumed. For sensitivity analysis with a focus on socio-economic conditions (Scenario B), a high technology improvement scenario accompanied by high economic growth and corresponding low population growth is assumed.

Table 10.4 shows assumptions on GDP and population in Scenarios A and B. The global per-capita GDP growth for 2010–2050 is projected at 2.6 per cent per annum (p.a.) and 2.9 per cent p.a. respectively in Scenario A and Scenario B. Scenario A and B both assume moderate and low population growth in the relationship between per-capita GDP and

Table 10.4: Global Population and GDP Scenarios in Baseline Scenarios.

	Population (in billions)			GDP (MER) (% p.a.)		
	2030	2050	2100	2010–2030	2030–2050	2050–2100
A: Base Scenario						
World	8.31	9.15	9.25	2.9%	2.2%	1.4%
Asia	*4.44*	*4.68*	*4.41*	*4.2%*	*2.8%*	*1.4%*
Japan	*0.12*	*0.10*	*0.08*	*1.3%*	*0.1%*	*0.1%*
China	*1.44*	*1.40*	*1.19*	*6.5%*	*3.3%*	*0.8%*
India	*1.48*	*1.61*	*1.54*	*6.5%*	*4.3%*	*2.2%*
B: High Economic Growth Scenario						
World	8.08	8.55	7.36	3.2%	2.6%	1.7%
Asia	*4.32*	*4.37*	*3.40*	*4.3%*	*3.1%*	*1.9%*
Japan	*0.11*	*0.10*	*0.07*	*1.3%*	*0.5%*	*0.5%*
China	*1.41*	*1.31*	*0.89*	*6.7%*	*3.7%*	*1.3%*
India	*1.44*	*1.50*	*1.18*	*6.5%*	*4.5%*	*2.9%*

Source: Compiled by the Authors.

population, which is in line with historical trends. The global population in 2050 is projected at 9.15 billion and 8.55 billion respectively for Scenario A and Scenario B; while the figures for 2100 are 9.25 billion and 7.36 billion respectively. Accordingly, the global real GDP at market exchange rate (MER) in 2050 is estimated at US$113 trillion and US$129 trillion respectively for Scenario A and B.

Energy security issues usually have very high priority in most countries. Substituting coal with natural gas lowers CO_2 emissions and contributes to mitigation of climate changes, but it may heighten vulnerability in energy security. Finding ways to achieve a balance between the two issues will be important. In order to assess the balance, Scenario C which places a higher priority on energy security is also used in our studies. For quantitative analysis, higher CIF prices of oil and gas are assumed in Scenario C, as outlined in Table 10.5. The sensitivity analyses in Scenarios B and C will be discussed in Section 5.

Assessments for Emission Reduction Scenarios

This chapter discusses the assessments for different emission reduction scenarios as outlined in Table 10.2 using several of the indicators listed in Table 10.1.

Table 10.5: CIF Prices of Oil and Gas in Baseline Scenarios (Scenarios of No Specific Policy for GHG Emission Reduction).

	2010	2030	2050
Oil (US2000$/toe (US2000$/bbl))			
A: Base scenario	399 (63)	702 (110)	818 (128)
C: Energy security prioritised scenario		877 (138)	1022 (160)
Gas (US2000$/toe)			
A: Base scenario	308	530	569
C: Energy security prioritised scenario		662	711

Source: Compiled by the Authors.

Greenhouse gas (GHG) emissions

Different global CO_2 emission and atmospheric concentration pathways are being assessed in the study. All the stabilisation scenarios except for the baseline require CO_2 emissions to be below the current level by 2150. Global average per-capita CO_2 emissions stood at 5.2 tCO_2 in 2005. In 2050, the emissions will be 7.5, 6.8, 4.6, 2.9, and 2.0 tCO_2 for the Baseline, CP6.0, CP4.5, CP3.7, and CP3.0 scenarios respectively. In 2100, the emissions will be 11.2, 4.6, 1.9, 0.6, and -1.2 tCO_2 for Baseline, CP6.0, CP4.5, CP3.7, and CP3.0 respectively. All the stabilisation scenarios except for Baseline require per-capita CO_2 emissions to be below the current level by 2100. In order to achieve the CP3.0 scenario, global CO_2 emissions are required to be negative through afforestation or reforestation measures and the use of biomass power and carbon dioxide capture and storage (CCS).

In the Baseline scenario, the share of Asian regions in global GHG emission will increase and be almost double in 2050 compared with that in 2005, as shown in Figure 10.2. On the other hand, the cumulative energy-related CO_2 emissions for 1971–2050 in China, India and other Asia will be slightly lower in 2050 at 23 per cent, 7 per cent, and 7 per cent.

Mitigation costs

The global marginal abatement costs of CO_2 (or carbon prices) in 2050 are US$6, US$30, US$140, and US$380/tCO_2 for CP6.0, CP4.5, CP3.7 and CP3.0 respectively. The costs in 2100 are US$100, US$180, US$230, and US$600/tCO_2 respectively. The marginal abatement costs in this study will be at levels comparable with those of the IPCC RCP scenarios.

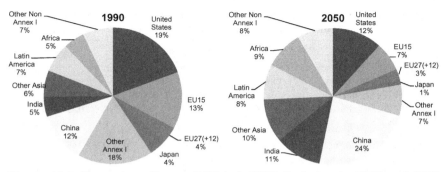

Figure 10.2: Percentage Share of Global GHG Emission in 2005 and 2050 under Baseline Scenarios.

Source: IEA (2011a) for 2005; estimated by the Authors for 2050.

Estimated GDP losses due to climate mitigation measures in 2050 for CP6.0, CP4.5, CP3.7 and CP3.0 compared with 0.0 per cent, 0.7 per cent, 1.9 per cent, and 3.1 per cent, respectively for the Baseline scenario. The GDP losses in 2100 for CP6.0, CP4.5, CP3.7 and CP3.0 are 1.2 per cent, 2.2 per cent, 2.8 per cent, and 4.3 per cent, respectively. It should be recognised that Africa's current share of global GDP is about 2.2 per cent (World Bank, 2011) and that a global GDP decline of even a few percentage points would have enormous impact on countries in this region.

Aggregated macroeconomic impact of climate change

Climate change will have huge impact on several sectors worldwide though the extent at macroeconomic levels remains uncertain despite great efforts being made at quantification. Estimations should be and will improve with progress in research. This study basically focuses on assessments of the impact of climate change on specific sectors, and how to seek ways to tackle issues relating to sustainable development. The aggregated macroeconomic impact due to climate change is also evaluated here based on past studies and includes several indicators such as mitigation costs in terms of GDP. This study estimates the aggregated impact using the functional equation provided by Nordhaus (2010) shown below:

$$\frac{D(t)}{GDP_{Base}(t)} = a_1 T(t) + a_2 \left(T(t)\right)^{a_3}$$

- $D(t)$: aggregated macroeconomic impact due to climate change;
- $GDP_{Base}(t)$: GDP excluding climate change impact;
- $T(t)$: global mean temperature;
- a_1 and a_2: coefficients depending on 12 countries and regions into which the world is divided (refer to Nordhaus (2010));
- a_3: coefficient of 2 for all countries.

Table 10.6 shows the aggregated macroeconomic impact of climate change in Scenario A. The global average aggregated impact of climate change in 2100 is 3.1 per cent and 0.8 per cent of GDP in the Baseline and the CP3.0 scenarios respectively. Thus, the benefit by mitigation from Baseline to CP3.0 is projected at about 2.3 per cent of GDP in 2100. (As noted previously, the mitigation cost is 4.3 per cent of GDP in 2100 for CP3.0, according to our mitigation model analysis.)

Poverty

Per-capita GDP in 1990 was US$23, US$2.3, US$0.6, and US$2.1 billion in OECD90, Russia and East Europe (REF), Asia excluding OECD90 countries (ASIA), and Africa & Latin America (ALM), respectively. The figures in 2005 were US$29, US$2.5, US$1.3, and US$2.5 billion. For the baseline scenario under scenario A — the figures for 2050 will be US$57, US$19,

Table 10.6: Aggregated Macroeconomic Impact Due to Climate Change (% of GDP in Baseline Scenario).

	2030	2050	2100	2150
A-Baseline (Global)	0.56%	1.11%	3.14%	5.56%
China	*0.51%*	*0.94%*	*2.44%*	*4.38%*
India	*1.26%*	*2.08%*	*4.63%*	*4.74%*
Other Asia	*0.82%*	*1.47%*	*3.63%*	*6.41%*
A-CP6.0 (Global)	0.55%	1.01%	2.15%	2.84%
A-CP4.5 (Global)	0.51%	0.87%	1.55%	1.83%
A-CP3.7 (Global)	0.49%	0.77%	1.14%	1.29%
A-CP3.0 (Global)	0.47%	0.67%	0.84%	0.77%
China	*0.43%*	*0.57%*	*0.62%*	*0.57%*
India	*1.09%*	*1.39%*	*1.48%*	*1.38%*
Other Asia	*0.69%*	*0.92%*	*0.99%*	*0.91%*

Note: The 12 regional impact have been aggregated into a world average impact using regional GDP in this table.
Source: Estimated by the Authors.

US$11 and US$8 billion. For 2100, it will be US$104, US$54, US$38 and US$27 billion. The GDP for ALM in 2100 will be close to the 2005 level for the OECD90 countries. The annual growth rate for 2005–2100 is 1.3 per cent, 3.2 per cent, 3.5 per cent, and 2.5 per cent in OECD90, REF, ASIA and ALM respectively.

The MDGs call for a reduction in the number of people living in poverty to halve the number in 1990 or 0.9 billion by 2015. Figure 10.3 shows numbers of people living in poverty under Scenario A. The estimates are conducted assuming a constant Gini coefficient for all countries in the future. Two types of poverty lines are assumed: 1) a constant line of $1.25 per day for the future; and 2) a variable poverty line which is based on future oil prices with elasticity of 1.0. Basically, poverty will be reduced greatly and the number of people below both poverty lines will fall in line with higher global economic growth. There were about 1.6 billion people in the world living in poverty in 2000. There are expected to be around 0.4 billion people in 2030 living under $1.25/day. On the other hand, if the poverty line is assumed to change in accordance with oil price (poverty line = $2.83/day in 2050), about a billion people will be living in poverty in 2030. Given this

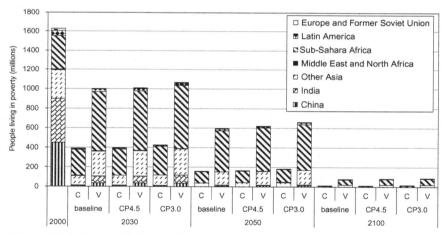

Figure 10.3: People Living in Poverty under Scenario A.

Note: "C" and "V" denote a constant poverty line of 1.25$/day and a variant poverty line determined using future oil price, respectively. The estimates are made assuming a constant Gini coefficient for all countries in the future. If distributions in income change in the future, the estimates will also change.

Source: Estimated by the Authors.

threshold for poverty, the number of people living in poverty in sub-Sahara Africa will see a rise by 2050 compared with the figure for 2000.

The benefits from reducing the impact of climate change will be smaller than mitigation costs up to 2050 at least, and the expected economic growth in developing countries is much greater than the expected impact of climate change on the macro-scale. Therefore, the effects of emission reduction levels on people living in poverty will be low.

Energy

Energy consumption has been drastically increasing on a global scale since the industrial revolution. The provision of modern energy services is recognised to be critical for sustainable development (UN-Energy, 2005; UNDP, 2005). This section assesses the use of energy in an efficient manner while ensuring security of supply.

Energy access

Access to energy is a critical factor in inducing economic growth and vice versa. Figure 10.4 shows people who do not have access to electricity in 2009 and 2050 under the Baseline Scenario A. Access will be enhanced in most

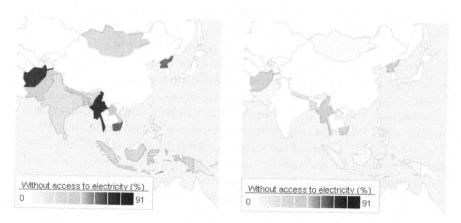

(a) Year 2009   (b) Year 2050

Figure 10.4: People with no Access to Electricity in 2009 and 2050 under Baseline (Scenario A).

Source: Estimated by the Authors.

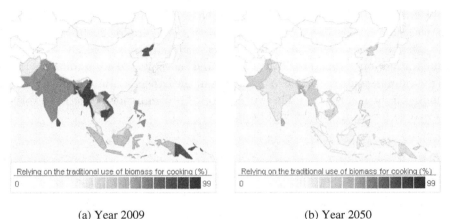

(a) Year 2009   (b) Year 2050

Figure 10.5: People Relying on the Traditional use of Biomass for Cooking in 2009 and 2050 under Baseline (Scenario A).

Source: Estimated by the Authors.

Asian countries by the middle of this century but as Figure 10.5 shows, the access to clean cooking facilities will improve at a slow pace.

Sustainable energy use

The world is currently highly dependent on fossil fuels for energy. In terms of sustainable energy use, there is a strong consensus that it is important to reduce fossil fuel consumption. Our assessment of sustainable energy use scenarios and cumulative fossil fuel consumption figures shown in Table 10.7. The global fossil fuel consumption between 2000 and 2030 is about 1.5 times of what it was in 2000, in almost all the emission reduction scenarios. Fossil fuel consumption will still be rising after 2030 in the Baseline and CP6.0 scenarios. The consumption in other scenarios (CP4.5, CP3.7, and CP3.0) is almost the same as or lower than that over 2000–2030. These three scenarios assume that there will be no drastic rise in fossil fuel consumption, but it should be noted that they do not guarantee sustainable energy use at all because of limited supply of fossil fuels.

Efficient energy use

The primary energy consumption per capita and per GDP in the world for five scenarios with different emission levels are shown in Table 10.8. The

Table 10.7: Cumulative Global Fossil Fuel Consumption from 2000 (in gigatons of oil equivalent or gtoe).

	2000–2030	2000–2050	2000–2100
A-Baseline	372 (1.5)	735 (1.8)	1732 (2.2)
A-CP6.0	364 (1.5)	708 (1.8)	1458 (1.8)
A-CP4.5	354 (1.5)	659 (1.6)	1238 (1.5)
A-CP3.7	346 (1.4)	619 (1.5)	1107 (1.4)
A-CP3.0	337 (1.4)	571 (1.4)	997 (1.2)

Note 1: Parentheses denote average consumption during the relevant periods compared with total global fossil fuel consumption in 2000 (8.0 gtoe/year).

Note 2: The numbers were estimated with the DNE21+ model up to 2050, and thereafter, they were estimated with the DNE21 model.

Source: Estimated by the authors.

Table 10.8: Primary Energy Consumption Per Capita and Per GDP.

	Per Capita (toe per capita)				Per GDP (toe per thousand US2000$)			
	1980	2005	2050	2100	1980	2005	2050	2100
A-Baseline (Global)	1.63	1.78	2.35	3.28	0.402	0.311	0.190	0.134
Japan	*2.95*	*4.08*	*4.79*	*5.88*	*0.123*	*0.105*	*0.075*	*0.070*
China	*0.62*	*1.32*	*3.70*	*4.45*	*2.481*	*0.814*	*0.213*	*0.144*
India	*0.30*	*0.48*	*1.35*	*2.80*	*1.302*	*0.834*	*0.266*	*0.175*
Other Asia	*0.46*	*0.90*	*1.25*	*2.42*	*0.607*	*0.467*	*0.239*	*0.152*
A-CP6.0 (Global)			2.22	2.61			0.180	0.107
A-CP4.5 (Global)			2.06	2.50			0.166	0.103
A-CP3.7 (Global)			1.98	2.61			0.161	0.107
A-CP3.0 (Global)			1.89	2.64			0.153	0.108
Japan			*4.27*	*4.81*			*0.067*	*0.057*
China			*2.53*	*3.22*			*0.146*	*0.104*
India			*0.88*	*0.71*			*0.173*	*0.044*
Other Asia			*1.16*	*0.87*			*0.222*	*0.055*

Note: The numbers for 2050 and 2100 were estimated with the DNE21+ and DNE21 models, respectively.

Source: IEA (2011b; 2011c) for 1980 and 2005.

average growth rate of primary energy per capita was 0.35 per cent p.a. between 1980 and 2005. The growth rate between 2050 and 2100 will be 0.62 per cent, 0.32 per cent, and 0.13 per cent p.a. respectively for Baseline, CP4.5, and CP3.0 scenarios. The rate for CP4.5 is almost the same as the historical evidence for the period between 1980 and 2005. The average growth rate of primary energy per GDP was −1.0 per cent p.a. between 1980 and 2005. The growth rate between 2005 and 2050 will be −1.4 per cent, −1.7 per cent, and −1.9 per cent p.a. respectively for Baseline, CP4.5, and CP3.0 scenarios in our models. The rates for 2005–2050 are expected to be higher than those for 1980–2005 in all the scenarios for different emission levels. Primary energy consumption figures in 2100 for CP3.7 and CP3.0 scenarios are slightly higher than those for CP4.5 as energy efficiencies will dip due to carbon capture and storage (CCS) being deployed resulting in the energy use to lower emissions exceeding energy saved.

Energy security

Figure 10.6 shows the energy security index for selected countries and regions under Scenario A. The energy security index is basically based on the IEA data (2007) (Oda *et al.*, 2012). Energy insecurity increases when imported oil and natural gas account for a large proportion of total primary energy consumption for a nation. Energy supply and demand, as well as related trade figures are projected under the DNE21+ model which represents 54 regions/countries with cost minimisation factored into the assessments. There will be greater energy security vulnerabilities in 2050 compared to 2000 for most countries but not Japan. Future energy security vulnerability in the US and Western Europe will rise due to a decline in domestic oil production by 2050. Energy security in Japan will increase in CP3.0 due to a projected dip in fossil fuel consumption as a result of falling

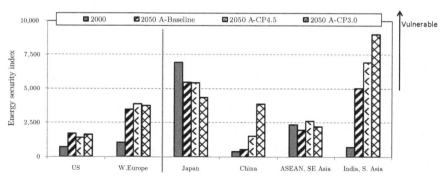

Figure 10.6: Energy Security Index.

Source: Estimated by the Authors.

population and more efficient use of energy. On the other hand, China, India and South Asia will see increases in vulnerability.

Water

Water demand will be affected by not only socio-economic conditions such as population shifts and changes in GDP but also land use for agriculture and industries under the DNE21+ model. The number of people subjected to water stress in selected countries and regions is shown in Figure 10.7. The indicator for water stress is based on the widely acceptable withdrawals-to-availability ratio of over 0.4 (Alcamo, 2007; Oki and Kanae, 2006). The number of people living in areas with figures over the threshold will increase by the middle of this century. The figure was about 2 billion in 2000, and is projected to increase by about 80 per cent in Scenario A. South Asia and the Middle East are particularly expected to be home to large numbers of people under water stress due to population and economic growth. The number of people under water stress globally in climate stabilisation scenarios will be greater than those in the Baseline scenario. One major factor will be a decline in annual water availability in South Asia under the climate stabilisation scenarios. Scenario B assumes higher economic growth than Scenario A. Water stress levels will increase by 2050, but will taper off sharply due to population decline after 2050 in the wake of high

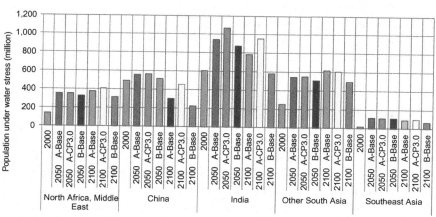

Figure 10.7: People under Water Stress.
Source: Estimated by the Authors.

economic growth. The analysis also shows clearly that water stress levels have a strong correlation with both population and economic growth.

Food and land-use change

Global food consumption rose by 2.5 per cent p.a. and 1.5 per cent p.a. for the periods 1961–1990 and 1990–2005 respectively. (The global average per-capita growth rates are 0.7 per cent p.a. and 0.2 per cent p.a. respectively for these periods.) According to our estimates, global food consumption for Scenario A (moderate GDP growth and moderate population growth) will be 0.9 per cent p.a. and 0.1 per cent p.a. for 2005–2050 and 2050–2100 respectively. (The global average per-capita growth rates are 0.1 per cent p.a. and 0.0 per cent p.a. respectively, for these periods). Global food consumption in 2050 will increase by about 50 per cent compared with consumption levels in 2005 in Scenario A. Figures for Scenario B (high GDP growth and low population) will be 0.7 per cent p.a. and −0.3 per cent p.a. for 2005–2050 and 2050–2100 respectively. The results for Scenario A in this study tallies with the FAO projections for global food consumption growth at 1 per cent p.a. for 2000–2050 (FAO, 2006).

Long-term food prices have generally been on a downward trend as productivity rises have exceeded increases in demand. Crop prices in the Baseline scenario will see a decrease in the future according to our estimates which also corresponds with FAO projections. This is because the average growth rates in population and food demand will be lower due in part to improvements in crop productivity.

This chapter conducted an analysis of crop productivity based on indicators such as water availability, land use for crop and bio-energy production, afforestation and reforestation, income changes and impact of climate change mitigation efforts (see Section 4.2) and their results (see Section 4.3).

Land use for food production

In the baseline scenario under Scenario A, land area for food production will need to increase by an additional 18 per cent by the middle of this century to satisfy a projected 50 per cent increase in global food consumption by 2050. The increase for sub-Saharan Africa will be prompted by an increase in food consumption exceeding productivity rises. In some regions such as China and India, land area will decline due to increases in productivity. The projections including the baseline scenarios assume changes in varieties

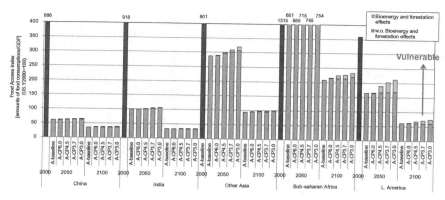

Figure 10.8: Food Access Index — Food Consumption Per GDP.
Source: Estimated by the Authors.

of crops and planting times to optimise productivity. On the other hand, almost no additional area for food production will be needed under Scenario B due to lower food demand.

Food access

Figure 10.8 shows food consumption per GDP as indicator of food access which basically mirrors Engel's Law which states that the proportion of income spent on food will dip as income rises. Hunger will be more widespread in areas where incomes are low while food prices are high as noted by the FAO (2009). The food access indices will fall drastically in the future for most Asian countries but will still be high for sub-Saharan Africa in 2050, exceeding current levels in most developed countries.

Food security

Food security is defined as food import per GDP in this study. Figure 10.9 shows the estimated import per GDP, including the effects of rises in crop prices. High income countries are able to purchase food while it will be more prohibitive for low-income countries at times when prices are elevated in global markets. The results are similar to those for the food access index. The index in the baseline scenario is better than that in CP3.0. Effects of lower crop productivity due to climate change are smaller than those stemming from net income declines due to climate change, mitigation costs

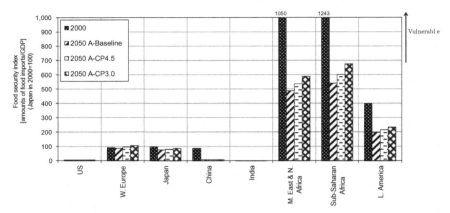

Figure 10.9: Food Security Index Based on Food Imports Per GDP.
Source: Estimated by the Authors.

as well as price increases stemming from bio-energy use and CO_2 emission reduction measures such as afforestation and reforestation.

Ocean acidification

The rise in atmospheric CO_2 concentrations will lead to an increase in ocean acidification resulting in damage to calcite and aragonite deposits which contain $CaCO_3$ or calcium carbonate, usually found in limestone and marble. The damages are a major concern in the field of ocean biodiversity. Aragonite is unsustainable under the baseline scenario in areas at N60° Latitude. In areas with lower temperatures than those found in N60°, the damage is more severe. The model for ocean acidification is based on the assessment done by the Royal Society (2005). The current ocean pH or acidity level is around 8.05. According to the model analysis, the pH levels in 2100 for Baseline, CP4.5 and CP3.0 will be around 7.85, 7.95 and 8.01 respectively. The figures for 2150 are projected at 7.71, 7.93, and 8.02 respectively.

Summary of assessments

Scenarios for different GHG emission levels are assessed using several indicators in this section. The CP3.0 scenario, which is expected to likely lead to a global mean temperature change of up to 2°C above the pre-industrial level, is expected to have a smaller environmental impact such as ocean acidification for example. However, several indicators assessed under CP3.0

are not necessarily better than those for other scenarios when it comes to reduction in emission levels, particularly for Asian countries. On the other hand, some of the indicators for the Baseline scenario are better than some of the others, but some of the indicators, such as those for sustainable fossil fuel use and ocean acidification are the worst among the assessed scenarios and would be unacceptable in terms of sustainable development. The desirable emission reduction level cannot be determined without value judgments, and this chapter does not treat value judgments or address desirable levels. However, an important implication of this study is that features relating to sustainable development and climate change are very complex when various indicators and country differences are taken into account.

Sensitivity Analysis

Socio-economic scenario

This chapter assesses two socio-economic scenarios: Scenarios A and B (see Table 10.3). Scenario B is assumed to entail higher economic growth brought on by advances in technology and a smaller population base compared to Scenario A. As shown in Figure 10.7, the number of people under water stress was greatly reduced under Scenario B. In addition, much less land is required for crop production in Scenario B compared to Scenario A due to lower food demand as a result of a smaller population base. The marginal abatement cost of CO_2 in 2050 under Scenario B is about US$320/t$CO_2$ for the CP3.0 scenario, while that under Scenario A is about US$380/t$CO_2$. High economic growth can provide higher emission reduction potential including deployment of bio-energy and afforestation/reforestation measures due to the fact that less land is required for crop production, although the overall energy demand in Scenario B is expected to be slightly higher than that in Scenario A. Economic growth might present obstacles to sustainable development in some areas, but it can certainly be expected to reduce several vulnerabilities that are disruptive to sustainable development in the future, if proper measures are implemented.

Energy security prioritised scenario

The energy security indices under Scenarios A and C (energy security prioritised scenario) for the US, Western Europe and Asia are compared in Figure 10.10. CO_2 marginal abatement cost will increase slightly under

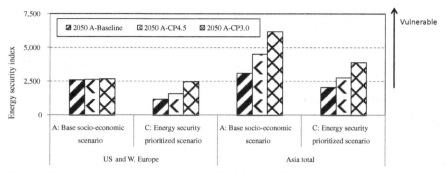

Figure 10.10: Energy Security Index (Scenario C).
Source: Estimated by the authors.

Scenario C compared with Scenario A due to the higher-cost mitigation measures such as switching from coal to gas. On the other hand, energy security in Scenario C is higher than that in Scenario A, as seen in Figure 10.9.

Implications for Asian countries

The increase in access to electricity will be vital in South Asian countries in order to raise economic growth, lower poverty levels and enhance healthcare. Reduction in CO_2 emission will be made possible by lowering of carbon intensity through more fuel-efficient power plants. This will require not only technology transfer and upgrade but also greater cooperation between developed and developing countries. The water stress will be more severe in many Asian countries particularly South Asia due to population growth. Better water management infrastructure will be needed with the cooperation and assistance of developed countries including those with the design capability to cope with precipitation increases and intensity of Asian monsoon brought on by rise in temperature due to climate change. These investments in infrastructure will be necessary to provide economic growth as well as create opportunities for sustainable development in response to climate change.

Conclusions and Policy Recommendations

This study show some of the complex trade-offs among several models over variables such as CO_2 emission reduction levels, energy security and food access. Deep GHG emission cuts by themselves, will not lead to sustainable development, but at the same time, neither can high levels of economic development do so. Balanced measures will be needed. Most of the indicators do show that sustainable development will improve with economic growth. However, some of the indicators such as ocean acidification point to severe outcomes under the baseline scenario. Efforts to lower GHG emission are hence necessary especially if they cap temperature increases at less than 2°C which will prevent ocean acidification and other climate related changes. On the other hand, issues related to food access and energy security can result in greater vulnerabilities. In short, there is no one-size-fits-all solution or policy for sustainable development.

Further Research Needed

This chapter assesses some of the key factors that can affect climate change and sustainable development with high consistency. However, there are still numerous limitations due to difficulties in quantitative analyses on variables such as the effects of extreme events and disasters caused by climate change. Other issues regarding the impact of distribution of wealth and water, food, energy resources are not covered in this chapter. Further research will be required.

Endnote

[1] See Moss *et al.* (2008).

References

Akimoto, Keigo, Toshimasa Tomoda, Yasumasa Fuji and Kenji Yamaji. "Assessment of Global Warming Mitigation Options with Integrated Assessment Model DNE21." *Energy Economics* 26 (2004): 635–653.

Akimoto, Keigo, Fuminori Sano, Junichiro Oda, Takashi Homma, Ullash Kumar Rout and Toshimasa Tomada. "Global Emission Reductions through a Sectoral Intensity Target Scheme." *Climate Policy* 8, 1 (2008): S46–S59.

Akimoto, Keigo, Fuminori Sano, Takashi Homma, Junichiro Oda, Miyuki Nagashima and Masanobu Kii. "Estimates of GHG Emission Reduction Potential by Country, Sector, and Cost." *Energy Policy* 38, 7 (2010): 3384–3393.

Alcamo, Joseph, Martina Florke and Michael Marker. "Future Long-term Changes in Global Water Resources Driven by Socio-economic and Climatic Changes." *Hydrological Sciences Journal* 52, 2 (2007): 247–275.

FAO (Food and Agriculture Organisation of the United Nations). "Interim Report (2006): World Agriculture: towards 2030/2050." 2006. Available online at http://www.fao.org/fileadmin/user_upload/esag/docs/Interim_report_AT 2050web.pdf. Last accessed on 20 July, 2012.

FAO (Food and Agriculture Organisation of the United Nations). "Key Messages". *The State of Food Insecurity in the World 2009.*" 2009. Available online at ftp://ftp.fao.org/docrep/fao/012/i0876e/i0876e00.pdf. Last accessed on 21 August, 2012.

Fischer, Gunther, Harrij van Velthuizen, Mahendra Shah and Freddy Nachtergaele. "Global Agro-ecological Assessment for Agriculture in the 21st century." 2002. Available online at http://www.iiasa.ac.at/Research/LUC/ SAEZ/index.html. Last accessed on 20 July, 2012.

Fujii, Yasumasa and Kenji Yamaji. "Assessment of Technological Options in the Global Energy System for Limiting the Atmospheric CO_2 Concentration." *Environmental Economics and Policy Studies* 1 (1998): 113–139.

Hayashi, Ayami, Keigo Akimoto, Fuminori Sano, Shansuke Mori and Toshimasa Tomada. "Evaluation of Global Warming Impact for Different Levels of Stabilization as A Step Toward Determination of the Long-Term Stabilization Target." *Climatic Change* 98 (2010): 87–112.

Hayashi, Ayami, Keigo Akimoto, Toshimasa Tomada and Masanobu Kii. "Global Evaluation of the Effects of Agriculture and Water Management Adaptations on the Water-Stressed Population." *Mitigation and Adaptation Strategies for Global Change* 18, 5 (2013): 591–618.

IEA (International Energy Agency). *Energy Security and Climate Policy: Assessing Interactions.* Paris: OECD/IEA, 2007.

IEA (International Energy Agency). "CO2 Emissions from Fuel Combustion Statistics." 2011a. Available online at http://www.oecd-ilibrary.org/energy/ co2-emissions-from-fuel-combustion-2011_co2_ fuel-2011-en. Last accessed on 21 August, 2013.

IEA (International Energy Agency). "Energy Balances of Non-OECD Countries." 2011b. Available online at http://www.oecd-ilibrary.org/energy/energy- balances-of-non-oecd-countries-2011_energy_bal_non-oecd-2011-en. Last accessed on 21 August, 2013.

IEA (International Energy Agency). "Energy Balances of OECD Countries." 2011c. Available online at http://www.oecd-ilibrary.org/energy/energy- balances-of-oecd-countries-2011_ energy_bal_oecd-2011-en. Last accessed on 21 August, 2013.

IPCC (Intergovernmental Panel on Climate Change). "Summary for Policymakers." In *Climate Change 2007: The Physical Science Basis. Contribution of Working Group I to the Fourth Assessment Report of the Intergovernmental Panel on Climate Change,* edited by Susan Solomon, Dahe Qin, Martin Manning, Melinda Marquis, Kirsten Averyt, Melinda M. B. Tignor, Henry

LeRoy Miller, Jr., and Zhenlin Chen, p. 12. Cambridge; New York: Cambridge University Press, 2007.

IPCC. *Towards New Scenarios for Analysis of Emissions, Climate Change, impact, and Response Strategies.* Geneva: Intergovernmental Panel on Climate Change, 2008.

K-1 Model Developers. "K-1 Coupled Model (MIROC) Description." In *K-1 technical report*, edited by Hiroyasu Hasumi and Seita Emori. Centre for Climate System Research, University of Tokyo. 2004. Available online at http://ccsr.aori.u-tokyo.ac.jp/~hasumi/miroc_description.pdf. Last accessed on 21 August, 2013.

Meinshausen, Malte, Tom M.L. Wigley and Sarah C.B. Raper. "Emulating coupled atmosphere-ocean and carbon cycle models with a simpler model, MAGICC6−Part 1: Model description and calibration." *Atmospheric Chemistry and Physics* 11, 4 (2011): 1417–1456.

Nordhaus, William D. "Economic Aspects of Global Warming in a Post-Copenhagen Environment." *Proceedings of the National Academy of Sciences* 107, 26 (2010): 11721–11726.

Oda, Junichiro, Keigo Akimoto, Fuminori Sano, Miyuki Nagashima, Kenichi Wada and Toshimasa Tomada. "Assessment of Asian Energy Security Index in the Context of Global CO_2 Mitigation." *Paper presented at IAEE Asian Conference.* Kyoto, February 20–22, 2012. Available online at http://eneken.ieej.or.jp/3rd_IAEE_Asia/pdf/paper/085p.pdf. Last accessed on 21 August, 2013.

Oki, Taikan and Shinjro Kanae. "Global Hydrological Cycles and World Water Resources." *Science* 25, 313 (2006): 1068–1072.

Oki, Taikan. "Total Runoff Integrating Pathways (TRIP)." 2001. Available online at http://hydro.iis.u-tokyo.ac.jp/%7Etaikan/TRIPDATA/TRIPDATA.html. Last accessed on 20 February, 2010.

The Royal Society. *Ocean Acidification Due to Increasing Atmospheric Carbon Dioxide.* Cardiff: The Clyvedon Press, 2005.

UNDP (United Nations Development Programme). *Energizing the Millennium Development Goals: A Guide to Energy's Role in Reducing Poverty.* New York: UNDP, 2005.

UN-Energy. *The Energy Challenge for Achieving the Millennium Development Goals.* New York: UN-Energy, 2005.

van Vuuren, Detlef P., Jae Edmonds, Mikiko Kainuma, Keywan Riahi, Allison Thomson, Kathy Hibbard, George C. Hurtt, Tom Kram, Volker Krey, Jean-Francois Lamarque, Toshihiko Masui, Malte Meinshausen, Nebojsa Nakicenovic, Steven J. Smith and Steven K. Rose. "The Representative Concentration Pathways: An Overview." *Climatic Change* 109 (2011): 5–31.

World Bank, *World Development Indicators 2011.* Washington, DC: World Bank, 2011.

Concluding Thoughts

Future Environmental Challenges for Asia

Shreekant GUPTA

This century is the 'Asian century' — of that there can be no doubt. Indeed, as Asia regains its primacy in the world economy, a position it has occupied for much of human history (certainly from 1 AD) barring the last 300 years, it is more meaningful to speak of the re-emergence of Asia. A key motivation for this volume is this re-emergence, centred on the rapidly growing economies of China and India, but in no less measure on other already developed as well as rapidly growing economies of Japan, Singapore, Malaysia, Indonesia and Vietnam, to name a few. In fact, with regard to rapid economic transformation, countries such as Singapore and China have in recent times, witnessed the most dramatic rise in per capita incomes in human history, with the former going from a third world to a first world country within the span of one generation.

The key question Asia faces is whether this gravitational shift can be sustained. With almost 60 per cent of the world population, the aspiring Asian countries generate about 30 per cent of global GDP. In another 20 years or so this share is expected to be around 50 per cent. But this achievement is far from assure — these countries face several challenges which if not successfully met "could lead to economic, social and even political instability and, in turn, derail economic development and growth" (ADB, 2011: xv). Two centuries ago, a rapidly growing country invoked its 'Manifest Destiny' to expand across a continent from one ocean to another. In doing so, it deployed human ingenuity and effort to overcome a number of challenges, albeit in a far less complex world. The emerging Asian countries, already spanning oceans as they do, must similarly meet and surmount challenges to achieve their own destiny.

In this volume the challenge under consideration is that of environmentally sustainable growth. As mentioned in the Introduction by Huang Jing, after accounting for the costs of environmental degradation, Asian growth rates look less impressive. He rightly flags a long-term and serious concern whether Asia is 'eating up' its natural capital (forests, biodiversity, mineral wealth, water resources and so on) and converting it into Gross Domestic Product (GDP) growth that will not sustain into the future. But on the flip side, given the economic, institutional and environmental diversity of countries, Asia offers a crucible of experience and polices within which the way forward can be forged and the challenge of environmentally sustainable development met.

It was with this in mind that the chapters in this volume considered a variety of environmental issues in seven Asian countries from the perspective of various stakeholders. Common themes that resonated across all chapters were the key role of sound institutions, of sensible policies and of good governance. While these findings are intuitive and hardly surprising, it is important to note they cut across countries at very different levels of economic and institutional development and also across a range of environmental issues from industrial pollution and natural resource degradation to climate change. Further, these findings are based on careful and detailed studies by well-regarded experts of specific environmental issues within a range of Asian countries.

Looking Ahead to the Future — Four Major Environmental Challenges for Asia

So where do we go from here? The chapters in this volume describe environmental conditions and challenges in the Asia of today or in the near future. But just as the Asia of 2014 looks vastly different from the Asia of the 1990s, less than a quarter century ago (and very much within living memory of many Asians), the Asia of 2030 or of 2050 will be again very different. It will be (in all likelihood) a more prosperous continent and certainly with many more people, doing very different things from what they do now and living in different ways.

It may be useful to gaze into the crystal ball to discern major environmental challenges Asia will face and how these might be met as well as the underlying drivers of these challenges. In doing so, we transcend national boundaries and instead develop broad brush assessments of these challenges. Looking at the future, this is helpful as Asian countries converge in their development pathways as well as in levels of economic development. Sharing of best practices and experiences, and evolving a common approach to global and regional environmental problems, is imperative if Asia is to continue its re-emergence.

We begin this look into the future by first examining the underlying trends and drivers of these environmental challenges, namely, a burgeoning Asian population increasingly concentrated in towns and cities and with rising income and consumption levels. Thus, in the year 2050, while Asia's share of world population is likely to remain in the vicinity of 60 per cent, this percentage will be of a much larger total: at least 9 billion people on the planet as compared to 7.1 billion now. Despite the inherent uncertainty of long range population projections, it may then be safely assumed there will be at least a billion more Asians then as compared to now. In other words, by 2050 there will be total of 5.2 billion Asians. A majority of them will live in towns and cities which will absorb all the additional one billion or more Asians on the planet. Worldwide far more people will live in urban than rural areas and Asia will be no exception — according to the United Nations (2012) Asia's urban population will soar from 1.9 billion to 3.3 billion (whereas it will see 480 million fewer people in rural areas). In fact, urbanisation and its attendant challenges and opportunities will be a defining feature of the Asian century.

Given their population density, "cities are where the pressures of migration, globalisation, economic development, social inequality, environmental pollution and climate change are most directly felt. Yet at the same time they are the engines of the world economy and centres of innovation where many solutions to global problems are being piloted" (United Nations, 2012). While this unprecedented increase in urban population will provide opportunities to improve education and public services in Asia, as more concentrated populations become easier to reach, this will also pose new challenges of providing jobs, housing, energy and infrastructure to mitigate urban poverty, expansion of slums and a deterioration of the urban environment.

The largest increases in global urban population are expected in India, China, Nigeria, the United States and Indonesia. Over the next four decades (2010 to 2050), India will add another 497 million to its urban population; China — 341 million, Nigeria — 200 million, the United States — 103 million and Indonesia — 92 million. Thus, there will be about a billion or more Asians living in cities.

Accompanying this defining feature of the Asian century will be a series of major environmental challenges at least in the medium term up to 2030. A study commissioned by the Asian Development Bank grouped them under four themes: *climate change, water management, deforestation and land degradation* and *air pollution* (Howes and Wyrwoll, 2012) and we draw on it in the discussion that follows. While other issues such as marine ecosystems and resources, biodiversity, waste management, etc. are also important, these four areas present the most pressing challenges to Asia's development over the next two decades and perhaps beyond.

What these environmental challenges have in common is their complexity. Borrowing from the social planning literature, they can be thought of as "wicked problems" (Howes and Wyroll, 2012). One characteristic of wicked problems is there are no easy solutions. And these problems may worsen as Asia grows — the 'environmental Kuznets curve' (EKC)[1] may not work — though more resources may become available to tackle them as incomes rise. This once again underscores the importance of sound institutions, of sensible policies and of good governance that the chapters in our volume highlight.

Climate change subsumes global warming in that an increase in global surface and ocean temperatures is accompanied *inter alia* by a rise in sea levels, melting of polar ice caps, ice shelves and glaciers and an increase in the frequency of extreme weather events such as cyclones and floods. Climate change is caused by emissions of heat trapping gases (greenhouse gases or GHGs), largely carbon dioxide but also methane and other gases. The implications of climate change have been discussed in several chapters in the volume including those on China, Vietnam and Japan. At a regional level Asia is highly vulnerable to the effects of climate change and this vulnerability is likely to increase with a large number of cities in low-lying and coastal areas.[2] In addition, Asian agriculture is at particular risk from higher temperatures, more erratic rainfall, rising sea levels and also stresses on the water sector. For example, it is estimated yields of important crops will decline in parts of Asia by 2.5 per cent to 10 per cent by the 2020s and 2030s (IPCC, 2007; Lobell *et al.*, 2008). Similarly, a study by International Food Policy Research Institute (IFPRI) on behalf of Asian Development Bank (ADB), of climate change impacts on Asian agriculture has predicted a fall in both irrigated rice production and wheat production by 2050 with concomitant rise in global food prices (ADB and IFPRI, 2009).

The resource requirements for adapting to climate change will be massive and will run into billions of dollars. This will undermine other important areas of expenditure required for Asia's growth. For agriculture alone, the ADB-IFPRI study has estimated adaptation costs over the next ten years to be US$24 billion. This refers to investments in adaptation measures only and does not take into account losses from lost agricultural output or impacts on food prices. As mentioned above these latter impacts will be substantial as well. Thus, the big question Asia faces is how are these costs to be financed? How can Asian countries, particularly those struggling to reduce existing poverty and inequality, possibly afford the adaptation investments required to protect and 'climate proof' their economies? A coordinated strategy by Asian countries to secure and deploy climate finance in this regard is called for. More importantly, a new development paradigm is needed; one that holistically takes account of the physical, economic and political impacts of climate change.

In the long run, Asia will also play a decisive role in the mitigation of climate change. This is irrespective of how the intractable problem of 'common-but-differentiated-responsibility' of mitigation is resolved since GHG emissions from Asia, especially China and India, will be significant. In this context, it is clear that the process of lifting standards of living throughout Asia cannot follow the carbon-intensive trajectory of today's high-income economies: the limits of the climate system render such replication infeasible.

Switching to a 'green growth' or low carbon development path will reduce the impact of potentially major stumbling blocks for Asia arising from climate change, such as food and water insecurity, environmental refugees and conflict, among others. Not only does avoidance of major climate damages provide a firmer base for Asian growth beyond 2030, but there are significant economic opportunities in the short-term from Asia leading the way in areas such as renewable energy. Indeed, China and, to some extent, India and ASEAN countries are moving towards exploiting these opportunities. Asia has to lead the way in mainstreaming climate change adaptation and mitigation into economic development.

The *management of water*, its quantity and quality is another key environmental challenge for Asia. Water pollution generates huge economic costs through increased mortality and morbidity and lost productivity. As Asia adds a billion people to its cities by 2050, the demand for adequate and clean water for competing uses such as human consumption, industrial processes and agriculture will grow. Already by the year 2030, under current management policies demand for water will exceed supply in China and India by 25 per cent and 50 per cent, respectively (WRG, 2009). Given that the population will be increasingly concentrated in cities often far from sources of water the problem will be compounded.

On the supply side the challenge is also one by overexploitation and degradation of surface and groundwater resources. Excessive groundwater extraction, pollution from human waste and industry, poor infrastructure and dam-building are major factors contributing to degradation of Asia's fresh water sources. For instance, 28 per cent of rivers and 48 per cent of lakes in China are unfit for any use including industrial and approximately 300 million people in its rural areas depend on unsafe drinking water (World Bank, 2006). In India, over 200 districts in 19 states have severely contaminated groundwater (GoI, 2009). Though major improvements have taken place with regard to water access and sanitation in Asia over the last two decades, large numbers still have inadequate facilities.

The impact of climate change will also be directly felt on the global water cycle including key Asian weather systems such as the Indian and East Asian monsoons (IPCC, 2007). Within the next three decades, the pattern of increasing glacial melt during the dry season is likely to reverse and transform the major rivers originating in the Himalayas such as the Brahmaputra, Ganges, and Yangtze into seasonal rivers (Asia Society, 2009; Immerzeel *et al.*, 2010). In other words, the fragility of the water sector in Asia will be exacerbated by climate change.

The challenge thus will be of managing both demand and supply through better policies and through better implementation of these policies. These include a gamut of measures such as more rational pricing, reduction of transmission losses, sensible allocation among competing uses, better coordination across different sectors and levels of government and treatment of wastewater. The example of an Asian city, Phnom Penh capital of Cambodia, shows how millions of Asian city dwellers could actually benefit through good governance (Biswas and Tortajada, 2010). In that city a previously decrepit and war-torn water supply system was changed radically, from one with incompetent management which lost both water and customers, into a model public water utility providing 24 hour drinking water, subsidies to the urban poor and dramatic reduction in water losses (Chan, 2009; Chan *et al.*, 2012). Other successful examples such as Manila "illustrate that setting the right policies and strategies coupled with changes in behaviour (in terms of valuing water both physically and fiscally) and financial resources to implement these goals are tripartite keys to success — but the final piece that is always needed to complete the puzzle is, undoubtedly, *good management*." (Gunawansa, *et al.*, 2013: 32, emphasis added).

Widespread *deforestation and land degradation* in Asia are highly visible examples of the unsustainable use of natural resources and constitute yet another important environmental challenge. Natural resources are what Dasgupta and Mäler (1995) term 'natural capital' or 'natural resource base' of an economy. They have convincingly argued for inclusion of this form of capital in the overall capital stock that comprises manufactured and human capital (buildings, bridges, roads, plants, machinery, knowledge, R&D and so on) and constitutes the productive base of an economy. Further, they argue natural capital should be properly measured, valued and its depreciation should be accounted for in national income. This is something that those Asian countries which are richly endowed with forests, biodiversity and fertile land (and from which they derive great benefit) should take heed.

In Asia, deforestation is unfortunately happening apace in the biodiversity rich countries of Indonesia and Malaysia. This is especially tragic since as mentioned in the introductory chapter these countries are 'megadiverse' countries (a select group of 17 countries that harbour the majority of the world's plant and animal species). But deforestation is also happening in other countries such as Cambodia and Myanmar (FAO, 2011a). With regard to land degradation, 23 per cent of the total area of China and 18 per cent of the area of India is considered degraded (Bai *et al.*, 2008). Interestingly for India, official estimates put the figure even higher at nearly half of the country's land as degraded (GoI, 2009). The figures for Thailand and Indonesia are also alarming — 60 per cent and 54 per cent, respectively (Bai *et al.*, 2008). For ASEAN as a whole, Food and Agriculture Organization (FAO) estimates that in two-thirds of countries (excluding Singapore) 40 per cent of land is suffering either severe or very severe degradation due to human activities (FAO 2011b).

Looking into the future these trends could exacerbate in a business-as-usual-world and epitomise the concern articulated by Huang Jing in the Introduction as to whether Asia is 'eating up' its natural capital and converting it into (ephemeral) GDP growth that cannot be sustained.

Deforestation and land degradation are intrinsically linked[3] — unsustainable forestry practices such as clear felling lead to soil erosion and salinity and also affect the groundwater table. In dry lands, deforestation leads to transformation of fertile areas into barren land, a process known as desertification (which can also be caused by unsustainable farming practices such as intensive cropping). Once land is sufficiently degraded, it may be unable to support forests again, or even the agricultural use that often drives deforestation in the first place.

The causes of deforestation and land degradation in Asia include demand for timber products and palm oil, intensive farming, and urban sprawl. Poor regulation and corruption allow unsustainable practices to arise and persist. It is, however, increasingly apparent throughout the region that the long-term economic costs from unsustainable land-use ultimately outweigh more immediate gains. Once sufficiently degraded these ecosystems require time and large expense to recover (if at all), effectively eliminating future sources of wood and causing other problems that reduce the productivity of the natural resource base. Over cultivation of agricultural land is increasingly leading to declining soil productivity and, consequently, lower output and, in some areas, food insecurity.

The final major environmental challenge is *air pollution* a primary cause of illness and death both in the growing cities and the poorer rural areas of Asia. Air pollution comprises both indoor air pollution due to burning of biomass based fuels and outdoor particulate air pollution from industries and vehicles. The ubiquitous nature of this problem undermines the productivity and income of the labour force, exacting a heavy economic toll. For instance, a recent study estimated that in 2005 the annual welfare loss associated with air pollution in China amounted to US$ 151 billion (2010 dollars) (Matus *et al.*, 2012). Air pollution commonly exceeds standards across the cities of developing Asia. Emissions of noxious gas and particulate matter from motor vehicles, industry and other causes plus the rising urban population exposed to these emissions are increasing the regional burden of respiratory illnesses and cancer (HEI, 2010). In the year 2000 it was estimated 65 per cent of deaths from urban air pollution occurred in Asia (Cohen *et al.*, 2005). More recent estimates show developing Asia continues to contribute over 2/3 of the air pollution-attributable global burden of disease due to regional increases in pollution levels (The Lancet, 2012).

More important, as Asian economies grow, as its cities expand, as incomes rise and with more Asians owning vehicles (initially two wheelers and eventually cars) these problems could get further compounded unless appropriate policies and measures are put in place.

Should We Be Optimistic or Pessimistic?

The purpose of recounting the major environmental challenges Asia faces now and into the medium term future is to show what might be but then again what might not if it can 'get its act together' so to speak. Indeed, climate change may happen but with sound planning and finance the region can become more climate-resilient. Similarly it is not inevitable that water shortages and water pollution, deforestation and land degradation and air pollution proceed apace. The present is not always a guide to the future and history need not be destiny.

To avoid and mitigate some of these problems especially with regard to air and water, Asian countries need to put in place governance and regulatory structures that internalise the environmental externalities, so to speak. Inclusive growth and a green economy are possible as Asia looks to the future. The need is to restructure economic and financial systems, expand the use of market-based instruments to control pollution, introduce and implement legal and institutional reforms and above all strive for good governance.

Endnotes

[1] The eponymous Kuznets curve (after Nobel Laureate economist Simon Kuznets) postulates a stylised fact — as a country's per capita income rises (income) inequality first rises then falls in an inverted U shape. The EKC postulates a similar phenomenon for several environmental problems such as air pollution where concentrations of pollutants first rise and then decline as per capita incomes increase. This empirical generalization has spawned a vast literature in environmental economics especially because of its controversial policy implication that countries can 'grow their way out' of environmental problems or by corollary 'pollute-now-clean-up-later'.

[2] For example, 40 per cent of Ho Chi Minh City lies within one metre of current sea levels, and by 2050 as many as 11 million people will be at risk from sea level rise and extreme weather events.

[3] This discussion and the following one on air pollution is based on Howes and Wyrwoll (2012).

References

ADB (Asian Development Bank). *Asia 2050: Realizing the Asian Century*. Manila: Asian Development Bank. 2011.

ADB and IFPRI (International Food Policy Research Institute). *Building Climate Resilience in the Agriculture Sector of Asia and the Pacific*. Manila and Washington D.C.: ADB and IFPRI, 2009.

Asia Society. *Asia's Next Challenge: Securing the Region's Water Security*. Report by the Leadership Group on Water Security in Asia, 2009. Available online at http://asiasociety.org/files/pdf/WaterSecurityReport.pdf. Last accessed on 18 September, 2013.

Bai, Z.G., D.L. Dent, L. Olsson, and M.E. Schaepman. "Proxy global assessment of land degradation." *Soil Use and Management*, 24 (2008): 223–234.

Biswas, Asit K. and Cecilia Tortajada. "Water Supply of Phnom Penh: An Example of Good Governance." *International Journal of Water Resources Development*, 26, 2 (2010): 157–172.

Chan, Ek Somn, Michel Vermersch and Patrick Vaughan. "Water supply in Phnom Penh: from devastation to sector leadership." *Water Utility Management International*, 7, 3 (2012): 9–12.

Chan, Ek Sonn. "Bringing Safe Water to Phnom Penh's City." *International Journal of Water Resources Development*, 25, 4 (2009): 597–609.

Cohen, Aaron J. H. Ross Anderson, Bart Ostra, Kiran Diev Pandey, Michal Krzyzanowski, Nino Künzli, Kersten Gutschmidt, Arden Pope, Isabelle Romieu, Jonathan M. Samet and Kirk Smith. "The Global Burden of Disease Due to Outdoor Air Pollution." *Journal of Toxicology and Environmental Health* Part A, 68 (2005): 1–7.

Dasgupta, Partha and Karl-Goran Mäler. "Poverty, Institutions, and the Environmental-Resource Base." In *Handbook of Development Economics, Volume III, Part 1*, edited by J. Behrman and T.N. Srinivasan, pp. 2371–2463. Amsterdam: Elsevier Science B.V., 1995.

FAO (Food and Agriculture Organization). *State of the World's Forests 2011*. Rome: Food and Agriculture Organization of the United Nations, 2011a.

FAO. *FAOSTAT. Statistical Database of the Food and Agriculture Organization of the United Nations*, 2011b. Available online at http://faostat.fao.org/site/291/default.aspx. Last accessed on 18 September, 2013.

GoI (Government of India). *State of Environment Report for India 2009*. Ministry of Environment and Forests, 2009.

Gunawansa, Asanga, Lovleen Bhullar and Sonia Ferdous Hoque. "Introduction," In *Water Governance: An Evaluation of Alternative Architectures*, edited by Asanga Gunawansa and Lovleen Bhullar, pp. 1–43. Cheltenham: Edward Elgar, 2013.

HEI (Health Effects Institute). *Outdoor Air Pollution and Health in the Developing Countries of Asia: A Comprehensive Review.* HEI International Scientific Oversight Committee. Special Report 18. 2010. Available online at http://ehs.sph.berkeley.edu/krsmith/publications/2011/heiasiareview.pdf. Last accessed on 23 September, 2013.

Howes, Stephen and Paul Wyroll. "Asia's Wicked Environmental Problems." ADBI Working Paper 348. 2012. Tokyo: Asian Development Bank Institute. Available online at http://www.seachangecop.org/sites/default/files/documents/2012%2002%20ADBI%20WP348_asia_wicked_environmental_problems.pdf. Last accessed on 18 September, 2013.

IPCC (Intergovernmental Panel on Climate Change). *Climate Change 2007 — Impacts, Adaptation and Vulnerability: Contribution of Working Group II to the Fourth Assessment Report of the IPCC.* Cambridge: Cambridge University Press. 2007.

Immerzeel, Walter W., Ludovials P. H. van Beek and Marc F. P. Bierkens. "Climate Change Will Affect the Asian Water Towers." *Science*, 328 (2010): 1382–1385.

Lobell, David B., and others. "Prioritizing Climate Change Adaption Needs for Food Security in 2030." *Science*, 319 (2008): 607–610.

Matus, Kira, Kyung-Min Nam, Noelle E. Selin, Lok N. Lamsal, John M. Reilly and Sergery Paltsev. *"Health Damages from Air Pollution in China."* Global Environmental Change, 22, 1 (2012): 55–66.

The Lancet. "The story of GBD 2010: A 'super-human' effort." Special Issue on Global Burden of Disease Study 2010. 380. December 15/22/29, 2012. Available online at http://download.thelancet.com/pdfs/journals/lancet/PIIS0140673612621746.pdf. Last accessed on 23 September, 2013.

United Nations. *World Urbanization Prospects, the 2011 Revision*: Press Release. United Nations, Department of Economic and Social Affairs, Population Division. 2012. Available online at http://esa.un.org/unup/Documentation/press-release.htm. Last accessed on 18 September, 2013.

WRG (Water Resources Group). *Charting Our Water Future.* Report of the 2030 Water Resources Group. 2009. Available online at http://www.mckinsey.com/App_Media/Reports/Water/Charting_Our_Water_Future_Full_Report_001.pdf. Accessed on 18 September, 2013.

World Bank. *China Water Quality Management: Policy and Institutional Considerations.* Washington D.C.: Environment and Social Development Department, East Asia and Pacific Region. 2006. Available online at http://siteresources.worldbank.org/INTEAPREGTOPENVIRONMENT/Resources/China_WPM_final_lo_res.pdf. Last accessed on 23 September, 2013.

Index